Labour Law and Climate Change

Studies in Employment and Social Policy

VOLUME 57

Editors

Professor Alan Neal (founding editor of the *International Journal of Labour Law and Industrial Relations*, and Convenor of the European Association of Labour Law Judges); Professor Manfred Weiss (past president of the International Industrial Relations Association); and Professor Birgitta Nyström (professor of private law at the Law Faculty, University of Lund, Sweden, and member of the European Committee of Social Rights).

Objective

Studies in Employment and Social Policy series seeks to provide a forum for highlighting international and comparative research on contemporary areas of significance for evaluation and regulation of the world of work.

Introduction

Launched in 1997, the Studies in Employment and Social Policy Series now boasts over fifty titles, addressing key policy and development issues in the fields of industrial relations, labour law, social security, and international labour regulation.

Content

With contributions from leading figures in the field, the series brings together key policymakers, academics, and regulators, providing a unique context in which to analyse and evaluate the rapid and dramatic work and social policy developments taking place around the globe.

The titles published in this series are listed at the end of this volume.

Labour Law and Climate Change

Towards a Just Transition

Edited by

Adalberto Perulli & Tiziano Treu

Wolters Kluwer

Published by:
Kluwer Law International B.V.
PO Box 316
2400 AH Alphen aan den Rijn
The Netherlands
E-mail: lrs-sales@wolterskluwer.com
Website: www.wolterskluwer.com/en/solutions/kluwerlawinternational

Sold and distributed by:
Wolters Kluwer Legal & Regulatory U.S.
920 Links Avenue
Landisville, PA 17538
United States of America
E-mail: customer.service@wolterskluwer.com

ISBN 978-94-035-0877-1

e-Book: ISBN 978-94-035-0887-0
web-PDF: ISBN 978-94-035-0897-9

Editors

Adalberto Perulli is a Full Professor of Labour Law at the Ca' Foscari University of Venice and Visiting Professor at the University of Paris Ouest Nanterre La Défense since 2000. He is the Director of a First Level Master in Global Economics and Social Affairs and Scientific Director of a First Level Master in Labour Law at the Ca' Foscari University of Venice. He did research and studies for the European Commission and for the International Labour Organization (ILO) of Geneva. Prof. Perulli has been rapporteur to the XVIII World Congress of Labour Law on 'Labour Law and productive decentralization' in Paris, in 2006; he is Master EMA Director at EIUC (European Inter-University Centre for Human Rights and Democratisation).

Tiziano Treu is a Professor Emeritus of Labour Law at the Catholic University of Milan, Law School, and former President of CNEL (National Council for Economics and Labour). Previously he has been President of the Italian Association of Labour Law and Social Security and the International Society of Labour and Social Security Law (ISLSSL). During his political experience Prof. Treu has been Minister of Transportation and Minister of Labour and Social Security in the Italian Government, and more recently President of the XI Commission (Labour and Welfare) of the Italian Senate.

Contributors

Marzia Barbera, Professor of Labour Law at the Department of Law at the University of Brescia, Italy.

Manfred Weiss, Professor emeritus of Labour Law, and until 2008 Professor at the Law School of the Goethe University in Frankfurt, Germany.

Pablo Arellano Ortiz, Labour Law Specialist at ILO (Geneva) and Professor at Pontificia Universidad Católica de Valparaíso, Chile.

Giuseppe Casale, Director a.i. of ITCILO, Director of the Turin School of Development.

Margarita Miñarro Yanini, Professor of Labour and Social Security Law at the Universitat Jaume I, Spain.

Tonia Novitz, Professor of Labour Law at the University of Bristol Law School in the UK.

Elena Buoso, Professor of Administrative Law at the University of Padova, Italy.

Elena Gramano, Assistant Professor of Labour Law at the Department of Legal Studies of Bocconi University of Milan, Italy.

Frank Hendrickx, Professor of Labour Law at the Faculty of Law of the University of Leuven, Belgium.

Brian Langille, Professor of Law at the University of Toronto Law School, Canada.

Sophie Robin-Olivier, Professor of Law at La Sorbonne School of Law, Paris 1 Panthéon-Sorbonne University, France.

Summary of Contents

Table of Contents

Towards a Green Labour Law

Adalberto Perulli

1 LABOUR LAW IN THE PRISM OF THE MAN-NATURE CONFLICT

This book deals with a very important and difficult topic, which is starting to be studied also at the academic level but is still in its early stage of analysis within the field of labour law: climate change and its relationships, its influences on the labour market and on the regulation of labour relations, at the individual and collective level.

The historical phase we are in is characterized by major events, on which the very fate of humanity depends. I am referring to the increase in CO_2 emissions, global warming, and natural disasters produced by climate change. This type of impact requires an equally proportional response, at the level of legislative method. Yet this type of political method is rarely assimilated and adopted by modern democracies. Actually, they are generally known for adopting only a short-term view with little programmatic vision, especially concerning climate issues. The political consequences of climate change are disruptive but above all long-term: they create a clear boundary between those who decide on the choices to be made and those who will suffer the consequences (at least the most serious ones) in the years and centuries to come.

The political decision to combat climate change can no longer be based on the hypothesis of a selfish-rational subject who acts driven by fear, like the one hypothesized by modern realism, from Hobbes: climate change created a fracture that is not only methodological, legislative and normative but also constitutional and regulatory. The disruptive effect of the phenomenon, in addition to acting on the physical and environmental level, is also and inevitably acting on the level of sources and visions of the system. Consequently, law in general (not only labour law) should reconsider its functions and objectives; it should be rethought on the basis of scientific discoveries concerning the relationship between humans, the planet they live in, the environment and climate. But above all, law must help the values that are in place (environment, work, the human person) to find – thanks in particular to the 'law of balancing' among interests, in a perspective attentive to the claims of justice[1] – an effective synthesis.

This law of balancing is above all possible in systems that have constitutionalized the environment as a fundamental right. For example, in Italy: the new paragraph 3 of Article 9 of the Constitution, in providing that the Republic – therefore, all the entities of the Republic – 'protects the environment, biodiversity and ecosystems, also in the interest of future generations', dictates a general criterion for action by public authorities based on environmental protection.[2] However, such a balancing principle can also operate in the absence of a direct constitutionalization of the environment. Many years before the change made to Article 9, the Italian Constitutional Court n. 641/87 had already established that the environment is protected as a determining element of the *quality of life*. Its protection does not pursue abstract naturalistic or aesthetic aims but expresses the need for a natural habitat where humans may live and act, that is necessary for the community and citizens. This is imposed above all by constitutional precepts (Articles 9 and 32 of the Constitution),[3] according to which environment stands as a primary and absolute value. At the supranational level, a constitutionalization of the environment has been implemented with the Charter of Fundamental Rights of the European Union according to which (Article 37) 'A high level of environmental protection and the improvement of the quality of the environment must be integrated into the policies of the Union and ensured in accordance with the principle of sustainable development.'

However, as we shall see, this balancing process is by no means simple, neither at national nor at supranational level.[4] As a matter of fact, the relationship of labour law with environmental issues is very problematic.

First of all, we need to consider a basic problem, which concerns the relationship between Work which opposes humans to Nature: as Kojève wrote, no human being can play the role of 'impartial and disinterested third' party in this relationship, nobody

1. In the perspective indicated by R. Alexy, *A Theory of Constitutional Rights*, Oxford, OUP, 2002.
2. *See*, in this Volume, M. Barbera, *Just Ecological Transition and Inequalities*: such action will now be made possible in the Italian legal system by the modification of Art. 9 of the Constitution, as well as by the constraints arising from the international climate agreements, and, on the level of inter-private relations, by the constraints connected to the protection of health, environment and the inviolable rights of the person introduced by the recent reform of Art. 41 of the Constitution.
3. Article 9: 'The Republic promotes the development of culture and of scientific and technical research. It safeguards natural landscape and the historical and artistic heritage of the Nation'; Art. 32: 'The Republic safeguards health as a fundamental right of the individual and as a collective interest, and guarantees free medical care to the indigent. No one may be obliged to undergo any health treatment except under the provisions of the law. The law may not under any circumstances violate the limits imposed by respect for the human person.'
4. The concept of a high level of protection can advance the effectiveness of environmental law. It plays a role in the case law of the ECJ, in relation to environmental and health-related issues, even if with varied outcomes. Recent ECJ case law demonstrates the high level of protection requirement as a possible ground for reviewing legality of European acts or boosting its interpretations in reviewing a measure's legality, especially when assessing proportionality; *see* C. Voigt (eds) *International Judicial Practice on the Environment*, Cambridge University Press, 2019, in particular Ch. 8, *The Court of Justice of the European Union and the High Level of Environmental Protection: Transforming a Policy Objective into a Concept Amenable to Judicial Review.*

will want to defend *until the end* Nature's interests against those of human beings.[5] Kojeve's observation fits perfectly with the history of the relationship between labour law and Nature. Labour law has long taken part in the regulation of production processes based on the transformation of Nature into non-durable objects of consumption, with the concern of protecting people in the work environment (think to health and safety in the workplace), *certainly not the Earth.* In fact, all the regulatory powers of labour law concern the places, times and ways of organization of this entropic process of production, that is totally indifferent to the 'laws of Nature', as evidenced by numerous corporate cases involving environmental issues (for example, *see infra*, paragraph 7). This being the case, it is easy to understand why - as Tiziano Treu observed in this Volume - the impact of the green transition on industrial activities is creating strong tensions among the social parties and difficulties of the public powers which are asked to sustain massive processes of enterprises restructuring and the relocation of thousands of workers, to the point that some observers and trade unions are inclined to argue that the reasons of the environment are incompatible with those of employment.[6]

How can the relationship between labour law and the environment be interpreted differently? How can we consider the relation between labour law and the Earth where humans live, which they have at the same time largely contributed to destroy? In order to change this path, it is necessary to put forward a different paradigm, capable of introducing new values that may positivize the Work-Nature relationship. What Nietzsche called the 'love of the remote' is characteristic of the critique of traditional values.[7] Well, precisely *the love for the remote is the basis of the responsibility of the present man for the future and for the generations to come.* It is a responsibility that falls on the living generation at all times: the need for superior solidarity, not only towards our contemporaries but towards those who will reap all the good and bad sowing of the present.[8] Isn't this, in the end, the concern that underpins the Sustainability paradigm? Within this paradigm, which combines different instances including those of the natural environment, it is possible to imagine a new type of balance in the conflict between values: no longer the balance between Capital and Work, as traditionally happens, but between Capital, Work and Nature. This perspective obviously presupposes, in turn, a renewed ability of labour law for strategic thinking. As rightly observed by Frank Hendrickx in his contribution to this Volume, this legal domain is essentially open to change. Labour law is a 'preeminently strategic-juridical area', and it is therefore probable that this sector of law can be receptive to environmental demands.[9]

But to best develop this strategic thinking, it is perhaps appropriate, before any strictly legal consideration, to start from a philosophical-anthropological reflection, on

5. A. Kojéve, *Esquisse d'une phénoménologie du droit*, Gallimard, Paris, 1981, p. 197.
6. T. Treu, *The Impact of the Green Transition on Employment, Labour Law and Industrial Relations*, in this Volume.
7. F. Nietzsche, *Thus Spoke Zarathustra*, Cambridge University Press, 2006.
8. N. Hartmann, *Grundzüge einer Metaphisik der Erkenntnis*, Walter de Gruyer & Co., Berlin, 1949 (fourth edition).
9. F. Hendrickx, *Climate Change and Labour Law: Redefining the Collective Interest*, in this Volume.

the relationship between humans and the Earth, and then, put forward some points on the necessary changes in labour law.

2 THE MANY MEANINGS OF 'EARTH': SOIL, GLOBE, AND GAIA

First of all, it is necessary to understand what the word Earth means, a word that has a multiplicity of meanings:[10] Earth as soil, Earth as globe, Earth as *Gaia*.

2.1 The Earth as *Soil*

The Earth is the *soil* of the earthly orb, which in the legal logic applied to production plays a fundamental role as it expresses, at the same time, appropriation and localization, hence the concept of 'ordering'.[11] The land, as being soil (and sub-soil, source of minerals and diamonds, oil and fossil energies) is part of the Trinity formula that Karl Marx placed at the basis of the Theory of Capital,[12] and which Karl Polanyi has compared to work and money to unmask the fictitious use that humans make of these elements in the artificial construction of the market.[13]

Humans take possession of the soil and locate productive activities there. In this context, the *homo oeconomicus* does not manifest a belonging to Nature, but rather a detachment from it in order to implement the so-called civilization, which is essentially an abandonment of the natural world. Paradoxically, the destruction of the human environment is, therefore, a moment of self-affirmation of the *anthropos* on earthly soil. Anthropocene is above all the act of trampling on the ground, delimiting its (private) property and (public) domain, but also the act of claiming the (completely unnatural) right to spoil the environment that makes human life possible. As a matter of fact, today this soil is constantly polluted by heavy metals, pesticides, poisons, and plastics (forming islands in the Pacific Ocean): in Europe, 70% of the soil is now unhealthy due to poor management practices, pollution, climate change and urbanization,[14] and the situation could get worse.

We should therefore ask ourselves where the genetic relationship between Earth and human work has ended up. Virgil described it as the relationship between humanity procreated by work and work that is generously repaid by the righteous Earth (the verse says '*the righteous Earth, unbidden, pours forth from her soil an easy sustenance*'[15]). The theme of the equity of the Earth, giving back to humans the fruit of

10. Here I am freely inspired by B. Latour, *Facing Gaia: Eight Lectures on the New Climatic Regime*, Polity Press, 2017.
11. *See* C. Schmitt, *Nomos of the Earth in the International Law of Jus Publicum Europaeum*, Telos Press, 2003.
12. K. Marx, *Capital Volume 3, Chapter 48: The Trinity Formula.*
13. K. Polanyi, *The Great Transformation: The Political and Economic Origins of Our Time*, Beacon Press, 2001; on the relationship between nature and work, Karl Polanyi states that land and work are not separate: work is part of life, the land remains part of nature and life and nature form an articulated whole.
14. Source: European Commission, *Life on Earth Depends on Healthy Soils*, March 2022.
15. Virgil, *Georgics* II 458-542.

the efforts made, is combined in Virgil with the epicurean motif of *autárkeia*, which is the value of those who, like the wise or the farmer, place the principle of happiness inside and not outside the self and who therefore knows how to live according to balance and measure. But this is not enough, because it still concerns subjective moral choices. A systemic and global action is needed, such as that proposed by a study by the European Commission (*Caring for Soil*, 2020), according to which the main goal of mission *Caring for Soil* is caring for life: By 2030, at least 75% of soils in each EU Member States should be healthy, or show a significant improvement towards meeting acceptable thresholds, to support ecosystem services.

Where does labour law fit in this context? It is clear that it should be re-modelled in order for it to promote the co-creation of new market mechanisms, corporate and governance models, as well as educational tools, which support sustainability within the production, including in it the well-being of the soil. Labour law must also be placed in the perspective (also indicated in *Caring for Soil*) of the creation of shorter value chains, and in the creation of a circular bio-economy.

The systematic problem of labour law, therefore, consists in dealing with the quest for a new balance in the relationship between economic production and the Earth, which is also the 'mother of the law'.[16] And here we have a problem because labour law was first conceived as an Anthropocene right, indifferent to the ecological issue (except for it being the discipline of the working environment, to protect workers). But it is quite clear that the work environment is too narrow a concept, and too self-referring to humans, to take on a real ecological connotation: that is to say, to ensure that labour law can be a discipline capable of internalizing behavioural models aimed at directly protecting (not the workers but) the Earth as a whole. What is missing, and should be advocated for is a new regulatory framework explicitly placing the ecological issue among the values to be arbitrated in the complex legal regulation of work, to ensure that labour law is able to contrast any work or production organization ignoring the requirements of ecological justice.

2.2 The Earth as 'Globe'

Second, the Earth is a 'globe', a geo-political concept of which globalization is today the icon. Globalization expresses a different conception of the Earth and of Nature, a vision of an Economic Nature imposing its steel cage and its rationality. Globalization led to the deconstruction of social systems, as being the result of an exacerbated competition between companies, producers, and workers: this Earth-globe is the world of calculation, global production, and consumption on a world scale. In fact, global competition is the basis of the global value chain production model, creating a global division of

16. Originally the idea of 'natural law' expresses the concept of Justice conceived as the highest and supreme law deriving from the Nature of the Universe, that is, the law of God and of Nature; we find this idea in the Stoic doctrine based on the 'return to nature': *see* A. Passerin d'Entrèves, *Natural Law*, Hutchinson University Library, 1951; *see also* L. Strauss, *On Political Philosophy. Responding to the Challenge of Positivism and Historicism*, University of Chicago Press, 2018, p. 193, who reminds us that 'in *status naturalis*' the state of nature is the old meaning of the state of nature according to which the state of nature is the state of health, of perfection.

labour in the production of negative externalities in social and environmental terms (as well as people's health, product safety, social rights, etc.).

In this geopolitical context, the Earth (and its ecology) is almost completely neglected by labour law, as the ecological objectives are not actually part of the labour law scope.

There is a lack of effective tools for regulating global economic processes and the negative externalities of these processes. Environmental awareness has been raised within the codes of conduct of multinational companies, applying specific labels to green and fair trade products, under the sphere of Corporate Social Responsibility. Further, International trade has been developed in order to internalize social and environmental aspects in the paradigm of Sustainability,[17] also in the perspective of supranational governance, as Tonia Novitz has analysed in this volume.[18] In both cases, these are largely questionable processes in terms of effectiveness. However, there have been some positive outcomes, as in the case of the AfCFTA (Continental African Free Trade Area) agreement signed by 54 African states, which provides for the reduction of tariffs and other trade barriers to help member countries move from extractive products (oil and minerals) to a more sustainable production, made up of manufacturing and agriculture.

From this global perspective, it is important to remember that (on 23 February 2022) the European Commission finally published the proposal for a directive on due diligence, which hopes, at least in the programmatic intentions, to introduce into the EU legal order an obligation of due diligence on human rights and environment for European businesses. The contents of the directive show profiles of primary interest: once (and if) it enters into force it will be applicable not only within the EU area but will also be applied along all the supply chains of European companies at a global level. It would therefore be the first and unprecedented regulatory instrument of the European Union (EU) containing human rights due diligence obligations for the private sector to be applied horizontally to all productive sectors and with extra-territorial effects. If this were to be adopted, the future regulation would therefore operate in the wake of the creation of a 'level playing field' in the legal systems of the Member States. Such 'level playing field' would, on the one hand, implement the obligation to protect human rights from violations attributable to private sector activities enshrined in the first Pillar of the UN Guiding Principles (UNGPs) on business and human rights and, on the other hand, would give normative 'concreteness' to the responsibility of companies to respect human rights governed by the second Pillar of the Guiding Principles. Of extreme interest, then, are the principles pertaining to corporate governance which introduce the obligation (so-called duty of care) for the directors of companies falling within the scope of application of the proposed directive to take into consideration the consequences of their decisions on matters related to sustainability, including human

17. *See* A. Perulli, T. Treu (eds), *Sustainable Development, Global Trade and Social Rights*, Wolters Kluwer, 2018.
18. T. Novitz, *Challenges when Combining Labour and Environmental Objectives: Trade and Sustainable Development Chapters and Beyond.*

rights, the environment and climate change.[19] The central element of the proposed directive, therefore, lies in the obligation imposed on the EU Member States to introduce legislative disciplines into their respective internal systems aimed at forcing large companies operating in the European internal market to adopt obligations related to human rights and environmental diligence, designed to identify, prevent, mitigate and account for actual or potential adverse human rights and environmental impacts in relation to their operations and along supply chains. The legislation, which will basically apply to all productive sectors, will therefore oblige these companies to identify and assess a potentially wide range of risks, for example, the exploitation of child labour, the use of forced labour, discrimination in the workplace, environmental pollution, etc.

The Earth as *globe*, therefore, requires a renewed capacity of national states (and their aggregations of continent-states) to intervene in global economic processes. Corporate Social Responsibility, with its voluntary and soft law tools, is not enough.

2.3 The Earth as *Gaia*

Finally, the Earth is *Gaia*, a mythical and pluriverse concept to which humans also belong, and in which Science, Politics and Nature coexist, in the name of a new ecological regime. *Gaia* does not so much mark the irruption of a 'metaphysical' or ideal nature into the public space, but the end of the idea of Nature as a 'fact' separated from 'values' (ethics, culture, politics, law), according to a line of thought that brought us to the ancient distinction (and contrast) between nature and convention, between *Physis* and *Nomos*.[20] In other words, we should be aware that the ecological crisis necessarily requires a new cultural and normative approach to Nature, where elements of 'fact' and 'law' are contaminated in a complex both top-down and bottom-up project, made up of government actions and politics and at the same time through the mobilization of local *consciences* and *knowledge* to protect the environment. In this new perspective, *Gaia* pushes us towards a new social and institutional 'ecumene': think about, for example, the environmental and energy policy objectives that need to be widely shared and agreed upon among different public bodies, economic operators and the public, as emerged in the Italian experience analyzed by Elena Buoso in this Volume, during the consultation procedures for the Strategic Environmental Assessment of the Plan.[21]

What law, then, does *Gaia* generate? What is its new *Nomos of the* Earth? For sure a law that is opposite to that of globalization, of the separation between *Physis* and *Nomos*, between nature and politics. For sure not the law of Trisimachus, where justice is the profit of the superior (in the sense of the strongest) (as Plato writes, in the

19. With specific reference to climate change, Art. 15 introduces the obligation to assess the risk of negative impacts on the climate deriving from company operations and in particular in relation to the achievement of the 1.5° limit set by the Paris Agreements.
20. *See* L. Strauss, *On Political Philosophy. Responding to the Challenge of Positivism and Historicism*, University of Chicago Press, 2018.
21. E. Buoso, *The Role of Public Administration in Italy's Integrated National Energy and Climate Plan*, in this Volume.

Republic, 1095). From this perspective, as Sophie Robin-Olivier rightly observed, the fight against climate phenomena must take place within a strategy of distributive justice, to prevent new categories of vulnerable workers from paying the cost of the green transition.[22]

Gaia produces laws that recognize Nature as the *autonomous sovereignty* that has been challenged by the 'will to power' of human beings, and which directs the resources accumulated by production towards a new climate regime, forcing finance to support the environmental transition. Can labour law be part of this regulatory process? And how? In the first section (I) I am going to try to provide some indications of this matter, while in the second section (II) I am going to develop a series of problematic considerations with reference to the European dimension, to highlight the difficulties encountered by EU policies in this complex matter, which must combine social, economic and environmental aspects.

SECTION I LABOUR LAW AND GAIA, A COMPLEX RELATIONSHIP

3 THE COMPONENTS OF A NEW ECO-SOCIAL LABOUR LAW

The *ILO Guidelines for a Just Transition towards Environmentally Sustainable Economies and Societies for All* (2015) provide some valuable indications to answer the question of how labour law can participate in the process of redefining the relationship between human beings and Nature. In workplaces, both employers and workers may intervene to put in place practices to make their enterprise sustainable and resilient to environmental degradation and climate change. The ILO *Guidelines* stipulate that 'Sustainable development is only possible with the active engagement of the world of work' and that 'Governments, employers and workers are not passive bystanders, but are rather agents of change, who are able to develop new ways of working that may safeguard the environment for present and future generations.' The *Guidelines* express the aspiration that 'Greening all enterprises and jobs by introducing more energy and resource efficient practices, avoiding pollution and managing natural resources sustainably leads to innovation, enhances resilience and generates savings which drive new investment and employment.' They also emphasize cooperation and social dialogue among employers, workers and their representatives, and governments, on the means to achieve such a goal while at the same time creating and protecting employment. Governments play a crucial role in fostering such enterprise-level transition towards Sustainability, including the creation of a conducive environment through laws and regulations. On the basis of these very general indications, let us now try to articulate some reconstructive proposals for an ecologically oriented labour law.

3.1 New Labour Rights

First, the environment and its protection require the creation of *new labour rights*, that are calibrated on existing ones (for example, rights to information, training,

22. S. Robin-Olivier, *Energy Poverty, Fair Transition and Labour Law.*

notification, etc.) but adapted to the new ecological context. As the most recent ILO report indicates,[23] the workers' environmental or environment-related rights comprise the rights: (a) to ask the employer for environmental information; this rights-based approach to accessing environmental information is also found in an increasing number of national legal systems, in particular in laws on freedom of information; (b) to notify employers of any risk to the environment. French labour legislation requires workers to notify the employer immediately if they consider, in good faith, that the products or manufacturing processes being used by the establishment may represent a serious risk to public health or the environment; (c) to refuse to work when there is a risk to the environment. It is matter-of-factly possible to argue that the general right to suspend the provision of labour under the Occupational Safety and Health Legislation (OSHL) can also be used to protect the environment indirectly.[24] For instance, a certain level of air pollution or environmental degradation may harm the health of the worker; and (d) to the protection of environmental whistleblowers who report potential or actual threats to the environment. Some countries, as well as the EU, have enacted dedicated whistleblower protection laws containing specific provisions to protect environmental whistleblowers.[25] The protection of whistleblowers has received increasing attention. These rights have so far mostly been adapted from OSH legislation and are part of the broader framework of ensuring safety and health at work.

In addition to these rights connected to the fight against climate change, I believe we must also reconsider other rights which are much discussed but which sometimes fail to emerge fully and clearly: I am thinking, in particular, of the right to professional training. As Elena Gramano pointed out in her contribution to the Volume, in consideration of the extension of the duties that an employee might be asked to perform, the importance of training can be extended to preserve professionalism not only as a set of competencies but also as an extension of the employee's concrete chances to stay active on the labour market. In this sense, as Margarita Miñarro Yanini observes, it is an essential condition for the transition of the model to be successful, the training of workers in the new skills, in relation to the work that was being developed or to the one that will be developed in the future, as well as in internships companies and technologies from the standards of sustainability and respect for the environment, including, where appropriate, requalification.[26]

23. *Greening Enterprises Transforming processes and workplaces*, ILO, 2022.
24. *Greening Enterprises Transforming processes and workplaces*, ILO, 2022.
25. The *Chancery Lane Project* makes available to all users the so-called Net Zero Toolkit, a set of practical tools to help professionals implement climate-conscious clauses in their organization; among these the clause Net Zero Within Company Whistleblowing Policies (Sasha's Clause). This clause provides a formulation to be used within the whistleblowing policies to guarantee coverage from possible repercussions to the employee who reports the non-compliance or non-adherence by the company to climate or sustainability policies. The clause also provides employers with guidance and considerations relevant to the implementation of their whistleblowing policy. For example, it encourages employers to collect statistics on the number of reports and to verify the effectiveness of the policy in order to make corrective changes if necessary.
26. Margarita Miñarro Yanini, *The Labour Instruments of Internal Flexibility at the Service of the just Ecological Transition in the Context of the Next Generation EU.*

3.2 New Concept of Human Work

Second, labour law should promote *a new concept of human work capable of recomposing the fracture with the 'iustissima tellus'*: valorizing cultural work, promoting permanent research education and the forms of autonomous, creative and dis-alienated work (and therefore attentive to the ecological consequences of the action), and the work producing long-lasting projects, as opposed to things subject to the wear and tear of time. The more work becomes autonomous from the production processes typical of industrial society, the more it regains control of the procedures and purposes that de-alienated human work is capable of carrying out. This is completely evident in the case of intellectual work, cognitive work, and in work that takes on the task of transforming the way in which men relate to Nature with scientific research and technology. In the alarming scenario of the climate crisis, professions, and scientific and technical knowledge must acquire a new social power through work, imposing the necessary changes on the ruling class and the elites.

3.3 Translating the Sovereign Demands of the Earth into Norms and Regulations

Third, labour law can participate in the reconversion of capitalist production itself in an ecological sense, if it is capable of *translating the sovereign demands of the Earth into norms and regulations*. This means not only imposing severe penalties on those who pollute but, *ex ante* redesigning production organizations in order to re-think the production processes (implementing resource efficiency measures and green technologies, *id est* 'greening processes', greening outputs, in terms of green products and services) and valorizing local staff and local raw materials. In contrast to the 'business-as-usual' paradigm, which is based on a purely economic view of enterprises, sustainable business models allow enterprises not only to take into consideration social and environmental interests but also to integrate these concerns into their organizational processes and ensure they are represented in the final output of their activities.[27] To create an institutional basis for such an approach to doing business, some countries have promoted sustainable business models such as 'benefit corporations' through legislation and regulations. In this perspective, the 'greening of business' implies the greening of output and/or the greening of process. The greening of products and services belongs to 'output', while efforts to reduce energy and raw material fall under the 'process'. Enterprises in sectors that do not provide green products or services can contribute to the green transition by implementing strategies that reduce their environmental footprint. Enterprises can also choose to use environmentally friendly materials and renewable energy as 'inputs' or to take 'marketing' action that drives consumers' behaviour towards more sustainable consumption.[28] 'Green enterprises' therefore can be defined as those that have successfully introduced any of these

27. *Greening Enterprises Transforming processes and workplaces*, ILO, 2022.
28. *Greening Enterprises Transforming processes and workplaces*, ILO, 2022.

measures into their business strategy and operation. We need to write a new labour law for communities and people, based on the commons (water, land, air, data, knowledge) to achieve complete decarbonization. In this perspective, the ILO Report on *Greening Enterprises Transforming processes and workplaces* estimates that firms offering green products and services are key drivers of the green transition. Outputs of the firms surveyed include recycled plastic bottles, electricity produced through renewable energy, electric cars, and a consultancy providing green training.

3.4 New Work Organization

Work organization is also very important. Some countries are introducing remote working or teleworking in their environmental regulations and highlighting its benefits to the environment. Working time is another strategic topic: recently time policy has become of significant interest in debates on sustainable societies and workplaces. Although research on time policy is still at an early stage, environmental research has found that sustainability is intertwined with time and that, in turn, time is closely connected to patterns of consumption. Accelerated work processes and technological advances have led to greater consumption. From this standpoint, labour and employment policies 'are always also time policies, and sometimes also environmental policies', given that 'more work also means more energy and environmental consumption and more harmful emissions'.[29] As environmental economists have suggested, the time dimension of sustainability, particularly when related to working time, involves a strong correlation between working hours and environmental degradation. It is argued that 'a successful path to sustainability must confront our commitment to growth and will ultimately entail a stabilization of consumption through reductions in working hours'.[30]

3.5 Climate Migration Law

Labour law should be able to manage the phenomena of mass migration related to environment. According to the ILO, 150 of the 244 million migrants in the world are workers who can contribute to the growth and economic development of the countries of destination and of origin. However, there is to date no ad hoc international convention that protects those who migrate due to the effects of the climate crisis. The United Nations High Commissioner for Refugees believes that the term 'climate refugee' cannot be used as it is not based on any rule of international law. In fact, the 1951 Geneva Convention on refugees and the subsequent 1967 Protocol restrict this status to those who are threatened in their own country by persecutions related to ethnicity, religion, political opinions, and nationality, but do not contemplate environmental issues. Furthermore, climate migrants basically never flee abroad: very often the movement takes place within the borders of their own country (in this case, we

29. *Greening Enterprises Transforming processes and workplaces*, ILO, 2022.
30. *Greening Enterprises Transforming processes and workplaces*, ILO, 2022.

speak of progressive migration). For the law, therefore, it is as if they did not exist. When called upon to resolve concrete cases, the international courts of justice have had to refer to other flexible juridical mechanisms: such as the Universal Declaration of Human Rights of 1948, or the International Covenant on Civil and Political Rights of 1966. The stimuli for legally defining the status of climate migrants are few, also because it would be a process that would open up the possibility of applying for asylum to millions and millions of people. Anyway, such a phenomenon of environmental migrants represented one of the first insights into the reality that industrial relations are experiencing in terms of climate change. In fact, among the indirect effects of the climate crisis, we certainly have that of migratory flows determined by the increasing hostility within the environment due to climate change. Such phenomenon of environmental migration shall then need to be analysed: we are talking about human beings that have not yet found a place within the law, to whom the international community is demonstrating that it is not in line with their changing needs. We will therefore have to turn our gaze towards European policies, and in particular to some national and supranational jurisprudential cases on environmental migration which have proposed the most concrete answers to the gaps in the legislation. But a *climate migration law is still to be conceived.*

3.6 New Environmentally Friendly Labour Market

The labour market undoubtedly represents one of the most important labour law issues in the context of the transition towards a climate-neutral economy. Labour law should advocate for a new environmentally friendly labour market model. The transition to a coal-free economy implies a radical reorganization of the labour market and therefore a just transition for the workers involved. In fact, if the climate crisis triggers a necessary transformation of an immense range of sectors, the birth of new professional figures will be consequential, while others will be replaced and others redefined. As Giuseppe Casale has clearly pointed out in his contribution to this Volume, to guarantee that skills needs are satisfied and climate pledges are effectively executed, action planning on skills development must be integrated with important climate and environmental policies and regulations, including the nationally determined contributions (NDCs).[31] It will be necessary to promote and support green employment, deal with the training and retraining of workers and foresee the changes in the workplace of the future. The European climate plan – at least from a programmatic point of view – is certainly the European action that first and most effectively has focused on policies of encouraging businesses and organizations to participate in the pact for skills in order to retrain workers and to participate in the dissemination of good practices in the various European programmes. Further, it promoted the use of the European Social Fund, which will enable the training of five million people in green jobs and in green recovery. Finally, it encouraged stakeholders, local authorities and communities to make full use of the Just Transition Mechanism to promote the reskilling and active

31. G. Casale, *The Green Transition and New Skills in Occupation*, in this Volume.

inclusion of workers and jobseekers and the creation of new local job opportunities in the regions concerned. As Pablo Arellano Ortiz noted in his contribution, we should not think of the link between labour and environment as a problem: it should be considered as an opportunity, as it always has been, to restructure the labour market, protections for the worker, and the way employers work and produce.[32]

3.7 The Employment Contract to Accommodate Ecological Demands

The employment contract should also be reconsidered. After all, the employment contract is the first terrain for an individual action that recalls the juridical-moral responsibility of the company that employs human resources in the entropic processes of production. The contract represents, in general, a field for the negotiation of private - at times conflicting - interests. In labour law, the contract is not limited to organizing the exchange between corresponding services, but it carries out a broader organizational function because the work performance does not end in the performance of certain tasks, but it concerns the obligation to perform these tasks in view of the organization's purpose.

Therefore, we must ask ourselves the following question: is the employment contract ready to accommodate ecological demands, thus becoming an instrument for a new environmental ecumene? It is time to think in these terms: to include the ecological rationality of *Gaia*, in its complex cultural identity, into the employment contract. In order to do this, it is necessary to de-construct the employment contract understood as an intersubjective relationship of exchange, and to develop a new form of co-regulation, overcoming the dichotomies of the labour law system (private vs public, state vs market, individual vs collective) in favour of an eclectic combination of environmental concerns, interests and rationalities. In this perspective, the employment contract should reflect the new ecological identity of the company, resulting in no longer being indifferent to the environment.[33]

---

32. P. Arellano Ortiz, *Policy and Regulatory Implications of Current Debates on Labour Market and Climate Change: Southern Perspective,* in this Volume.
33. The first timid signs of an ecological use of the employment contract can be found in the clauses prepared in the *Chancery Lane Project*. Consider, for example, the Employee Climate Engagement Provisions (Athena's clause). Employee Climate Engagement Provisions is a clause to be included in the employment contract aimed at regulating the provision, by the employer, of training courses as well as the possibility of participating in them for employees in terms of education and awareness on Environmental, Social and Governance (ESG) issues. It includes training for company employees, participation and active involvement in the climate ambitions and Net Zero goals of their employer (the term 'Net Zero' refers to a state in which greenhouse gases released into the atmosphere are balanced by the removal of gases from the atmosphere.

    Another clause is the ESG Based Performance Conditions for Employee Incentive Awards (Scarlett's clause). The clause ties the performance standards for employee incentive awards to ESG issues and incentivizes and rewards the long-term decision-making necessary to take sustainable and climate-aligned actions to reduce the company's greenhouse gas emissions by 2050 or first, in line with the objectives of the Paris Agreement.

    Another interesting clause is the Employer - Employee Environmental Obligations (Eric's clause).

    Eric's Clause allows you to rethink periods such as the so-called employee gardening leave as an opportunity to volunteer with environmental organizations. This formulation allows

3.8 Industrial Relations and Participation of Workers

Further, we should develop ecological industrial relations, on the following matters: (a) health and safety, considered by the ILO as strictly connected to the environmental issue and affected by phenomena such as thermal stress and the aggression of atmospheric agents increasing the risks of incidents at work; further, also regarding the problems related to the productive sectors most exposed to climate change or dependent on resources; (b) the environmental organization of work, becoming the face of the same coin with the ecological footprint; (c) the development of Green-Jobs in the most suitable sectors (energy, transport, design, agriculture, tourism) through the creation of new tasks and professionalism linked to the effective reduction of energy and raw material consumption, the limits of gas emissions, the reduction of waste and contamination, the protection of ecosystems, etc. In this perspective, the acquisition of new green skills, as well as the management of sustainability, that is the development of managerial skills relating to the environmental, social and economic sustainability of companies, acquire major relevance; (d) the recognition of decent work development opportunities in the transition to sustainable economies; (e) the contrast of an economic eco-modernization based on the acceptance of the logic of growth and efficiency, in favour of a labour law of sustainability.[34]

---

employees (for example) on leave or sabbatical to use the time available to volunteer at an environmental organization, in order to address climate change issues. Companies can incentivize their employees and contribute to the Just Transition through the different use of the time of suspension of work performance.

In addition to the *Chancery Lane Project*, several professional associations are promoting the introduction of new practices sensitive to the issue of climate change within the workplace and in the profession in general. Among these, the Australian Legal Sector Alliance, Lawyers for Climate Justice in Canada, Lawyers for Climate Action in New Zealand.

34. At the European level, there is a renewed ferment regarding trade union action in terms of environmental impact and the climate crisis. Definitely active as regards the monitoring of the policies undertaken, the European trade unions are also giving various inputs in the form of associations and concrete proposals. The *Agreement: A Green Mentality for Collective Bargaining* project, which investigated the role of representation and collective bargaining in the promotion of Just Transition, is definitely interesting. Here are some virtuous cases that emerged:

    1. France

        A) In 2018, the French trade union federations of the construction sector negotiated and concluded an agreement in the Limousin region with the regional federation of employers in the public works sector (FRTP-EFPW) on workers' rights in the field of health, safety and working conditions in the event of heat and heat waves. The agreement includes a series of preventive measures to be implemented in the workplace when the outside temperature reaches 30°C. Such measures include: the possibility of obtaining unemployment benefits for the interruption of work in the event of hot weather; the obligation for employers to monitor weather forecasts, adjust workload, working conditions and working hours in case of heat waves; the supply of suitable work clothes and a special room to accommodate workers in the event of climatic conditions that could compromise their health.

        In June 2019, the government and employers were asked to extend this type of agreement to all French regions, as the relevant national legislation has a binding effect on the rights of workers and their representatives.

        B) In 2009, the German group Bosch decided to close the production plant in Vénissieux, France. Following a strong mobilization of the union, after negotiations with the board of directors (among others also at the level of the

European Works Council), the decision was taken to set up a commission composed of representatives of the company and of trade unions at national and local levels. The objective was to identify the solution to maintain employment at the site (search for an external partner, alternative productions). After a year of work, the plant was turned into a solar panel production facility. A worker retraining program was therefore launched. In total, 400 of the total 900 jobs were retained at the site.

2. Germany

Companies such as RAG and ThyssenKrupp have started diversification processes by investing in plant technologies, environmental technologies and control services. The Ruhr has been turned in recent years into the center of environmental technology research for all of Germany, developing a comparative advantage in energy supply and waste disposal. Social dialogue and co-determination have played an important role in the political process, during which four key policies have been defined: 1) wage subsidies for the reintegration of the unemployed and for those at risk of unemployment; 2) support of labour market policies to support business development; 3) combined promotion of employment and infrastructure; 4) integrated development of problematic urban areas.

3. Spain

A research team from the Pompeu Fabra University has highlighted how, in the Spanish context, collective bargaining represents a valid option for the transformation of production models in a broadly sustainable sense. Think not only of the key role in the transition to a green economy played by the reduction of working hours, but also of the strengthening on these issues of the promotion of lifelong learning, in particular through training, research, innovation and the use of new technologies, as well as the need to equip employers' representative bodies and trade union organizations with new skills, in the light of their driving function towards sustainable work models.

Specifically: ITAS has implemented the Salutdapt project, aimed at contributing to the development of territorial plans and strategies for adaptation and health protection in the face of climate change. Within this framework, the Institute has developed a wide range of proposals aimed at improving the protection of workers' health. The final document is aimed at public authorities, social partners and businesses. Among other things, ITAS proposes to improve the communication of occupational contingencies related to high temperatures (including them in the categories of accidents at work) and to encourage companies to adequately assess the occupational risks due to thermal stress;

In Catalonia, Life Clinomics was a three-year project (June 2016-June 2019) led by the Provincial Council of Barcelona and partially funded by the European Union (60%) which aimed to increase the resilience to climate change of selected territories and economies within the within the Province of Barcelona. The proposed actions were in line with the Spanish climate change strategy. The project involved local administrations and workers in the agriculture, forestry, fishing and/or tourism sectors. The main objective was to build the resilience of local authorities in the Mediterranean through interventions in the counties of Montseny, Alt Penedès and Terres del Ebro in the province of Barcelona. The specific objectives of the project were the elaboration of action plans and strategies for adaptation to climate change, equipping local authorities with tools that allow them to effectively start processes of adaptation to climate change, develop adaptation planning models to climate change, attract investments for adaptation measures, improve the competitiveness of agricultural, forestry, fisheries and tourism enterprises, as well as create new jobs and raise awareness among citizens, stakeholders and local authorities. CCOO Catalunya and UGT Catalunya were members of the project.

4. Italy.

The case of Luxottica stands out in the panorama of company-level bargaining. In 2011, Luxottica launched the Zero Waste project, aimed at reducing the greenhouse gas emissions produced by the Luxottica plants. As part of this project, which includes a

Last but not least, is the issue of workers' participation in the decisions that the company must take to combat climate change. As Manfred Weiss rightly observed in his contribution, the fight against climate change will lead to a whole set of decisions which may have serious, often negative short-term effects for employees (stop certain types of production, change production patterns, reconstruct parts of the company or the company as a whole, closing parts of the company or of the whole company, etc.).[35] Workers' participation significantly increases the chances of acceptability of these changes by workers.

4 A MATTER OF VALUES

All these solutions imply a precise *choice of value*. Creating a new climate regime is possible if we start to build a new 'natural' labour law, an eco-social labour law where the relationship between human action and nature on the one hand, and between law and Nature on the other find a virtuous synthesis, capable of balancing different but no longer conflicting interests.

The values of labour law, Freedom, Solidarity and Equality should be constantly reinforced through a new interdisciplinary dialogue with the ecological dimension of work. Although they find themselves in a disenchanted world and they are accustomed to translating values of relativism into polytheism, to the point of embracing the eradicating nihilism of the Economic, these values have demonstrated the (juridical, not only moral) ability to acquire their own normative life and become positive factors of

Life Cycle Assessment and recycling programs for different waste streams (cardboard, office paper, stationery, etc.), company management and employee representatives have agreed to link part of variable remuneration to a composite index called 'zero waste', originally built in turn on two indicators relating to the consumption of electricity and paper and toner for printers. With the renewal of 30 October 2015, the structure of the bonus was updated, also through the redefinition of the sustainability index. The new bonus associates a portion of salary increase with an index that measures the annual reduction in electricity consumption in CO2 equivalent. The percentage of the reduced electricity index generates an average bonus value per worker which varies according to the percentage of reduced waste containment. Basically, as the percentage of waste reduction increases, there is an increase in the bonus paid to each worker. Alongside the reduction of electricity, the new performance bonus has included three other parameters associated with the reduction of pollution: 1. reduction of prints: the agreement provides for salary increases linked to the reduction compared to the previous year in the number of hard copies in A4 format; 2. increase in the use of public transport and zero-car means: this index rewards the increase compared to the previous year in the indicator that measures the ratio in percentage terms between zero-car users and subscribers to public transport services such as metro and bus, and the average strength of the period; 3. reduction in the consumption of indirect materials: the agreement rewards the reduction compared to the previous year in the cost of indirect materials based on production volumes (e.g., cutters, tumbling material, containers and packaging, tools, etc.). The achievement of objectives such as the reduction of prints, the increase in the use of zero-car public transport means and the reduction of indirect materials generates a 20% increase in the deliverable value based on the results of the electricity consumption.

35. M. Weiss, *The Fight against Climate Change: Implications for Labour Law and Industrial Relations*, in this Volume.

rationalization of the economic sphere. But these values of eco-social justice need social and institutional 'bodies' to be carried forward, to effectively become part of the fundamental principles of global law. However, as we shall see later, the old twentieth-century institutions promoting interdependence in social matters (such as the ILO, WHO, and FAO) have been marginalized – in a process that is by no means linear and indeed full of contradictions – by the institutions of the economy (WTO, IMF and World Bank). The latter are matter-of-factly in a state of profound crisis and should be profoundly reformed and placed in close regulatory correlation with social institutions to make them suitable for responding to the eco-social challenges of the Anthropocene. Even the European social model, while standing out with its extra-mercantile values as a real 'beacon' within an economic cosmopolitanism that has risen to a global religion, has experienced a progressive loss of regulatory authority, serving economic imperatives and competitiveness of businesses, both in the internal market and in relations with countries characterized by levels of job protection not comparable to those of the EU.

In this perspective, the exchange with environmental law can be useful, in order to get new institutional tools and raise awareness, such as the principles of precaution, preventive action, priority correction at source, the damage caused to the environment, and responsibility ('polluter pays principle'). In other words, labour law must be part of a new 'ecological law' that interfaces society and Nature, in a symbiotic and organic connection between the environmental and the social sphere:[36] it should be capable of guiding the ecosystem changes, in order to promote a permanent process of adjustment to changing biological times, necessary to safeguard the life of *homo faber* on the Earth.

SECTION II POLICIES AND ACTIONS IN THE EUROPEAN PERSPECTIVE

In this second section, I am going to try to articulate some reflections which, on the one hand, prove the necessary interrelationship between social and environmental issues and, on the other hand, show that ecological thinking in labour law encounters difficulties in translating into policies suited to the challenge of climate change. I am going to analyse the following aspects: (a) the relationship between the social and environmental sphere and their comparison with the economic sphere; (b) the awareness that this integrated vision should be pursued in EU policies on climate and social matters; (c) the difficulties that these relationships actually present, with the risk of conflicts between social and environmental spheres and with all the weaknesses of the regulatory instruments in order to progress on such matters.

5 THE NECESSARY LINKAGE BETWEEN THE ENVIRONMENT AND THE SOCIAL SPHERE

Regulation is trying to put the social sphere and the environmental sphere in an inter-regulatory relationship with the dynamics of the market and production, on the

36. Cfr. T. Novitz, *Engagement with Sustainability at the International Labour Organization and Wider Implications for Collective Worker Voice*, in *ILR*, 159, 4, 2020, p. 465.

assumption that the first two spheres are interrelated with each other and that both of them must confront and coordinate with economic rationality: this is, in a nutshell, the essence of the sustainable development paradigm.

Now that the social and environmental spheres are interrelated is a rather evident observation. Environmental considerations refer to the mitigation of climate change and the adaptation to it, as well as in a broad sense the adaption to the environment and related risks, such as natural disasters. Social considerations, on the other hand, refer to issues of equality, inclusiveness, fairness of employment relationships, and investments in human capital and communities. Let's take some easy examples of interconnection.

One first interconnected element is that climate change tends to widen social inequalities. There is growing evidence that the negative impact of global warming is greater for poorer countries, both because they do not have adequate resources to face climate issues and because they are already hot geographic areas, where further warming is harmful to the health of workers and the productivity of the economic system.

A second interconnected element is the link between climate change and gender discrimination: in 2018, the European Parliament adopted a resolution on women, gender equality and climate justice to integrate the gender perspective into strategies to face climate change. The resolution recognizes that men and women are affected differently by the impacts of climate change and that women are more vulnerable, in terms of inequality of access to education, job opportunities, social and cultural norms, health, and migration.

A third example of interplay concerns the relationship between climate change and the labour market: the European Climate Pact launched in 2020 has set the goal of giving priority to actions focused on four areas that entail immediate benefits not only for climate and environment but also for the health and well-being of citizens: green spaces, green mobility, green skills. The latter undoubtedly represents one of the most important issues in the context of the transition to a climate-neutral economy. In fact, the climate crisis will trigger a necessary transformation of a vast range of production sectors, with the advent of new jobs, while others will be replaced and others will be redefined. It will therefore be necessary to promote and support green employment, to take care of the training and retraining of workers as well as to foresee the changes induced by climate change in the workplace and in businesses.

However, the close connection between the social and environmental spheres clearly emerges – in relation to the economic sphere – because they are both affected by the negative externalities produced by the economic system. For example, waste and emissions from the production cycle are, at the same time, negative environmental and social externalities: just think about the issue of workers' health and more generally about the population in highly polluting production areas.

Therefore, we can affirm that the social and environmental spheres must go along in the face of market failures in conditioning economic rationality to reduce or eliminate the negative externalities of the economy. Today we talk about ecological transition to indicate a path of transformation of our societies that may be able to combine the fight and adaptation to climate change and the need for a more comprehensive reflection on our way of producing and living our relationship with nature.

6 SOME EUROPEAN EXAMPLES

The interrelation I am referring to is clearly expressed in the documents of the EU and, more generally, in the action of the EU, in its external relations (especially in the commercial ones). To give some easy examples, think of the 2018 EU action plan to strengthen the role of finance in creating an efficient economy that also achieves environmental and social objectives. Moreover, think of the social and environmental clauses in international trade treaties, with which the EU promotes compliance with social and environmental standards through conditionality techniques, with an integrated approach between the social and environmental spheres.

Here is another example. Achieving climate neutrality is promoted as the main objective of the *European Green Deal*. The Commission specified the conditions in order to achieve it: the ecological transition process must *preserve the welfare and social cohesion of European citizens and represent an opportunity to rethink and modernize the models of economic and social development and organization*. Indeed, the Commission has more than once stressed the importance of achieving a 'socially just ecological transition' that is capable of ensuring that the cost of the transition is not borne by the most vulnerable populations as a precondition for a successful transition to a zero-emission economy. In this context, the European Pillar of Social Rights is presented as the reference framework to ensure that '[...] *no one is left behind*'.[37]

And again, the two spheres appear integrated into the *Next Generation EU* which aims at stimulating '*a robust recovery of the European economy in the name of ecological transition, digitization, competitiveness, and training, social, territorial and gender inclusion*'. Thus the EU has set the ambitious goal to start an unprecedented process of transformation that allows new competitiveness and renews the European social model, at the same time.

More than other EU actions, the European Climate Plan has for sure focused on a policy of encouraging companies and organizations to participate in the Skills Pact to contribute to the updating and retraining of workers, to participate in the dissemination of good practices and exemplary stories collected in the various European programmes. Moreover, it has promoted the use of the European Social Fund, which will allow the training of five million people in green jobs and green recovery. Finally, it encouraged stakeholders, local authorities and communities to make full use of the Just Transition Mechanism to promote the retraining and active inclusion of workers and job seekers and the creation of new local job opportunities in the regions involved.

37. The principle 'Left no one behind' is also one of the key principles of 2030 Agenda.

7 THE DIFFICULTIES OF AN INTEGRATED APPROACH AND BALANCING: THE ILVA CASE

And here we get to the point: the difficulties in putting forward an integrated strategy. As a matter of fact, this process of integrated regulation is by no means easy. And the relationship between social sphere and environmental issues is often very much problematic and it often leads to conflicts between the two spheres. The steel plant ILVA in Taranto (Italy) is an exemplary case highlighting all the difficulties of reconciling the expectation of a community to lead a dignified and free existence through work, with the not less important one, to live in a healthy environment. This conflict between work and the environment has raised a series of delicate legal issues, which have been the subject of rulings, as well as on the part of the ordinary judiciary, the Italian Constitutional Court, the European Court of Justice (ECJ) and the European Convention on Human Rights (ECHR), which has condemned the Italian State for the absolute inability to identify and implement suitable solutions to ensure adequate and effective protection of social rights and the environment.

With the Cordella ruling, the European Court of Human Rights recognized the violation of the right to private life (Article 8 ECHR) and the right to an effective remedy (Article 13 ECHR) of the inhabitants in the areas next to the steel plants.

As a consequence, the first section of the ECHR, with a sentence of 5 May 2022, condemned Italy for violating Articles 8 and 13 of the ECHR, which protect the right to respect for private life. The applicants, residing in Taranto and employed at that company, complained that the State had not taken legal and regulatory measures to protect their health and the environment and did not provide them with information on pollution and the related risks to their health. The European Court of Human Rights has yet again ascertained the persistence of the violations – already ascertained in the Cordella judgment – because the Italian authorities have omitted and persist in omitting the adoption of measures in order to protect the health of citizens from the harmful effects of noxious emissions from the steel industry and to implement effective remedies in order to obtain the reclamation of the area. The opinion of the Court is that the Italian authorities are not taking any action in order to solve the problem and thus extending this situation of impasse in the management of the environmental issue with respect to the production activities of Taranto. At the same time, this situation of serious environmental pollution persists, endangering not only the health of the applicants but more generally that of the entire population residing in the neighbouring areas.

The Court also found that the execution procedure of the aforementioned Cordella judgment is still pending before the Committee of Ministers of the Council of Europe which complained about the absence of information on the part of the Italian government regarding the implementation of the environmental plan, an element considered essential by the European Court so that the steel plant can operate without presenting health risks.

Finally, the Court reiterated the urgency of adopting the remediation measures and implementation of the environmental plan approved by the national authorities in order to safeguard the environment and the health of citizens.

8 THE INSTRUMENTS OF REGULATION AND THEIR EFFECTIVENESS

What the impact of climate change requires from international sources is that the link of reciprocity between environmental sustainability and sustainability of work – established in the socio-economic literature on the origins and on the (hypothetical) decline of industrial capitalism[38] – begins to find a response in the political agendas in order to be justified and developed, also on a legal level in terms of responsibility and planning for the future. Therefore, the second critical aspect concerns the instruments of regulation and their effectiveness. On several occasions, the European Commission has specified that '*at the heart of the Green Deal are people*' and that '*the European pillar will guide interventions aimed at ensuring that no one is excluded from this process*'. This is to highlight that in order to achieve the objective of the economic and social component of the transition, it will be a priority to combine social equity, sustainability and economic growth, which 'will be dissociated from the use of resources'.

However, although such a statement of principle is revolutionary, the tools intended to actualize these rulings lead to the risk of making it remain on paper.

One of the first tools that the Green Deal project has activated to monitor the green transition process on the part of the Member States is the Open method of coordination. However, such an approach characterized by the adoption of soft-law acts bears strengths and weaknesses: most Member States, in fact, are often unable to spontaneously implement EU recommendations, especially when this requires important economic and social reforms capable of affecting consolidated national interests. The progressive deterioration of public finances in many countries, as well as the disappointing results in the implementation of the major European plans for economic and social progress (think of the 'Lisbon Strategy' or 'Europe 2020'), have already shown the limits of such a method of coordination based essentially on non-binding instruments and peer comparison.

A further risk factor on the effectiveness of the Open method of coordination concerns the confusion caused by the proliferation of supervisory rules and procedures. Taking into consideration the issue of environmental protection, there are several governance tools at the European and international levels which Member States have decided to submit to: from the 'Europe 2020' strategy to national plans for climate action and energy, from long-term national strategies under the Paris agreement to river basin management plans, from the implementation of the directives on the conservation of natural habitats to the strategic plans of the common agricultural policy. The overlapping of rules and commitments has made it very difficult for Member States to organize coherent and effective action to achieve environmental protection objectives. Conversely, the hypertrophy of the discipline and the fragmentation of the procedures managed by different parties have made it hard to effectively stigmatize the breaches on the part of national authorities as well as to take sufficient measures to tackle them.

38. *See* W. Streeck, *How Will Capitalism End?*, in *New Left Review*, 2014, 87, p. 50.

In order to overcome these structural problems, the strategy could be for governments to evaluate some reforms of the environmental governance model. For example, an interesting approach could be that of adopting the so-called Closed method of coordination based on the assumption of legally binding obligations by the Member States and, more importantly, based on the use of coercive tools in case of violations (as it has recently happened in the framework of the strengthening of the preventive supervision of public budgets in the framework of economic governance).

The rationalization and reasoned unification of legal instruments could also facilitate the management of the green transition: amortizing the risk deriving from the overlapping of procedures and environmental policy commitments represent a useful tool especially in the face of the various and different procedures provided for by the EU governance of energy and climate action governed by Regulation (EU) no. 2018/1999.

Finally, the methodological orientation behind all European action appears even more critical. The approach that has emerged so far, in fact, is mostly focused on what the economic crisis produces as an environmental impact. But analysing the climate crisis only from the point of view of the impact on the environment as an abstract concept is scientifically problematic. As a matter of fact, this perspective considers the natural environment as an abstract and *ex se* existing element, and not as a whole with the living environment and the working environment. With such a distinction, we face a partial, non-resolving perspective of a problem that deserves to be treated as a unit, devoid of ideological and irremediably abstract statements.

The ongoing ecological transition, as we know, does not only involve a mere rise in temperatures with a probable crisis of manpower and/or the prosperity of certain sectors or technologies. It will be an epochal and transversal transformation, in intensity and speed, '*similar in nature to the shift from horse-drawn to steam and then electric power*'. It will affect all the subjects of industrial relations, as well as all sectors of the market as a whole, and will have substantial effects on the quantity and composition of the workforce, as well as on the way of perceiving work and, therefore, labour law.

Such a process cannot be faced with only a single imperative (to prevent the Earth's temperature from rising by more than 2°C) and timid and generic protection of social rights through provisions that risk remaining only principles, without leading to, on the contrary, a symbiotic and organic connection between the two spheres.

Rather, European action should be built on a more sensitive and attentive labour law perspective that takes into account the incisive legal and social-economic implications, involving all the actors concerned, with a method that labour law has more than once proved effective.

In fact, it will be necessary to understand that work, understood as a productive activity, is the most important instrument of alteration of nature by humans, in an ever more affecting way along with the progress of technique and technologies and with the market expansion. The sector of the legal system that studies individual labour relations and trade union relations not only can but must play a greater role in the debate on the climate crisis.

9 FINAL REMARKS

'Work', understood as a productive activity, is the humans' most important tool for altering Nature. People do not 'humanize' Nature through their own work. As Hans Jonas wrote, the idea of humanization of Nature is a hypocritical euphemism to designate its total submission on the part of humans.[39] In an increasingly penetrating way, with the progress of technique and technologies and with the expansion of markets, work increasingly comes into conflict with Nature. However, at the same time, human work can represent the keystone for opening a new chapter in the difficult and conflictual relationship between man and the Earth. However, in order for work to play a new and positive role within this dialectic, people must 'humanize themselves' and, in doing so, 'naturalize' Nature.[40] In this way, they both will simultaneously be freed from their alienation on the part of humans. In this perspective of human responsibility towards Nature, it is precisely work – which is the main poietic activity of mankind – that can bring about a decisive change. Labour law, that is the sector of the legal system that studies the regulation of individual employment relationships and union relations not only can, but absolutely must, assume a greater role in the debate on the climate crisis and move towards a new eco-friendly labour paradigm.

To this end, it will be necessary to legislate with a view to overcoming, on the level of concepts as well as in actuality, the first 'stumbling block' that traditionally characterizes the subject: the discrepancy (or better, *the conflict*) between work and the environment. At the cost of a decisive simplification, this can be summed up in the consideration according to which, from the industrial revolution onward, the acquisition and transformation – in a word: the exploitation – of natural resources in the field of production represents one of the prerequisites for economic development and the creation of wealth that derives from it, and such wealth is, in turn, shared more or less unequally between the parties to the industrial conflict. More than anything else, it will be a matter of understanding why, in cases where the protection of nature interferes with the performance of production activities, workers and union organizations sometimes get in the way (as in the ILVA case): they defend not the economic initiative of the company or a sort of freedom to pollute but the right to sustenance through work, sometimes of entire local communities.[41]

But human work, occupation, and interest in production as a precondition of social citizenship can no longer be indifferent to Nature and humans can no longer fail to assume full responsibility towards the Earth where they live. It is time for humans to recognize the *autonomous status of nature in labour law* as well. If not for Nature, for the love of the remote, for the generations to come.

39. H. Jonas, *Das Prinzip Verantwortung, Insel Verlag*, Frankfurt am Main, 1979.
40. H. Jonas, *Das Prinzip Verantwortung, Insel Verlag*, Frankfurt am Main, 1979.
41. *See* S. Barca, *Greening the Job: Trade Unions, Climate Change and the Political Ecology of Labour*, in *The International Handbook of Political Ecology*, ed by L.R. Bryant, Edward Elgar Publishing, 2015, p. 387; A. Rosemberg, *'No Jobs on a Dead Planet': The International Trade Union Movement and Just Transition*, in *Just Transitions. Social Justice in the Shift Towards a Low-Carbon World*, ed by E. Morena, D. Krause, D. Stevis, Pluto Press, 2020, p. 32.

Part I Environmental Humanities, Labour Law and Economy: An Interdisciplinary Dialogue

CHAPTER 1

The Impact of the Green Transition on Employment, Labour Law and Industrial Relations

Tiziano Treu

1 THE IMPORTANCE AND THE CHALLENGES OF THE GREEN TRANSITION

The decision to devote an international seminar in Venice to the challenges of climate change to labour law and labour policies is very timely, given the dramatic urgency to adopt climate policies and actions needed for the very survival of the planet. The seminar is particularly important because it draws the attention, so far insufficient, of our discipline to the implications of climate change for the world of work and indeed for our future destinies.

This lack of attention is not limited to our area of studies but is common to other social sciences and has been shared until recently also by the main representative social actors, whose primary preoccupation has been to bargain (only) about the results of growth and in particular about its distribution.

This has been true also for the trade unions, whose action has rarely raised issues concerning the scope and quality of production. When this has been done, it was for verifying the impact of production and of the economy on the conditions of work and not on the safeguarding of the environment.

Even when the international agenda[1] and the new course of the European Commission[2] have highlighted the objective of sustainability as a central guideline for

1. United Nations Development Programme, *The SDGS in Action. Sustainable Development Goals* (*see*_undp.org); ASVIS, *L'Unione europea e gli obiettivi di sviluppo sostenibile* (cfr. www.asvis.it). Communication from the Commission, *A strong Social Europe, for just transitions*, Bruxelles, 14

our future public and private policies, the attention of the social parties and of most experts has been on the social aspects of sustainability, and (sometimes) on how to find a possible compromise between economic and social sustainability.

The reasons for the environment have been by and large disregarded or marginalised until recently.

The fact of the matter is that including respect for the environment in the essence of sustainability implies drastic changes in the structures of our productive and economic systems which have been prevailing during the industrial era for a century.

The impact of the green transition on our industrial activities is already creating strong tensions among the social parties and difficulties of the public powers which are asked to sustain massive processes of enterprises restructuring and the relocation of thousands of workers.

Some observers and trade unions are inclined to argue that the reasons for the environment are incompatible with those of employment. In any case, the targets fixed by the European authorities with the Green Deal and the objective fit for 55 are considered by many too ambitious and possibly disruptive of the European industrial system, particularly in countries like Germany and Italy.

A most important challenge for the policymakers of our countries is to provide positive evidence that the objectives and practices of the green transition can be reconciled with the safeguard of production and of employment

.Even more important is to demonstrate that the new model of production envisaged by the Next Generation EU (NGEU),[3] based on the twin transitions of green and digital, may not only promote a more sustained growth but also be favourable to a better quality both of the environment and of employment. The institutions responsible for social policies and the collective parties should be the first drivers in showing that quality of work and quality of development are reciprocally functional.

2 CHANGING THE EXISTING ECONOMIC STRUCTURES FOR SUSTAINABLE DEVELOPMENT

The ambitious targets set by the European programs Indeed the NGEU is based on this assumption, namely that the three dimensions of sustainability, economic, social and environmental, can go together and can reinforce each other.

The investments and the reforms provided by the National recovery and resilience plans following the NGEU are in fact finalised to support Member States in pursuing these ambitious and interconnected objectives.

The first implementation of these plans however has proved quite difficult not only due to the complexity and the tight schedule fixed for the execution of the various

January 2020, COM (2020) 14 final; SDG Watch Europe, *Manifesto for a Sustainable Europe for its Citizen. The need for action* (sdgwatcheurope.or).

2. Comunicazione della Commissione, *Il Green Deal europeo*, Bruxelles, 11 December 2019, COM (2019)640 final.
3. Regolamento UE 2021/241 del Parlamento Europeo e del Consiglio del 12 febbraio 2021 che istituisce il dispositivo per la ripresa e la resilienza. F. Fabbrini, *Next generation EU. Il futuro di Europa e Italia dopo la pandemia*, Bologna, il Mulino, 2022.

projects but also because the pursuance of the digital and the green transition requires a drastic change of most economic and industrial practices prevailing in the industrial era.[4]

This process of change will prove particularly difficult in the short period because its introduction will produce shocks in many existing productions, while alternative solutions are not immediately available. That is why a long-term perspective will have to be taken by both public authorities and social parties in implementing the various aspects of the transitions in order to reduce the negative impact of this time gap.

Time will be necessary to implement the combination of innovative policies necessary to adapt the industrial structures to the new scenario and to promote the welfare measures needed to compensate for the damages caused during the transition to the workers.

The implications of these changes are wide-ranging and not yet fully understood by the public and private actors who must implement them.

The enterprises are requested to change their governance and strategies in order to make them consistent with the objectives of sustainable development and to enable them to contribute to their attainment, in particular to the prevention and the mitigation of the negative environmental impact of the traditional activities.

Specific European guidelines and proposed directives require that companies report their plans to ensure that these objectives are being pursued. Moreover, companies active in the international markets are asked to control not only their operations but also those of the subsidiaries and units of their supply chains to minimise the adverse impact on the environment and on human rights.

These requirements go beyond the traditional contents attributed to corporate social responsibility and are being monitored by national and European authorities in order to prevent greenwashing practices.

Moreover, the European regulations concerning the implementation of the National recovery plans (2020/852 Article 17) have provided even more rigorous conditions on the activities financed with the NGEU funds.

3 THE PRINCIPLE NOT SIGNIFICANT HARM AND POSITIVE CONTRIBUTIONS TO A JUST TRANSITION

All these activities must respect, as a major condition for receiving the funds, the principle do not significant harm (DNSH) i.e., do not affect negatively the status of the environment and guarantee basic compliance to the European green strategy.

Respect for this principle is required for all projects under the National recovery plans. The conformity to it must be evaluated in advance by the public institutions responsible for the projects, but it will impose obligations on all enterprises implementing the activities.

4. The first experience is analysed and commented on the discussions of the partnership table of social parties and organised civil society: T. Treu, *Relazione del coordinatore del Tavolo permanente per il partenariato economico, sociale e territoriale*, 26 agosto 2022.

Even though the impact of this requirement is yet to be fully evaluated, its implementation appears to be very complicated and might create quite a few difficulties in company practices.

A critical issue will be how to balance the respect of the DNSH principle with normal activities and the freedom of action of private business

A recent document of the ILO,[5] based on extensive research, has stated that the conduct of enterprises is crucial to the natural environment and for a just transition and has indicated how their conduct can positively contribute to this end.

Most areas of the enterprise strategy and organisation will have to be changed: from the use of renewable energy and sustainable raw materials to the adoption of technologies capable to produce more with the same level of input, to greening the places of work and promoting less consumption of resources and sustainable transportation.

The research indicates that a large majority of enterprises have already taken some initiative in this direction, but more must be done, particularly by Small Medium Enterprises (SMEs), in order to adopt a systematic long-term approach to the green strategy, particularly by SMEs.

This new approach is in fact present in many NGEU projects and in the available resources which are aimed at supporting the adoption of green practices in production and services.

These practices, together with the adoption of digital technologies, will imply radical changes in many aspects of employment relations, individual and collective: from the organisation of work to its evaluation and reward systems, to the prevention and safeguarding of health and safety.

This opens a new area of research for both practitioners and experts in industrial relations, including labour law scholars.

We are challenged to understand which kind of innovations the new green and digital environment of production will introduce in the design and contents of employment: a new context (*terra incognita*) where our acquired categories will not be sufficient and might possibly be misleading.

4 THE IMPACT OF THE GREEN DEAL ON THE QUANTITY AND QUALITY OF WORK

So far the prevailing attention of labour lawyers has been devoted to the impact of the digital platform on the legal qualification of employment.

To this question is addressed the proposed European directive on platform work[6] which establishes a presumption of subordination for those employment relations which present some objective characters, mostly in line with those adopted to the same end by many courts of our states.

But the impact is far more widespread, because both the digital and green transitions will greatly influence the future quantity and quality of work.

5. Greening enterprises 2022.
6. Eur. Commission dic. 9, 2021. Com (2021) 762 final.

On the first aspect, the opinions (mostly of the economists) and the forecast are uncertain, ranging from extreme pessimism to moderate optimism.

Some National recovery plans, including the Italian, are rather optimistic and estimate that their full implementation will contribute to a considerable increase in the rate of employment (in Italy 3.6%).

The ILO projections present a similar outlook and estimate that by 2030 the green transition will greatly affect employment with approximately 25 million new jobs created and over 7 million present jobs disappearing

All estimates indicate that the transition will greatly influence the quality of employment. Even though the characteristics relevant to the qualification of green jobs are variously appreciated by the national labour statistics and experts, most of them will require skills quite different from those prevailing in the traditional economy.

According to Italian estimates shared between CNEL and the information system of the chambers of commerce a great majority of future jobs (60%) will require green skills of an average level and 37% at a high level.[7]

The ILO estimates[8] underline the great need for new skill in order to tap into the job opportunities offered by the green transition and the urgency to face with appropriate policies, the serious skill shortage.

The presence of green jobs will be distributed, although unevenly, in many sectors including traditional industries and constructions; urban renewal and energy efficiency of public and private buildings will be a major source of them. But similar new skills will be needed also in many service sectors, beginning with services of personal care.

Meeting these new needs will require not only major investments in education and in continuous training but also a renewal of their contents aimed at linking them to the needs emerging from the implementation of the two transitions.[9]

According to a recent Recommendation of the European Council (14.1. 2022, COM 2022 final), 'learning for environmental sustainability' and integrating the principles of environmental sustainability in all the programs and processes of education and training is essential to develop the skills and abilities necessary to support the green transition.

This recommendation is the need for a coherent approach to the competences skills and attitudes of people for promoting sustainability.

5 CONTINUOUS TRAINING AND ACTIVE LABOUR POLICY TO MANAGE THE TRANSITIONS

Moreover, these transitions will change the geography of the economy with the rapid growth of new sectors and the decline of others, which will require relocation of

7. C. Gagliardi, C. Lucifora, *Occupazione e PNRR. Cambiamenti e mismacth nella struttura dell'occupazione*, Cnel, Rapporto sul mercato del lavoro, 2022, p. 325.
8. ILO Conference, *Shaping skills and lifelong learning for the future of work*, 109th Session, 2021.
9. ILO, *Skills for a Greener Future: Challenges and Enabling Factors to Achieve a Just Transition*, Geneva, 2019; Cedefop, *Understanding technological change and skill needs: skills surveys and skills forecasting*, Cedefop practical guide 1, Luxembourg 2021.

material and human resources of great dimensions and consequently an unprecedented challenge to our systems of training and active labour policies.

The Italian National recovery plan devotes significant resources to support both the investment in training and economic assistance to the displaced employees. But the dimension and novelty of the challenge will require not only more economic resources but new institutions dedicated to finalising the new educational and labour policies to successfully manage the transitions. This is particularly the case in Italy where the existing instruments of active labour policies have proved inadequate also to perform their ordinary functions The National plans assign to the State and the local governments the major responsibility for the management of the various projects. At the same time the European regulation (2021/241, Article 18), calls for a true and continuous involvement of the social parties and of the organised society in their implementation.

The activities needed for this implementation are so numerous and decentralised in the various sectors and territories that the success of the plan will depend on the mobilisation and common efforts of all the actors, private and private, of the country.

In particular, this is true for the innovation and management of active labour policies and continuous training which are the main instruments necessary to support the transitions of both workers and enterprises.

The impact of the two transitions on the labour market has destabilised the traditional relationship between the jobs and skills required by the enterprises and the competences traditionally offered by the school system.

This disconnection has dramatised the job skill mismatch and challenged the firms to reassess their recruiting and training programs, with or without agreement with the unions, with special attention to filling the gaps in digital and green skills.[10]

In order to prevent this mismatch structural measures are needed. One major project supported by the Italian national recovery plan aims at reinforcing the system of school guidance for better informing and directing young students in the choices of their studies.

The Italian unions' confederations and the central organisations of employers seem to have perceived the importance of these issues. A few national and decentralised agreements have set up bilateral bodies aimed at organising the reskilling of employees and at supporting their reallocation.[11]

However, the diffusion of these initiatives is still limited, whereas the dimension of the challenge would require a general involvement of the social parties together with the public authorities in the elaboration and management of training and active labour policies.

10. ILO reports indicate that in spite of recent progress the information on demand and supply for green jobs skills and the capacity to anticipate skills needs are still insufficient (*see* the paper by G. Casale in the seminar).
11. Extensive information about collective agreements on the various issues can be found in the periodical reports of Cnel, *Mercato del lavoro e contrattazione collettiva,* www.cnel.it., and ADAPT, *Rapporto sulla contrattazione.*

6 GREENING THE ORGANISATIONS

A most important area of common concern of both management and employees' representative is how to adapt to the green and digital environment in the organisation of business and of work prevailing in the industrial tradition.

As indicated in the ILO document,[12] changes will have to be introduced in most aspects of enterprise life, from the greening of the workplaces to the dematerialisation of many processes to the alteration of the very sense of time and place consequent to the use of telework.A major contribution to the greening of enterprises may come from the diffused use of the various forms of remote working allowed by digital technologies.

Intelligent work practices experimented with in many firms, usually following union-management agreements, have shown that this type of work particularly when implemented in a hybrid combination of activities partly remote and partly in presence, may favour not only a better work-life balance but also a more productive use of time and a reduction of energy consumption.

These positive results are most likely to materialise in firms which have a wider combination of innovative practices, concerning the organisation of work, investments in continuous training and labour mobility, and effective involvement of workers in the management of these issues.

Extensive research shows a possible positive impact of working time organisation on the sustainability of both social and environmental productive processes but warns that the outcome of these work patterns is not to be taken for granted and depends on the general management of employment relations in the enterprise.[13]

Improvements in these processes have been made possible by quite a few collective agreements signed, particularly at the enterprise level, which have adopted various regimes of flexible working time, possibly combined with the reduction of working hours. These win-win combinations can be maximised if the new regimes of work are extended to the majority of firms and connected with a parallel renovation of the systems of transportation and of city planning.

The regulation of this new set of issues is already present not only in some enterprise-wide collective agreements but also in some territorial accords between the social parties with the participation of local governments which tackle the wider implications of remote working in the external environment.[14]

The use of remote working presents uncertain traits and impacts both the conditions of employment and the management of the firms. For this reason, it is advisable to leave the regulation of its various aspects to collective agreements or, as proposed by the Italian Act 81/2017, to a combination of collective and individual contracts.

At least in this still experimental phase, the legislative intervention could more appropriately be limited to regulating some basic rights like that of disconnection and

12. ILO, *Greening enterprises*, quoted.
13. *See also* the remarks in the papers by M. Weiss and by F. Hendrick, in this seminar.
14. *See* the Reports of Cnel and Adapt, quoted.

the aspects of prevention and safeguarding of health and safety of workers operating in the variable spaces and context of remote digital activities.

7 HEALTH AND SAFETY IN THE WORK PLACES AND IN THE ENVIRONMENT: ONE HEALTH

The legislation on these latter issues has to face an aspect which has been barely considered so far, namely the connections between the quality and the risks of the workplace and the external environment.

The increased permeability allowed by technologies between the borders of the firm and the external space has made more clear than ever the importance of these connections, in both directions. It has shown that the negative consequences of dangerous and unhealthy conditions of work on the environment are more widespread than in the extreme cases of ecological disasters reported in many countries of the world (from Chernobyl to Fukushima) and consequently must be considered in the basic labour law regulation of the matter.

On the other direction, the experience of the COVID pandemic has given renewed evidence that the pollution of the environment not only threatens the health of the population, particularly of the weakest members, but may also endanger the workers by worsening their personal conditions and reducing their resistance to the conditions and burdens of work.

The importance of these bidirectional connections is signalled in the international documents in particular of the ILO report quoted by Hendricks, which remind us that workplace well-being relates to all aspects of working life, from the quality and safety of the physical place to the entire working environment.[15]

Even so, the implications for policy action have yet to be fully explored. A prerequisite in guiding this research should be to abandon the traditional approach still prevailing in our culture and legal systems which tends to maintain the separation between workplace and external regulations: a first challenge to this approach would be to leave the strict definition of the legal notion of professional risk and extend it to consider more general risks to which all persons who work are exposed

8 IMPACT ON THE EVALUATION AND REWARD OF WORK

The changes promoted by the various aspects of 'greening the enterprise' mentioned so far should have direct implications on the systems of evaluation and reward of the employees.

Innovations in both areas are present in some innovative management practices and collective agreements, but good examples are far from prevailing in actual practice.

15. ILO, *Workplace well being*, 2009; *see also European Agency for safety and health at work; creating a positive work environment*, ISSN, 1831 - 9351, 2013.

The systems of job classification adopted by firms and collective agreements have been rather resistant to innovation; recent agreements like that of the Italian metal-working industry, have been concentrated on reshaping the roles of the different categories of employees with the intent to respond to the need of flexibility and of internal mobility, without specific concern for environmental implications. But if the changes in the organisation of work mentioned above must be finalised to environmental improvements and the employees are requested to contribute to this end, this should have some impact on the classification and evaluation of the different jobs.

These changes and improvements may be reflected not only in the structure of basic wages but also and possibly more directly in the various systems of incentives and payments by result.

In the previous years, the number and quantitative importance of these payments by result, often connected with welfare benefits, have greatly increased, also due to the fiscal incentives that many legislators including the Italians have introduced to support them.

The Italian legislation[16] has distributed the incentives to these pay systems and to welfare benefits in a rather undifferentiated way, which has dispersed resources and reduced their impact.

In order to be consistent with the paradigm of sustainability the reward systems should be more selective and their emphasis should also move away from the traditional criteria of material productivity so as to give more weight to the indicators proposed by the sustainability agenda 2030 and to the individual and collective contributions that employees give to them.

9 CONCLUDING REMARKS

A reflexive analysis of the transformations undergoing in present times should draw our attention to some key points useful for future action.

First, it demands to be fully aware of the challenge posed by the two transitions to our economic and social institutions and of the need to change not only specific policies and regulations but the basic orientation of our development in line with the complex parameters of sustainability (Sustainable development goals (SDG) of the 2030 Agenda).

This awareness should sustain a comprehensive approach to future policy-making finalised to allow the transitions to be just and to mobilise to this end all public and private actors of our countries.

The public institutions which have a major responsibility in guiding the transitions together with the social parties and organised society which are requested to participate in this renovation of public policies must face some basic issues which have been for long eluded: namely what and how to produce, what and how to consume, in order to be consistent with the three dimensions of sustainable development.

16. Beginning with the budget law for 2016 (Act 208/2015) subsequently confirmed until the last (Act 197/2022) which has increased these tax incentives.

The two transitions have great technical and economic implications but are also a transformative force which is influencing our whole life and in perspective even our culture and mindset.

For this reason, the success and the very justice of the transitions will require not only comprehensive policies and regulations, implemented by coordinated efforts of all the public and social actors but also consistent changes in the priorities, approach and strategies of the same actors.

In short, the new paradigms of development and their implications for the justice of the transitions must be internalised by the actors to become effective.

CHAPTER 2
Just Ecological Transition and Inequalities*

Marzia Barbera

1 A NEW DIMENSION OF RESPONSIBILITY

The concept of a just ecological transition is a relatively new concept for labour law. With the worsening of the climate crisis, the concept has become more familiar but still needs to be explored, if only because a just transition means different things to different people. There is not much time to do this because the next decade will be crucial for tackling climate change.

When we talk about complex systems such as the biosphere, the changes that concern them are not achieved in progressive steps but in leaps. This means that, at a certain point, such systems can lose their equilibrium and, at the tipping point, fall towards a new condition, one that is qualitatively different. Hence the importance of acting before a trajectory of no return is triggered.

In other fields of scientific, economic and legal knowledge, reflection on these issues – on the links between decarbonization policies, market regulation, institutional structures and public policies – has been underway for some time. However, as mentioned, these issues have only recently begun to be discussed among labour lawyers.

Indeed, the traditional approach of labour lawyers has been to leave the issues related to the natural environment to environmental law scholars, while they dealt with the artificial environment constituted by the workplace. Conversely, the environmentalists left the task of taking care of occupational health and safety to labour lawyers.[1] Today the importance of the subject is no longer underestimated, driven by

* An extended version of this chapter has been published on the review *Giornale di diritto del lavoro e di relazioni industriali*, 2022, pp 339-357.

1. Tomassetti P., *Diritto del lavoro e ambiente*. Bergamo: Adapt University Press 2018, 36; Doorey D., Just Transitions Law: Putting Labour Law to Work on Climate Change. *Journal of Environmental Law and Practice*: 2017, 201 ff.

dramatic and inescapable transformations, so much so that it has been written that, while '(t)he twentieth century was the era of the "social question", the twenty-first century is the era of the new "geo-eco-social" question'.[2]

In the meantime, however, there has been a gradual approach to the issues of environmental sustainability and to the prevention techniques on which the legal protection of the natural environment is based, namely the principles of prevention and precaution, if only because these principles have contributed to strengthening the safety of the working environment.

Both the principle of sustainability and the principles of prevention and precaution have the characteristic of projecting themselves into a future temporal dimension, which also concerns the generations to come. It is an anticipatory rationale, which revolves around the problem of how to deal with the management of ecological risk for the future. This rationale differs from the 'retrospective and disillusioned gaze', with which the links between labour law and the environment were looked at by labour law.[3]

At the end of the 1970s, the philosopher Hans Jonas was among the first scholars to think of individual and collective responsibility in terms of a new forward-thinking ethics that centres not only on the artificial social institutions created by men but on nature itself.[4]

Traditional 'anthropocentric' ethics was interested in current circumstances, the *now* and the *here*. The spatial horizon included the places where people met their peers, as friends or as enemies. The required knowledge was limited to the circumstances in which the action took place: 'the short lever of human power did not require the long lever of predictive knowledge'.[5] It is the irreversibility of the changes produced by modern technology and their cumulativeness that continually forces us to face unprecedented situations, that makes accumulated knowledge vain and requires predictive knowledge, which is the basis of the principles of sustainability and precaution.

Modern technology has also introduced a new dimension of responsibility.

To the extent that, with the triumph of *homo faber*, the biosphere has also entered the domain of mankind, it now makes a moral claim to be preserved and cared for, on the basis of its own right. The transformation of human action thus alters politics; the boundary between *polis* and nature is erased. If it ever really existed, one may add. The great rift between nature and society, between nature and culture, on which the modern representation of the world has been built for at least three centuries, has been shattered, as Bruno Latour writes,[6] in the face of the proliferation of hybrids, of phenomena such as the hole in the ozone layer or the greenhouse effect that are human because they are of our making and are natural because they obey universal laws.

2. Perulli A., Speziale V., *Dieci tesi sul diritto del lavoro.* Bologna: Il Mulino, 2022, 146.
3. Tomassetti, 2018, 13.
4. Jonas H., *Il principio di responsabilità.* Torino: Einaudi., 2009.
5. Jonas, 2009, 8-9.
6. Latour B., *Non siamo mai stati moderni.* Milano: elèuthera, 2009.

Issues that had never been the subject of legislation have now become so in order to make it possible to have a world for future generations. The presence of humanity in the world, which before was an indisputable fact, now imposes a duty, that of ensuring the conditions for its survival. From a legal point of view, this duty is based on the principle of solidarity, enshrined in Article 2 of the Italian Constitution.

It is a duty that primarily concerns public authorities but which also concerns private agents, both as individuals and as social communities. It is not just a question of public policies and funds. A shared commitment on the part of citizens, consumers, workers, trade unions and businesses is required for a paradigm shift away from the model of economic and social development of the recent decades.[7]

The foundation of this new ethics of responsibility, in Jonas's view, rather than in Bloch's 'principle of hope' or Anders's 'principle of despair', is to be found in the 'heuristics of fear'. As long as the danger is unknown, no one knows what to safeguard and why. Knowing this arises from the perception of what it is necessary to avoid: '(w)e only know what is at stake if we know that it is at stake'. To know this, our conscience must consult our fears before our desires, and although what is feared is not necessarily what is actually to be feared, and although the heuristics of fear does not necessarily tell us something about the opposite of evil, about the good, and it is not, therefore, the last word on the search for the good, nevertheless it is an extremely useful first word (pages 35, 36). *In dubio pro malo* – when evil is projected into a future that is still uncertain, we should consider, operating a reversal of Cartesian doubt, what is so uncertain as possible. Adopting this attitude allows us not to consider human existence a stake. As a mark of this responsibility for what will be, of this duty towards future generations, caution becomes the core of moral action.

This idea of our duties towards future generations and, correspondingly, of the rights of those generations towards us contrasts with the classical idea of rights, which presupposes that the holder of rights already exists[8] and finds an echo in the ethics of caring for one's children, from which the dimension of reciprocity is absent. The same idea has also now taken on a constitutional form in the Italian legal system with the modification of Article 9 of the Constitution which in the third paragraph now states that the Republic '(p)rotects the environment, biodiversity and ecosystems, also in the interest of future generations'.

The principle of responsibility has taken on a greater value as the uncertainty and probability that Jonas spoke of 50 years ago have become more real.

In 2009, the journal *Ecology and Society* published an article in which 29 experts in Earth science and sustainability science, after identifying the processes that threatened the stability and resilience of the Earth system, proposed, for each of them, quantitative limits within which the Earth system can continue to maintain itself within the conditions that characterized the Holocene, i.e., the conditions that allowed the

7. Among the models of sustainable development proposed in the recent Italian labour law debate *see* Caruso B., Del Punta R., Treu T. (eds.), *Il diritto del lavoro e la grande trasformazione. Valori, attori, regolazione*. Bologna: Il Mulino, 2020, which try to hold together environmental, social and economic sustainability. On the relationship between labour law and sustainable development *see* Cagnin V., *Diritto del lavoro e sviluppo sostenibile*. Milano: Wolters Kluwer- Cedam, 2018.
8. *See* Monterossi M.W., *L'orizzonte intergenerazionale del diritto civile*. Pisa: ETS, 2020, 111 ff.

birth and development of human society. Of the nine interconnected planetary limits identified, the most critical are those related to climate change and biosphere integrity. Since the production of carbon now exceeds the absorption capacity and since, as a result, the planet's temperature has risen by more than one degree above pre-industrial values, the Earth has already crossed the planetary boundary of climate change: we are already beyond the Holocene. Similarly, the loss of biosphere integrity, with the reduction of species diversity, has already exceeded planetary boundaries in many cases. For example, the decline in the rate of insect diversity is such that it could lead to the extinction of 40 % of all species in the world in the next few decades,[9] a prospect that endangers not only the natural environment but also the man-made environment, primarily the agricultural one.

While it is difficult to predict what could be the tipping point beyond which an abrupt change in social systems, induced by the climate and biodiversity crisis, is triggered, what is certain is that all planetary limits are connected to the stability of human societies, influencing social and economic conditions and worsening existing inequalities.

2 WHAT JUST TRANSITION ARE WE TALKING ABOUT?

If we were to link the idea of a just ecological transition to the classical principles of sustainability and precaution, we could say that a just transition replaces their anticipatory rationale of risk under conditions of uncertainty with the rationale of a new ecological order, in which the main and irreversible risks must potentially be eliminated. These range from managing disequilibrium to the transition to a new equilibrium, in which the massive changes required in terms of decarbonization, creation of new transportation systems, agricultural and food policies, development of a circular economy, disappearance of some jobs, creation of others, transformation of still other jobs, do not occur at the expense of working people and the most disadvantaged communities. A just transition, therefore, aims to overcome the binary logic of the historical opposition between environmental and labour policies and to achieve the transition to a post-carbon economy through a socially just process.

The term 'just transition' first appeared in labour politics in the early 1990s, following on the heels of the demands of the environmental movement and a sector of North American trade unionism in previous decades,[10] and translated into a call for the alignment of labour, social and environmental goals so as to protect those whose jobs, income and livelihoods are at risk as a result of climate policies. It took nearly two decades for it to become an established international policy tool, included in the Paris Agreement of 12 December 2015, which affirms the need to 'take into account the

9. Butera F.M., *Affrontare la complessità. Per governare la transizione ecologica.* Milano: Edizioni Ambiente, 2021, 119.
10. Stevis D. & Felli R. Global Labour Unions and Just Transition to a Green Economy. *International Environmental Agreements*: 2015, *29 ff*; Stevis. D., Morena M., Krause D., *The Genealogy and Contemporary Politics of Just Transition.* In Morena M., Krause D., Stevis D. (eds.), *Just transitions. Social Justice in the Shift towards a Low-Carbon World.* London: Pluto Press, 2020, 9; Centamore G., Una *just transition* per il diritto del lavoro. *Lavoro e diritto*: 2022, 129 ff.

imperatives of a just transition of the workforce and the creation of decent and quality work in accordance with nationally defined development priorities'. They were integrated in subsequent years into the United Nations (UN) climate conference declarations and the Organisation for Economic Co-operation and Development (OECD) strategies, adopted by leading climate change non-governmental organisations such as Greenpeace and the World Wildlife Fund (WWF) and transposed into the language and policies of the institutions of the European Union (EU).[11]

The alignment of trade union and environmentalist policies with the just transition strategy not only marks a departure from the old conflict that separated them but also gives an indication of the willingness of both coalitions to work towards a common language and common goals.

There are two key features of the demand for a just ecological transition. The first is that there should be, first and foremost, as mentioned above, a public and collective responsibility to facilitate and actively support a process of change that is in the common interest of all; the second is that the transition to a decarbonized and sustainable economy is not just 'another transition' to be carried out together with the other major transitions of our century (globalization and digitalization). The different processes are taking place in the same fields – economy, work, social welfare – and this requires a holistic approach. Rather than a single transition, we should speak of 'twin' transitions, which are all part of a sustainable development framework.[12]

In labour law terms, just transition refers first and foremost to the goal of decent, sustainable work for all and, as to how to get there, to a socially participatory process that involves workers, unions and affected communities, and one that 'leaves no one behind'. Hence the ILO's Guidelines for a Just Transition Towards Environmentally Sustainable Economies and Societies for All,[13] which state that sustainable development is only possible with the active involvement of the world of work and the strategy adopted by the (International Trade Union Confederation (ITUC) since the 2009 congress, aimed at 'having a chair' at the table of climate negotiations and gaining the support of local communities and institutions.[14]

The right transition implies a shared vision of the trajectories to be followed and the measures to be taken and includes macro, sectoral, and micro policies; objectives related to occupational health and safety, social protection, and professional development; active labour policies; adequate social safety nets to support labour replacement processes and the transition from one occupation to another; redistributive interventions ('polluter pays' principle); and, at the level of method, the participation of workers and other stakeholders involved.

11. European Commission, *The European Green Deal*, COM (2019) 640 final; Council, *Recommendation on ensuring a just transition towards climate neutrality*, 7 June 2022; European Parliament, *A strong social Europe for just transitions*, 2021/C 445/11.
12. Verdolini E., Belpietro C., Giusta transizione ecologica. L'impatto delle tecnologie digitali. *Giornale di diritto del lavoro e di relazioni industriali*: 2022, 205 ff.
13. International Labour Organization, *Climate Change and Labour: The need for a just transition:* Geneva, 2010.
14. Rosemberg A., 'No Jobs on a Dead Planet': The International Trade Union Movement and Just Transition. In Morena M., Krause D., Stevis D. (eds), *Just transitions. Social Justice in the Shift towards a Low-Carbon World.* London: Pluto Press, 2020, 32 ff.

On closer inspection, however, a strategy that appears to square the circle between the need for change and the need for social protection, and which seems bound to bring everyone into agreement, has some contradictory aspects and runs the risk of being manipulated and used opportunistically. The rhetoric of a just transition, for example, was fully espoused by the Polish government at the 2018 UN Climate Conference (COP 25), but mainly with the aim of slowing down, at the domestic level, the process of reducing the use of energy produced from coal, which plays a primary role in the local economy. Moreover, the demands that lie under the umbrella of a just transition range from creating jobs in the green economy to more radical critiques of capitalist development and the rejection of market-driven solutions.[15]

The focus above all on the procedural steps towards a just transition, on the recognition and voice of the stakeholders involved, without a contextual redefinition of their interests; the redistributive but non-corrective character of the 'polluter pays' principle; the vagueness of the concept of justice underlying the adjective 'just' are some of the other critical aspects of this strategy. Is it possible to talk about justice in transition without asking what model of justice we are actually talking about?

We can put forward some answers to this difficult question by analysing the relationship between the climate crisis and inequalities.

3 THE RELATIONSHIP BETWEEN CLIMATE CHANGE AND INEQUALITIES

Some time ago, Tiziano Treu observed that traditionally labour law, being primarily concerned with the protection of workers and the distribution of income, has essentially been uninterested in the type of growth, assuming it to be a linear and self-sustaining process.[16] It is now clear that the limits to the sustainability of growth are both environmental limits and social ones. While, in the discussions on the climate crisis, attention initially focused on the physical effects of climate change, in the next phase, it shifted to the social effects and, in particular, to the relationship between climate change and inequalities.

These inequalities are first of all geographical and concern the division between underdeveloped and developing and low-income countries, on the one hand, and developed and high-income countries, on the other. In general, the former, for geographical and historical reasons, are more exposed than the latter to the negative effects of climate change. They are more susceptible to the harm caused by climate change and also have less capacity to cope and recover. As a result, climate change is worsening the relative position of low-income countries, thereby exacerbating inequality among nations.

Second, climate change is increasing poverty through its effects on agriculture, malnutrition, water supply and health.

15. Barca S., Greening the Job: Trade Unions, Climate Change and the Political Ecology of Labour. In Bryant R.L. (ed.), *International Book of Political Ecology*. London: Edward Elgar, 2015, 392.
16. Treu T., Labour Law and Sustainable Development. *WP CSDLE 'Massimo D'Antona'.INT*:, 130/2016, 2016, 2.

Finally, climate change weighs differently on social groups and individuals, worsening inequalities in conditions. As the IPCC's (UN *Intergovernmental Panel on Climate Change*) periodic reports show,[17] not only do the effects of the climate crisis tend to be regressive, hitting the poor more than the rich, but they also particularly affect people who suffer discrimination based on gender, age, race, social class, ethnicity or disability and in turn generate further discrimination against them. Slum dwellers are more likely to live in areas prone to natural hazards because many slums are located in urban districts at high risk of flooding or along hillsides exposed to landslides, which are becoming more frequent due to climate change. Economic and social factors often combine to increase exposure to climate risk. For example, prior to Hurricane Katrina, economic and racial reasons resulted in a large concentration in the lower districts of New Orleans of low-income African Americans, who were then found to be the most affected by the hurricane itself and, paradoxically, also the ones who received delayed relief and public recovery measures.

Age also affects exposure to climate risks: the youngest and oldest, for example, are the most exposed to damage caused by heat waves. Indeed, if we look at the younger generation, this is the group that is potentially the most disadvantaged. This factual finding has also recently found expression in the language of law. The civil suit filed in 2021 before the Civil Court of Rome against the Italian State by more than 200 plaintiffs to obtain compliance by the State, in the prescribed time and manner, with the positive obligations to combat climate change, contains, among other grounds of action, one based on the prohibition of age discrimination resulting from the combined provisions of Articles 14, 2 and 8 of the ECHR. According to the applicants, the younger generations are discriminated against by the Italian State's inaction on climate change because they belong, by reason of their age, to a group particularly vulnerable to the impacts of climate change and because such inaction shifts forward, and therefore mainly on them, the burden and the cost of the harmful consequences of public policy failure.

Finally, in general, exposure to climate risk tends to be determined not only by the location of the home but also by the nature of the work performed. For example, those who work in agriculture on marginal land are more exposed than others to climate-related risks and, in most cases, they are women.

Climate crisis and inequality are locked in a vicious cycle whereby climate change risks end up exacerbating inequality. While inequalities make disadvantaged groups more exposed to climate risks, when climate risks actually hit, disadvantaged groups suffer a disproportionate loss of income and assets. Climate change thus worsens inequality, perpetuating the vicious cycle.

In actual fact, there is also a feedback effect of inequality on climate change that makes the above vicious cycle even more worrisome. Studies show that among OECD countries, those that are wealthier and have higher rates of internal inequality tend to have higher per capita levels of waste generation, water consumption as well as meat and fish consumption, and, as a result, tend to have higher levels of greenhouse gas

17. *See* IPCC, *Climate Change 2022: Impacts, Adaptation and Vulnerability*, 2022, at: https://www.ipcc.ch/report/ar6/wg2/.

emissions per capita. Inequality, therefore, aggravates the climate crisis, with the greatest price being paid by those least responsible for it.[18]

It is understandable, then, that one of the goals of a just transition which is able to reduce inequality has been identified along the axis of the world's North-South relationship. There is a need for more developed countries to recognize their historical responsibilities in bringing about today's climate crisis and, as a result, to bear a greater cost and support the efforts of less developed countries towards transition.

However, in other cases, how exactly can a just transition address inequality is unclear. First, not all transition strategies have positive effects in terms of reducing inequality. An example of a problematic transition is the strategy of introducing a fuel tax which, if not balanced by appropriate correctives, risks having regressive effects on precarious and low-income workers.

Another example is the development of renewable energy. Many studies conducted nationally and globally have shown that the sector in question is labour-intensive and that the expected increase in renewable energy, particularly in the installation phase, will have a positive impact on job creation. However, from a just transition perspective, attention must be paid, in addition to the quality of the jobs created, to the fact that the employment rate for women in the renewable energy sector is still low, similar to that of the traditional fossil fuel sector[19]. Ensuring an increase in renewable energy without, at the same time, making an effort to improve the position of women in that particular sector of the labour market would mean making a transition that keeps existing inequalities intact.[20]

This raises the question of whether a just transition can really take place without the fight against climate change being conducted hand in hand with the fight against the structural inequalities that have been discussed so far. In turn, this reflection brings us back to the question from which we started, that is, what is the meaning of a just transition?

4 JUST TRANSITION AND PROTECTION OF HUMAN RIGHTS: FROM PRINCIPLES TO POLICIES

From a legal point of view, an initial answer concerns the link between just transition and the protection of fundamental human rights. The link between climate change and human rights (including the right not to be discriminated against) was enshrined in the Preamble of the Paris Agreement where, in Recital 11, it is recognized that 'climate change is a common concern of humanity, Parties, when taking action to combat it, should respect, promote and take into account their respective obligations to human

18. Islam S.N., Winkel J., Climate Change and Social Inequality. *DESA Working Paper No. 152, ST/ESA/2017/DWP/152*: 2017, 7.
19. Rosemberg A., Strengthening Just Transition Policies in International Climate Governance. *Policy analysis brief*: 2017, 1 ff.
20. Tiraboschi M., Rustico L., Le prospettive occupazionali della green economy tra mito e realtà. *Diritto delle relazioni industriali:* 2010, 931 ff; Casano L., Skills and Professions for a 'Just Transition'. Some Reflections for Legal Research. *E-Journal of International and Comparative Labour Studies*: 2019, 8.3.

rights, the right to health, the rights of indigenous peoples, local communities, migrants, children, persons with disabilities and persons in vulnerable situations, as well as the right to development, gender equality, the empowerment of women and intergenerational equity'.

But we are still at the level of a declaration of principles. Which policies, including policies of law, should be adopted to implement them remains an open question. While the transition to a de-carbonized economy implies in any case a radical change in the way we produce and consume, the underlying question is what kind of change and what model of justice the transition should strive for? Is it possible to decouple economic growth from the increased environmental impact of that growth,[21] which implies, in essence, the preservation of the current economic model or, vice versa, is it impossible to decouple economic growth from the increasing environmental resources necessary to produce it, and therefore what is required is a revision of the objective of an indefinite Gross Domestic Product (GDP) growth and the development of a circular economy? Is it enough to talk about redistribution, recognition, participation and representation of the different actors involved in the transition, above all workers, without reformulating identities[22] and redirecting the interests at stake?[23] Finally, what role can the law play in the transition?

The 2030 Sustainable Development Goals endorsed by all UN Member States in 2015, in particular, the goals related to fighting poverty and hunger (goals 1 and 2), reducing inequality and gender equality (goals 5 and 10), decent work and economic growth (goal 8), and the interconnected relationship that binds them, tell us that the vicious circle that connects climate crisis and social imbalances can only be broken if we intervene simultaneously on all the distorting aspects of development. However, within these goals, there is an intrinsic contradiction, relating to the actual possibility of combining social well-being, economic well-being, biophysical well-being of the planet and economic growth. Under the given conditions, many studies suggest that social, economic and environmental needs are not compatible in that the greater the amount of resources allocated to satisfy social needs and economic growth, the more the biophysical limits are exceeded.

Without exploring here the merits of this issue, it still seems difficult to deny that in order to secure the conditions of 'ecological sustainability', the redirection of

21. The objective declared by the European Green Deal is to achieve by 2050 a situation in which the European economy 'will not generate net emissions of greenhouse gases and in which economic growth will be decoupled from the use of resources' (Communication from the Commission of 11 December 2019).
22. *See* Barca S., The Just Transition and Its Work of Inequality. *Sustainability: Science. Practice and Policy*: 2020, 263, ff, who observes that, in the absence of the construction of an alternative identity, it is impossible for a miner to want anything other than being a miner.
23. Even experiences of participatory management of the transition, such as the German one, where the creation of a Commission on coal included a very large and varied number of stakeholders, have seen the more consolidated interests of different groups prevail, to the detriment of those of the actors most inclined to change. This has resulted in a convergence towards a minimum common denominator, which has prevented the adoption of truly innovative solutions (Reizenstein A., Schulz S., Eilmann F. The story of coal in Germany: A model for just transition in Europe? In Morena M., Krause D., Stevis D. (eds.), *Just transitions. Social Justice in the Shift towards a Low-Carbon World.* London: Pluto Press, 2020, 150 ff.

production processes must go hand in hand with a redistribution of resources from the richest to the poorest countries, as well as with intervention on the composition of GDP aimed at favouring public goods (i.e., accessible to all) over private ones. In other words, it means acting on all the distorting aspects that underlie the environmental crisis and its burden of inequality.

To return to Jonas, we must combine the heuristics of fear, the ethics of prevention and preservation, with a principle of hope and a utopian spirit, a spirit that tells us something not only about what not to want but also what to want, and about which social relations can reflect the aims of emancipation and enhancement of the dignity of the person.

And this was also at a time when one of the first effects of the war in Ukraine was that of questioning and sometimes reversing the transition processes that had just begun. It is difficult to predict how the ongoing conflict will change the interpretative categories and affect medium-term prospects, but the most unrealistic hypothesis is 'the idea that reality can indefinitely remain as it is'.[24] Therefore, we must in any case move towards change.

5 CLIMATE CHANGE LITIGATION AND REMEDIAL AND ANTI-DISCRIMINATION LAW

If the role that law can assume in the transition is above all that of 'marking the limits and establishing the bonds and commitments that public and private powers must respect in their economic, social and political action',[25] this role can be played through an array of different tools, often intertwined and ranging from hard law to soft law, from the changes made to Articles 9 and 41 of the Italian Constitution and from the system of protection of occupational health and safety to the tools of social responsibility, due diligence, promotional law and collective bargaining.[26]

Here, however, I want to focus above all on the role that remedial law[27] and litigation on the subject of human rights, discrimination and climate change can play in combating the inequalities that precede and coexist with the transition.

It is primarily a diagnostic role. As previously mentioned, the inequalities linked to climate change follow the lines marked by the various factors of discrimination: wealth, race and ethnicity, gender, age, disability, nationality and religion. The categories of anti-discrimination law allow, in the first place, to uncover specific phenomena of inequality from the indistinct terrain of the social injustices linked to the

24. Ferrajoli L., *Per una Costituzione della Terra*. Milano: Feltrinelli, 2022, 137.
25. Baylos A., Trabajo y ambiente: la necesidad del límite. *Lavoro e diritto*: 2022, 251.
26. For an analysis of the regulatory tools with which to address environmental issues, especially from the perspective of labour law, *see* the papers published in *Lavoro e diritto*, 2022, n. 2 and in Miñarro Yanini M. (ed.). *Cambio climático y derecho social. Claves para una transición ecológica justa e inclusiva*. Jaén: Uja Editorial. 2021.
27. On remedial law, *see* Treu T., Rimedi, tutele e fattispecie: riflessioni a partire dai lavori della Gig economy. *Lavoro e diritto:* 2017, 367 ff, and the other papers in issues 3 and 4 of Lavoro e diritto: 2017.

climate crisis and to identify exactly which groups are particularly disadvantaged both by climate change and by the transition processes.

Second, the law can play a remedial role starting from general principles and fundamental rights and making choices considered useful to meet the needs of society.[28] The case against the Italian state mentioned above is one of many 'climate lawsuits' being filed in countries around the world.[29] Through judicial action on the subject of human rights conducted in the guise of strategic litigation, the law proves it is capable of unifying the level of political and legal action and producing changes of a general nature and a collective scope that go beyond the traditional plan of individual redress.[30]

Such action will now be made possible in the Italian legal system by the modification of Article 9 of the Constitution, as well as by the constraints arising from the international climate agreements, and, on the level of inter-private relations, by the constraints connected to the protection of health, environment and the inviolable rights of the person introduced by the recent reform of Article 41 of the Constitution.[31] Moreover, the lawsuit before the Court of Rome shows the potential of anti-discrimination law.

If judges thus find themselves playing a substitute role in the search for adequate protection of the subjects harmed by the climate crisis, this will take place within a given legal framework, made up not only of specific legal rules (this applies to the French and German climate laws, which impose a ceiling on climate-altering gas emissions) but also, in the absence of those rules, by the principles present in national and supranational legal systems.

Moreover, these principles are often endowed with specifications, such as those, for example, which define in the Paris Agreement the maximum thresholds that the global average temperature must not exceed certain time limits (taken as a reference target by the German Constitutional Court and by the French Courts) or which define the commitments of the EU for the reduction of greenhouse gases[32] or which establish

28. On the role of principles concerning, in general, the remedial perspective, *see* Treu, 2017, 398.
29. The report by Setzer and Higham of 2021 gives an account of this climate change litigation. In 2020, 93 such cases were filed against governments, 16 against companies (see Setzer J., Higham C. *Global trends in climate change litigation: 2021 Snapshot*. London: Grantham Research Institute on Climate Change and the Environment and Centre for Climate Change Economics and Policy, London School of Economics and Political Science, 2021. At: www.lse.ac.uk/granthaminstitute/wpcontent/uploads/2021/07/Global-trends-in-climate-change-litigation_2021-snapshot.pdf.
30. On legal strategies as a form of social mobilization *see* Protopapa V., *Uso strategico del diritto e azione sindacale.* Bologna: Il Mulino, 2021. In the field of labour law, on the protection of collective interests in court, *see*, recently, Razzolini O., *Azione sindacale e tutela giurisdizionale.* Milano: Franco Angeli, 2018, Recchia G.A., *Studio sulla giustiziabilità degli interessi collettivi dei lavoratori.* Bari: Cacucci, 2018.
31. *See* Bin R., Il disegno costituzionale. *Lavoro e Diritto.* 2022: 115 ff, 125; Morrone A., Lavoro e ambiente nella Costituzione. Percorsi teorici per un nuovo contratto sociale. Giornale di diritto del lavoro e delle relazioni industriali, 2023, 1 ff.
32. Decision no. 406/2009/EC of the European Parliament and of the Council of 23 April 2009.

a classification of investments deemed environmentally sustainable by the EU Taxonomy Regulation.[33]

Even if the experimental nature of this 'remedial law' and the uncertainties deriving from the ups and downs of judicial litigation and the complexity of the issues involved make this legal apparatus still unstable,[34] its first successes allow us to glimpse some of the characteristics of the law of just transition.

SELECTED BIBLIOGRAPHY

Barca S. (2015). Greening the Job: Trade Unions, Climate Change and the Political Ecology *of Labour*. in Bryant R.L. (ed.), *International Book of Political Ecology*. London: Edward Elgar.

Barca S. (2020).The Just Transition and Its Work of Inequality. *Sustainability: Science. Practice and Policy*: 263 ff.

Baylos A. (2022). Trabajo y ambiente: la necesidad del límite. Lavoro e diritto: 247 ff.

Bin R. (2022). Il disegno costituzionale. *Lavoro e diritto*: 115 ff.

Butera F.M. (2021). *Affrontare la complessità. Per governare la transizione ecologica.* Milano: Edizioni Ambiente.

Cagnin V. (2018). *Diritto del lavoro e sviluppo sostenibile*. Milano: Wolters Kluwer-CEDAM.

Caruso B., Del Punta R., Treu T. (eds.) (2020*). Il diritto del lavoro e la grande trasformazione. Valori, attori, regolazione*. Bologna: Il Mulino.

Casano L. (2019). Skills and Professions for a 'Just Transition'. Some Reflections for Legal Research. *E-Journal of International and Comparative Labour Studies*: 8.3.

Centamore G. (2022). Una *just transition* per il diritto del lavoro. *Lavoro e diritto:* 129 ff.

Doorey D. (2017). Just Transitions Law: Putting Labour Law to Work on Climate Change. *Journal of Environmental Law and Practice*: 201 ff.

Ferrajoli L. (2022). *Per una Costituzione della Terra*. Milano: Feltrinelli.

IPCC (2022). *Climate Change 2022: Impacts, Adaptation and Vulnerability* available at https://www.ipcc.ch/report/ar6/wg2/.

Islam S.N., Winkel J. (2017). Climate Change and Social Inequality. *DESA Working Paper No. 152, ST/ESA/2017/DWP/152.*

Jonas H. (2009). *Il principio di responsabilità*. Torino: Einaudi.

Latour B. (2009). *Non siamo mai stati moderni*. Milano: elèuthera.

Miñarro, M. (ed.) (2021). *Cambio climático y derecho social. Claves para una transición ecológica justa e inclusiva*. Jaén: Uja Editorial.

Monterossi M. W. (2020). *L'orizzonte intergenerazionale del diritto civile*. Pisa:ETS.

33. Regulation (EU) 2020/852 of the European Parliament and of the Council of 18 June 2020 concerning the establishment of a framework that favours sustainable investments and amending Regulation (EU) 2019/2088 and subsequent delegated acts.
34. In general, on the 'unstable' nature of the legal framework of environmental sustainability *see* Baylos A., 2022, 247 ff.

Morrone A. (2023). Lavoro e ambiente nella Costituzione. Percorsi teorici per un nuovo contratto sociale. *Giornale di diritto del lavoro e di relazioni industriali*, 1 ff.

Perulli A., Speziale V. (2022). *Dieci tesi sul diritto del lavoro.* Bologna: Il Mulino.

Protopapa V. (2021). *Uso strategico del diritto e azione sindacale.* Bologna: Il Mulino.

Razzolini O. (2018). *Azione sindacale e tutela giurisdizionale.* Milano: Franco Angeli.

Recchia G.A. (2018). *Studio sulla giustiziabilità degli interessi collettivi dei lavoratori.* Bari: Cacucci.

Reizenstein A., Schulz S., Eilmann F. (2020). *The Story of Coal in Germany: A Model for just Transition in Europe?.* In Morena M., Krause D., Stevis D. (eds.), *Just Transitions. Social Justice in the Shift towards a Low-Carbon World.* London: Pluto Press, 150 ff.

Rosemberg A. (2017). Strengthening Just Transition Policies in International Climate Governance. *Policy Analysis Brief*: 1 ff.

Rosemberg A. (2020). 'No Jobs on a Dead Planet': The International Trade Union Movement and Just Transition. In Morena M., Krause D., Stevis D. (eds.). *Just Transitions. Social Justice in the Shift Towards a Low-Carbon World.* London: Pluto Press 32 ff.

Setzer J., Higham C. (2021). Global Trends in Climate Change Litigation: 2021 Snapshot. London: Grantham Research Institute on Climate Change and the Environment and Centre for Climate Change Economics and Policy, London School of Economics and Political Science, available at www.lse.ac.uk/granthaminstitute/wp-content/uploads/2021/07/Global-trends-in-climate-change-litigation_2021-snapshot.pdf.

Stevis D. & Felli R. (2015). Global Labour Unions and Just Transition to a Green Economy. *International Environmental Agreements*, 29 ff.

Stevis. D., Morena M., Krause D. (2020), *The Genealogy and Contemporary Politics of just Transition.* In Morena M., Krause D., Stevis D. (eds). *Just Transitions. Social Justice in the Shift Towards a Low-Carbon World.* London: Pluto Press, pp. 1 ff.

Tiraboschi M., Rustico L. (2010). Le prospettive occupazionali della green economy tra mito e realtà. *Diritto delle relazioni industriali*, 931 ff.

Tomassetti P. (2018). *Diritto del lavoro e ambiente.* Bergamo: Adapt University Press.

Treu T. (2016). Labour Law and Sustainable Development. *WP CSDLE 'Massimo D'Antona'.INT*, 130/2016.

Treu T. (2017). Rimedi, tutele e fattispecie: riflessioni a partire dai lavori della Gig economy. *Lavoro e diritto*, 367 ff.

Verdolini E., Belpietro C. (2022). Giusta transizione ecologica: L'impatto delle tecnologie digitali. *Giornale di diritto del lavoro e di relazioni industriali*, 205 ff.

CHAPTER 3

The Fight Against Climate Change: Implications for Labour Law and Industrial Relations

Manfred Weiss

1 INTRODUCTION

The dangers of climate change have become indisputable. The fight against this phenomenon has become a question of survival. Sustainability is the catchword to define the goal of this necessary transformation which, of course, also has and will have an impact on the world of work. There are no jobs on a dead planet. This is why reducing rapidly the effects of climate change has to be a top priority for labour law and industrial relations.

Decarbonisation, the substitution of fossil energies for renewable energies, will affect companies all over production patterns as well as products will change, work organisation will change, old skills will become obsolete and new skills will be required, the goal of companies will have to be redefined, old jobs will be lost and new jobs created. This transition undoubtedly is a big challenge for labour law and industrial relations.

Already in 2013 the ILO launched the green initiative and made later on environmental sustainability a cross-cutting policy driver (CCPD) for all its activities.[1] The ILO Centenary Declaration recognises climate and environmental changes as key drivers of the transformation of the world of work. Accordingly, the policies of the ILO are shaped by now. In the meantime, the ILO has developed 'Guidelines for a just

1. From the very beginning up to the action plan 2020-2021 *see* ILO Strategic frameworks in the area of environmental sustainability and climate change, https//www.ilo.org.global/topics/green-jobs/WCMS_744334/lang.

transition towards environmentally sustainable economies and societies for all'.[2] These guidelines are an action program for all actors who possibly might be involved, governments as well as administrations on all levels, employers and employers' associations as well as trade unions and NGOs.

Not only on a global but also on a regional level this approach has been followed, for example by the EU – long before the Green Deal was declared by the Commission. The social market economy as defined in Article 3 of the Treaty on the European Union (TEU) is not only characterised by competitivity and social progress but also by 'a high level of protection and improvement of the quality of the environment'.

According to Article 11 of the Treaty on the Functioning of the EU (TFEU), 'environmental protection requirement must be integrated into the definition and implementation of the Union policies and activities, in particular with a view to promoting sustainable development'. In other words: thereby the EU established also a cross-cutting policy driver in line with the ILO approach.

What this means in the EU's actual politics may be illustrated by two recent proposals. The Commission's proposal of the Corporate Sustainability Reporting Directive (CSRD) of April 2021[3] will require the companies to report their plans 'to ensure sustainable economy with a specific reference to the limiting of global warming to 1.5 degree Celsius in line with the Paris Agreement'. And equally impressive is the overall objective of the Commission's proposal of February 2022 for a Directive on Corporate Sustainability Due Diligence[4] to 'ensure that companies active in the internal market contribute to sustainable development ... through the identification, prevention and mitigation, bringing to an end minimization of potential or actual adverse human rights and environmental impacts connected with companies' own operations, subsidiaries and value chains'. This Directive is supposed to refer to human rights in the broadest sense, not only covering social rights but also a comprehensive catalogue of internationally recognised objectives and prohibitions included in environmental conventions.

In the debate on the future of labour law and industrial relations, it seems that the urgency and the dimension of this climate-related challenge for labour law and industrial relations is not yet understood to its full extent. It does not yet get the attention it deserves.

Before briefly sketching the impact of the fight against climate change on labour law and industrial relations it has to be stressed that it is the task of politics to develop a framework to promote the attractivity for investing in the green economy. States have to develop incentive schemes to stimulate enterprise innovation towards sustainable development, as recommended by the ILO guidelines. This is a task for politics on all levels: global, regional, national, sectoral and local. No area is excluded any longer from this ambitious task.

2. Geneva 2015.
3. Replacing Directive 2014/95/EU.
4. COM (2022) 71 final.

1.1 The Impact on Labour Law and Industrial Relations

To a certain extent, the challenges for labour law and industrial relations by climate change are similar to the challenges arising from digitalisation. This particularly will be the case in two areas: training and employee involvement in management's decision-making.

2 TRAINING

The need for skilling, re-skilling and up-skilling best can be illustrated by the automobile industry where electric cars are to be produced instead of cars driven by fossil energy. This evidently means that old skills become obsolete and new skills are needed. The only way to prevent unemployment is re-skilling. And this refers to a huge number of people. The automobile industry, of course, is only one example. Similar effects can be observed in many other branches of industry.

Law has to provide the framework for such opportunities of skilling, re-skilling and up-skilling to a bigger extent than ever. Not only governments but also the actors in collective bargaining are confronted with this task. Joint efforts of all these actors are needed.

Many questions have to be answered in this context: whether there should be an individual right for all employees to participate in such re-skilling programs, whether they should take place during working time without loss of remuneration, what incentives for employees and employers should be envisaged, how the costs are to be shared between employees, employers and the State and how the responsibilities are to be shared between legislation and collective bargaining. These are difficult questions, but they have to be answered.

The construction of this legal framework has become one of the top priorities of EU politics. Most important in this context are the Council Recommendation of 19 December 2016 on up-skilling pathways: new opportunities for adults[5] and the recent EU Commission's proposal for a Council Recommendation on learning for environmental sustainability of 14 January 2022.[6] The latter tries to 'develop a coherent approach to the competences, skills and attitudes that people need to act, live and work in a sustainable manner'. The strategies recommended by these EU initiatives are more or less in line with the skills development policies proposed in the already-mentioned ILO guidelines.

In short and to make the point: The de-skilling of employees by decarbonisation needs a tremendous effort of skilling, re-skilling and up-skilling in order to improve the chances of workers to either keep, gain or regain their jobs. Labour law has to significantly re-conceptualise the framework for such a strategy.

5. OJ 2016, C 484/1.
6. COM(2022) 11 final.

2.1 Employees' Involvement in Management's Decision-Making

As far as employees' involvement in management's decision-making is concerned, the starting point of all reflections has to be that the fight against climate change will lead to a whole set of decisions which may have serious, often negative short-term effects for employees: stop certain types of production, change production patterns, reconstruct parts of the company or the company as a whole, closing parts of the company or of the whole company, etc.

This may lead to problems of acceptability which only can be achieved if employees or their representatives somehow participate in the decision-making. Workplace democracy or workers' participation is of utmost importance in this context. Empirical studies which were made in view of technological innovations affecting employees demonstrate that workers' participation significantly increases the chances of acceptability.

Unilateral decision-making by management not only is inappropriate because of the acceptability problem. As already indicated, the goal of the company has to be redefined: it has to promote sustainability. So far the enterprise was understood in many countries as an entity to be exclusively characterised by ownership of the means of production. It only should be up to the owner what happens with the means of production. 'Shareholder value' was the result of this perception in company law. And in labour law, it still is 'management's prerogative'.

If this concept is put into question it, of course, does not mean eliminating private property of means of production. Or to put it differently: the idea is not to attack the system of private capitalism. It simply means that the traditional concept of property is to be reconsidered in the context of climate change. The company has to be shaped in a way which serves the common good of society, in line with climate protection policy. Only then the goal of sustainability has a chance to be achieved. This – in my view – implies that basic decisions on what and how to produce no longer can be left to unilateral management's power but need at least workers' participation in decision-making. After all: The future of the employees depends on the sustainability of the company.

It has to be stressed that these considerations not only have implications on workers' participation in a narrow sense but also on collective bargaining. Environmental issues, what and how to produce in line with the goals of climate protection, also should become a topic of collective bargaining. There are already empirical examples. It seems that Norway is somehow the forerunner in this context.[7]

These sketchy reflections lead to the delicate question of whether employees' representatives in the traditional schemes of institutionalised workers' participation or trade unions in the context of collective bargaining are conscious of the need on how to shape production in line with ecological goals and whether they are willing to do it if this might mean loss of short term advantages?

7. *See* B. Sjåfjell, *The Very Basis of Our Existence: Labour and the Neglected Environmental Dimension of Sustainable Development*, https://ssrn.com/abstract=1517393.

To just give you an anecdotal impression: I had the opportunity to ask the chairperson of the works council of a big airport in Germany: 'What are you doing to reduce the carbonite emissions, for example by reducing flights within the country?' His answer was: 'This is none of my priorities'. And this in spite of the fact that according to the Act on Works Councils, one of the general tasks of the works council is 'to promote the protection of the environment'.

After all, sustainability is a goal which might show positive effects for employees only in the mid or long-term perspective. Therefore, the question arises whether and how environmental organisations should be somehow integrated into these processes of workers' participation and collective bargaining. I have no answer and I am aware that I am touching on a taboo. And I am also aware that this would mean a dramatic change in labour law and industrial relations. But this may correspond to the dramatic dimension of climate change and the fight against it.

The question of integrating environmental organisations – by the way – not only may be posed for the micro-level of companies in a national context. It also may be posed on the international macro-level: Is the tripartite structure of the ILO still appropriate in view of the need for climate protection? Again I have no answer to this provocative question.

3 FURTHER IMPLICATIONS

Instead of ending this sketchy note with provocations and by raising taboos, it should be mentioned that climate change and the fight against it has many more implications on labour law which are important but less dramatic. Two examples may demonstrate what is meant:

3.1 Occupational Health and Safety

My first example refers to occupational health and safety which takes much room in the ILO guidelines. The effects of climate change on workers' health and on their ability to meet the requirements of the job still to a great extent are to be identified. Of course, we know already quite a bit about the effects of excessive heat and UV radiation on people working outdoors, for example, in the construction industries. But this is only a tiny part of the problem. Much research still has to be done and measures – again together with the employees and their representatives – are to be developed. Whatever the results of these research activities may be: the preventive and protective measures will be in line with the already well-known health and safety arrangements. So far this is an example where simply old patterns can be used to cope with new risks.

3.2 Home Office

Much more problematic is the second example for which already much empirical evidence has been gained in the pandemic: the opportunity to work online from home instead of working on the premises of the company. Whereas this so-called home office was chosen in the pandemic to prevent infection with the virus, it could help to reduce carbonite emissions caused by means of transport.

Home office, however, is a very complex phenomenon, raising many questions. Does it lead to isolation? What impact does it have on family life? Are standards of an ergonomic workplace met? Who is entitled to inspect and control the privacy of the employee? How can the communication between the employee and his/her representatives as well as with the trade union be guaranteed? etc. In short and to make the point: this example shows that the fight against climate change is only one - even an important - aspect which has to be balanced with many other considerations.

4 CONCLUSION

Climate change and the fight against it has all kind of implications for labour law and industrial relations. Some of them are far-reaching and challenge the traditional paradigm. This is true for the question of whether the traditional concept of management's prerogative can be maintained as well as for the question of whether the monopoly of representation by traditional bodies of workers' representatives and by traditional trade unions is still appropriate. Other impacts are less dramatic, they either can be integrated into traditional patterns (e.g., health and safety) or are to be balanced with other considerations (e.g., home office).

Part II Labour Market Facing with Climate Change: Critical Issues and Perspectives

CHAPTER 4

Policy and Regulatory Implications of Current Debates on Labour Market and Climate Change: Southern Perspective

Pablo Arellano Ortiz[*]

1 PREMISES OF THE CONTRIBUTION

It needs to be clarified from the very beginning that this contribution with not deal with ILO's international labour standards. This matter was covered during the seminar by other speakers who explained very well how these standards cover environmental issues.

It has been shared largely by academia that we are currently in a process of changes. In labour terms, these changes are known as the industrial revolutions, in short, these are first the introduction of the steam engine and other types of machinery, second standardization and mass production, third the introduction of the use of electronics and computers, fourth digital transformations and, for some the fifth the artificial intelligence. All industrial revolutions have transformed the labour market and the production mechanism of the occidental world. These transformations are not a global phenomenon, they may have a global impact and their starting point is Europe or the occidental world.

It is important to mention that climate change may also affect the way of production. As we also need to consider the environmental issues within the production process. This is not new this was also the case when the first industrial revolution

* Labour Law Specialist, Labour Law and Reform Unit, Governance and Tripartism Department, International Labour Office (ILO), and Researcher, School of Law, Pontificia Universidad Católica de Valparaíso. The views expressed are the sole responsibility of the author and do not necessarily represent the views of the International Labour Office or of the International Labour Organization Email: arellano@ilo.org.

started, as well as all industrial revolutions. Because all of them have transformed is a way the ways of production and labour, they also affect the environment. Now, we are more conscious of the way how it can be affected. This may lead to thinking toward a new type of revolution and perhaps skipping artificial intelligence. It can be proposed that the fifth revolution would be the environmental and labour revolutions. It represents a change in the way of production, as the other one, and as said we are now more aware of the impact of production and labour.

On the notion of climate change, now we can be more assertive that it can be understood as a crisis. And the crisis is at the heart of labour issues. They are also part of the idea of industrial revolutions. All these crises have led to an employment crisis and then the labour market has adapted to the new way of working. There is a crisis and climate change is creating tensions in the labour markets. On the way those labour markets are responding, in some cases it may lead to a rise in the unemployment rates or in other cases may be present as an opportunity for job creation. All this is in a very specific sector of the labour market and depends on how the issue of climate change is addressed.

It needs to be mentioned here, that crisis is also at the heart of the current time but it does not have to be a negative concept. It can also mean an opportunity and do something better. This is the way ILO proposed a way out of the COVID-19 crisis. During the crisis, ILO Director-General Guy Ryder published an open-ed calling for a better normal. Here is an extract:

> New normal? Better normal!
>
> With over 3 million cases and some 250,000 deaths from the virus to date globally, and the expected loss of the equivalent of 305 million jobs worldwide by mid-year, the stakes have never been higher. Governments continue to 'follow the science' in the search for the best solutions while foregoing the obvious benefits of much greater international cooperation in building the needed global response to the global challenge.
>
> But with the war against COVID-19 still to be won, it has become commonplace that what awaits us after victory is a 'new normal' in the way society is organized and the way we will work.
>
> This is hardly reassuring.
>
> Because nobody seems able to say what the new normal will be. Because the message is that it will be dictated by the constraints imposed by the pandemic rather than our choices and preferences. And because we've heard it before. The mantra which provided the mood music of the crash of 2008-2009 was that once the vaccine to the virus of financial excess had been developed and applied, the global economy would be safer, fairer, more sustainable. But that didn't happen. The old normal was restored with a vengeance and those on the lower echelons of labour markets found themselves even further behind.
>
> Now is the time to look more closely at this new normal, and start on the task of making it a better normal, not so much for those who already have much, but for those who so obviously have too little.[1]

1. For the full text *see* Op-Ed: New normal? Better normal! (ilo.org).

The message here is that if we are confronting a crisis, we should not try to get back to the status before the crisis. It can be possible to use this opportunity to effectively address the issues in the best way possible and restore the old normality differently. A better normality.

The environmental crisis can be taken in this sense. Positively is an opportunity that can give us the chance to address the link between labour issues and the environment. Aiming to have a better social and labour model. There is no thinking of labour and environment as a problem; it should be considered as an opportunity, as it always has been, to restructure the labour market, protections for the worker, and the way employers work and produce.

Considering all these ideas, the approach that we would like to propose is one focused not on Western developments and culture. We would like to propose a view on how to approach issues of global climate change and labour issues from the global south perspective. As we will explain the phenomenon of the Western world is there and they have an impact on the global labour market, particularly in the global south. The same applies to environmental considerations.

We will first develop arguments regarding the regulatory challenges. Afterwards, we will present a few labour market challenges. The labour climate changes will be then presented. In the end, we have some final reflections that are not meant to close the debate. On the contrary, we would like to consider this contribution as a different view in this global debate.

2 LABOUR REGULATION CHALLENGES

The environmental crisis and challenges required an appropriate regulatory framework to guide the work of government and social partners. However, this matter is not new,[2]

2. For example, *see*: Auvergnon, Philippe (sous la direction de) Les régulations sociales en devenir. Espaces, acteurs, modalités, collection de l'INTEFP, Editions de la Chronique Sociale, Lyon, 2008; Piore, Michael J. & Schrank, Andrew, *Root-cause Regulation. Protecting Work and Workers in the Twenty-First Century*, Harvard University Press, 2018; Collins, Hugh; Davies, Paul and Rideout, Roger (editors) *Legal Regulation of the Employment Relation*, Kluwer law International, 2000; Hardy, Tess and Ariyawansa, Sayomi, *Literature Review on the Governance of Work*, International Labour Office, October 2019. (It can be consulted at https://www.ilo.org/wcmsp5/groups/public/---ed_dialogue/---dialogue/documents/publication/wcms_731477.pdf); Howe, John, 'Labour regulation now and in the future: Current trends and emerging themes' in Journal of Industrial Relations, 2017, Vol. 59(2) 209-224 DOI: 10.1177/0022185616671352; Arellano Ortiz, Pablo, 'Teorías sobre regulación y protección del derecho del trabajo. Aportes a un debate en desarrollo', en Humberto Villasmil Prieto y César Augusto Carballo Mena (Directores Académicos) y Luis Alberto Torres Tarazona (Director de Publicación) Derecho laboural iberoamericano. Influencias del sistema normativo OIT, Universidad Libre (Colombia), Universidad Católica Andrés Bello y Academia de Ciencias Políticas y Sociales (Venezuela), Tirant lo Blanch, Bogota (Colombia) 2020, pp. 201-211; Arellano Ortiz, Pablo, 'La OIT y los desafíos de la regulación del derecho internacional del trabajo: reflexiones desde la perspectiva latinoamerica', en Moreira Gomes, Ana Virginia; Rodrigues de Freitas Júnior; Antônio y Siqueira Neto, José Francisco (Organizadores), O Centenário da Organização Internacional do Trabalho no Brasil, 1. ed. Belo Horizonte: Editora Virtualis, 2019, 543, pp. 289-312.

many theories have been developed,[3] and even a call for new forms of social regulations has been made.[4] Nevertheless, the overall approaches can be divided into two different visions, as Gomes and Verma described. On the one hand, the deregulation argument is based on neoclassical economic theory, which holds that trying to achieve equity or redistribution through regulatory means that disrupt or limit the competitive market process leads to a loss of efficiency, implying the existence of a trade-off between efficiency and equity. Labour standards, therefore, would potentially lead to a loss of efficiency that ultimately precludes the very promise of a fairer redistribution of wealth. On the other hand, defenders of labour regulation see labour legislation as a system of worker protection norms, which guarantees balance in labour relations. This vision of labour legislation dates back to and was consolidated in the first half of the twentieth century. The labour protection system was justified in the name of ideals of social justice as a restriction and/or limitation of market forces.[5] The question of regulation is not purely theoretical; it indeed has practical implications for daily life in any given country. Adoption of a position either to regulate or to deregulate should be in line with the development objectives of each country.[6]

For Collins, regulation theory has been 'used typically to justify deregulation of the labour market and the employment relations. Employment laws have been scrutinized and rejected on the ground that either they do not address a real problem, that they are ineffective to achieve their goal, or that the cost to business or employees exceed the benefits of the regulation. But it is possible to prise the regulation agenda apart from the deregulation movements in politics'.[7] Undeniably, political and economic views cannot be left out of the debate.

As pointed out by Gomes and Verma, labour legislation and policies, to be effective and accountable, need to share the concern for growth with other policy measures. They must demonstrate that they can contribute to the sustainability of development and human well-being.[8]

The question today is what regulation we need for labour issues, and how we will address environmental issues? Do we currently have those regulations? Do we need a new set of instruments? Do we need to give more flexibility to certain areas of law?

3. Hardy, Tess and Ariyawansa, Sayomi, *Literature Review on the Governance of Work*, International Labour Office, October 2019, pp. 6-38.
4. Auvergnon, Philippe (sous la direction de) Les régulations sociales en devenir. Espaces, acteurs, modalités, collection de l'INTEFP, Editions de la Chronique Sociale, Lyon, 2008, p. 12.
5. Gomes, Ana Virginia Moreira, and Verma Anil, 'Regulación "inteligente" en la economía disruptiva. Una crítica a las recientes reformas de la legislación laboural en Brasil', ANÁLISIS LABOURAL / ABRIL 2019, Dossier 500, p. 26.
6. Gomes, Ana Virginia Moreira, and Verma Anil, 'Regulación "inteligente" en la economía disruptiva. Una crítica a las recientes reformas de la legislación laboural en Brasil', ANÁLISIS LABOURAL / ABRIL 2019, Dossier 500, p. 27.
7. Collins, Hugh, 'Justifications and techniques of legal regulation of the employment relation', in Collins H.; Davis, P., and Rideout, R. (eds) Legal Regulation of the Employment Relation, Kluwer Law International, Netherlands, 2000, p. 5.
8. Gomes, Ana Virginia Moreira, and Verma Anil, 'Regulación "inteligente" en la economía disruptiva. Una crítica a las recientes reformas de la legislación laboural en Brasil', ANÁLISIS LABOURAL / ABRIL 2019, Dossier 500, pp. 26-27.

Thus, employers can develop more business, or give flexibility in general regarding environmental issues. The tension is clearly there.

However, in the latest development regarding the debate about regulation, we do not see the usual suspects, such as hiring and firing, or freedom of association. These are still key topics for new regulations. It is always good to have important content included in the regulation, but we also see that in important to have mechanisms of compliance and enforcement in the regulations.

Setting regulations will not solve all the problems raised by future work challenges. Regulations should be linked to the purpose and, in particular, to recipients' effective compliance. If the regulations are well designed, the recipients will naturally comply. However, a perfect regulation does not exist. They can all be improved to deliver better worker protection. Labour law regulation should fulfil the protective objective as it is stated by its historical narrative.[9]

Since natural compliance is not widely spread, enforcement mechanisms play a key role in achieving the regulations' objective. Howe identifies a recent trend in enforcement, as it can 'be attributed to a range of other factors, including a shift away from collective regulation of working conditions through industry or enterprise level to statutory individual legal rights, associated with a decline in union membership, and a growing interest in labour regulation in developing countries, where unions are often weaker and labour inspectorates play a more significant role in the observance of labour standards'.[10]

What is currently needed, in general, but also regarding environmental labour issues, is to make sure that regulations are complied with and enforced. That is the policy goal that was set when the regulation design is actually achieved, in particular regarding how to respond to climate change. Here important consideration should be given not only to public-private arrangements for regulation but also to enforce existing regulatory frameworks.

3 LABOUR MARKET CHALLENGES

If we take a close look at the scope of labour law regulation, they are meant to be applied only to the formal labour market. Which is not the general rule. Informality represents a large part of the categories of workers present in the global labour market. Hence, informality is one of the major issues in the labour market today.

A recent International Labour Organization (ILO)[11] report states that more than 60% of the world's employed population belongs to the informal economy; in some countries and regions this percentage is much higher. This notion, introduced by the ILO, points out that the 'term "informal economy" refers to all economic activities by

9. Gamonal, Sergio, 'Narrativa laboral y principios del derecho del trabajo chileno', in Revista de la Facultad de Derecho de México, Tomo LXIX, Número 273, Enero – Abril 2019, pp. 65-88 DOI: 10.22201/fder.24488933e.2019.273-1.68631.
10. Howe, John, 'Labour regulation now and in the future: Current trends and emerging themes', Journal of Industrial Relations, 2017, Vol. 59(2), p. 215 DOI: 10.1177/0022185616671352.
11. *See*: ILO, *Women and Men in the Informal Economy: A Statistical Picture* (*third edition* / International Labour Office – Geneva: ILO, 2018).

workers and economic units that are - in law or in practice - not covered or insufficiently covered by formal arrangements. Their activities are not included in the law, which means that they are operating outside the formal reach of the law; or they are not covered in practice, which means that - although they are operating within the formal reach of the law, the law is not applied or not enforced; or the law discourages compliance because it is inappropriate, burdensome, or imposes excessive costs'.[12] The origins of this ILO notion can be found in the works carried out about labour markets on the African continent in the 1960s and 1970s.[13]

The ILO Recommendation on the transition from the Informal to the Formal Economy, 2015 (No. 204), defines 'informal economy' in Article 1.2:

> (a) refers to all economic activities by workers and economic units that are - in law or in practice - not covered or insufficiently covered by formal arrangements; and
> (b) does not cover illicit activities, in particular the provision of services or the production, sale, possession or use of goods forbidden by law, including the illicit production and trafficking of drugs, the illicit manufacturing of and trafficking in firearms, trafficking in persons, and money laundering, as defined in the relevant international treaties.

The ILO has complemented the notion by giving guidance on which types of jobs are included, as follows:[14]

(i) own-account workers employed in their own informal sector enterprises;
(ii) employers employed in their own informal sector enterprises;
(iii) contributing family workers, irrespective of whether they work in formal or informal sector enterprises;
(iv) members of informal producers' cooperatives;
(v) employees holding informal jobs in formal sector enterprises, informal sector enterprises, or as paid domestic workers employed by households;
(vi) own-account workers engaged in the production of goods exclusively for their own final use by their household.

Formal working relationships are those that are formalized by a contract and are subject to legal and contractual rules. For some, informal working relationships are governed by more diffuse and hidden rules.[15] However, in our opinion, a particular

12. *See*: ILO, *L'économie informelle: permettre une transition vers la formalisation* (Document du travail, *Colloque interrégional tripartite sur l'économie informelle: Permettre une transition vers la formalisation*, Genève, 27-29 novembre 2007); ILO, *Rapport de la Commission de l'économie informelle* (Conférence internationale du Travail, 90e session, Genève, 2002); ILO, *Travail décent et économie informelle* (Conférence internationale du Travail, Rapport VI, 90e session, Genève, 2002).
13. ILO, *Employment Incomes and Equality: A Strategy for Increasing Productive Employment in Kenya* (International Labour Office, Geneva, 1972).
14. ILO, *Directrices sobre una definición estadística de empleo informal* (Adoptadas por la Decimoséptima Conferencia Internacional de Estadísticos del Trabajo, noviembre - diciembre de 2003).
15. José Luis Monereo Pérez, *Manual de teoría de las relaciones laborales* (Editorial Tecnos, Madrid, 2011).

status regulated by the legislation does not matter because these relations are often included in the regulation of dependent and subordinate work. This reasoning makes general labour regulations applicable and their protection to these precarious relationships.[16]

This leads to the legal debate regarding the role of subordination and the employment relationship definition, which is not a simple exercise. Although, it is an exercise of vital importance for comparative labour law.[17] Certain factors used as determinants of the employment relationship include dependence and subordination or work performed under the direction, authority, supervision or control of the employer; or under the orders or instructions of the employer; or given on his behalf.[18] The study of the parties has also been the subject of separate research by the labour doctrine. Among them is Davidov's work on the notion of worker[19] and Vacarie's study on the concept of employer,[20] just to mention some examples.

When we talk about addressing environmental issues through labour law, it refers to a very small number of workers that belong to the formal labour market, which globally is less than 40%. It needs to be mentioned that in the formal market, we find the public sector. So, in the end, the number of workers covered by labour law in the formal labour market is very low. An expansion of the coverage of labour law to all workers around the globe is much needed.

This is quite important because the southern hemisphere, where the consequences of climate change are felt more strongly than the north, is where the level of informality is much higher. Then, trying to propose solutions from the north without considering the particularities of the south would be ineffective.

The goal is to protect all workers and at the same time take into account the challenges posed by climate change. The particularities of the labour market in the south should be explicitly considered if the preservation of the planet is wanted. The south is the source of many products

4 LABOUR AND CLIMATE CHANGE CHALLENGES

Transformations are deeper in the global south. Labour market transformation as well as environmental ones have in general a deeper effect in the global south.

This statement has to be realistic and, for that, we have to be conscious that the state capacity, as well as social partners, are weaker in the global south. New forms of

16. *See* Arellano Ortiz, Pablo, 'Informal and self-employed workers in Latin America: from an excluded category to an example of innovative inclusive measures', in Mies Westerveld y Marius Olivier (eds) Social security outside the realm of the employment contract. Informal work and employee-like workers, Edward Elgar Publishing, 2019, pp. 141-161.
17. For a comparative view, *see*: Casale, Giuseppe, (ed.), The Employment Relationship. A Comparative Overview, Hart Publishing, Oxford and Portland, Oregon, International Labour Office, Geneva, 2011.
18. OIT, La relación de trabajo, Informe V (1), Conferencia Internacional del Trabajo, 95.a reunión, 2006, Quinto punto del orden del día, Oficina Internacional del Trabajo Ginebra. p. 21.
19. Davidov, Guy, 'Who is a worker?', in *Industrial Law Journal*, Vol. 34, No. 1, March 2015, pp. 57-71.
20. Vacarie, Isabelle, *L'empleyeur*, Sirey, Paris, 1979.

regulation are needed. Regulations that take into account the needs of the south. The big debate about deregulation should be put aside and consider cultural and environmental factors when political goals for regulations are set. At the same time, more awareness is needed to comply with regulations. Some sort of consensus of compliance and enforcement is required, which can include appropriate mechanisms.

It should be worth mentioning here, that we are aware that there is a link not only between labour law and climate change but also with development.[21] Labour issues are key to the development of a country. If we would like to achieve the development of all these goals, consideration should be given to this interaction between labour, environment, and development.

Just to reinforce my argument from the south, I would like to draw your attention to the book written by Ha-Joon Chang called *'Kicking away the ladder'*.[22] This Korean author tries to explain how developed countries achieved development and then compares the efforts of the now-developing countries. It is quite an impressive reading to understand the difference between the North and the South. The author explains how certain industries evolved over time and the reader can easily make the link that in this process environmental issues had a different approach. For example, the importance of the textile industry at the beginning of the 1800s. Even today textile sector is quite relevant, also in terms of environmental impact.

5 FINAL REFLEXIONS

A just transition,[23] a labour-just transition, would only be possible if the global south is considered as it is and not as it should be. It needs to be considered with the idiosyncrasies, characteristics, elements, culture, and the natural element of the south. Working with all these factors could be used to propose a new regulatory arrangement and policies to confront labour and climate change.

It needs to be understood that the labour markets have many shapes and structures in different regions. It is important to mention that the way that the western developed world considers the labour market is not necessarily the one used in other parts of the world. The interactions between regions need to be considered when solutions are proposed.

From the ILO perspective, tripartism has been showing its importance to face the effect of the crisis, lately, during the COVID crisis.[24] Thus, it can be also an important element to be considered in the discussion around climate change and just transition.

21. *See* Fenwick, Colin and Marshall, Shelley (eds), Labour Regulation and Development, Socio-Legal Perspectives, Edward Elgar, Cheltenham, UK, and Northampton, MA: Edward Elgar Publishing, 2016, 352 pp.
22. Chang, Ha-Joo, Kicking Away the Ladder: Development Strategy in Historical Perspective, Anthem Press; 1st edition (1 July 2002) 196 pp.
23. For the debate on the just transition please *see* Frequently Asked Questions on just transition (ilo.org).
24. Please *see* Flagship Report: Social Dialogue Report 2022: Collective bargaining for an inclusive, sustainable and resilient recovery (ilo.org).

The debate has been put on the agenda for the 11th Session of the International Labour Conference, and we extend an invitation to follow its developments.[25]

To conclude, a labour-just transition is only feasible if multiple factors are included, a complex analysis for a complex issue. In other words, an integrated approach is a must.

25. Agenda of the 111th Session of the International Labour Conference (ilo.org).

CHAPTER 5

The Green Transition and New Skills in Occupation

Giuseppe Casale

1 INTRODUCTION

Climate change, environmental degradation, technological innovation, demographic shifts, globalisation and other unprecedented transformations are having profound impacts on the world of work.

These changes will affect job availability and will lead to a growing mismatch between skills and jobs. Such changes, however, are both a challenge and an opportunity for job seekers. In this case, skill development can be a key factor in a productive transformation.

The transition towards a more sustainable pattern of economic growth will generate new jobs, cause some job losses and alter the skill composition of many jobs.

The International Labour Organization has provided projections of how the green transition will affect employment by the year 2030. Applying this study further reveals that worldwide, approximately 25 million new employments will be created while over 7 million existing jobs will disappear. Of the latter, 5 million are recoverable through labour reallocation, meaning that those who lose their jobs as a result of industry contraction will be able to find similar employment in another sector within the same country.[1]

This indicates that between 1 and 2 million workers are expected to be in occupations where jobs will be lost due to a lack of equal vacancies in other industries, necessitating re-skilling into other occupations. It also implies that significant investment will be necessary to train employees in the skills required for over 20 million new

1. ILO (International Labour Organization), *Shaping Skills and Lifelong Learning for the Future of Work*, International Labour Conference, 109th Session, 2021.

jobs. The transitions to these jobs, however, will not happen by default: people will need new skills in order to tap into these new job opportunities.

A sense of urgency and increased worry about the economic and social ramifications of climate change and environmental degradation has resulted in major agreements on climate change and sustainable development. In particular, 2015 saw the approval of the United Nations 2030 Agenda and its 17 Sustainable Development Goals, as well as the Paris Climate Agreement, which underlined the significance of a just transition and decent work.

The availability of appropriate skills facilitates the transition to carbon-neutral, environmentally sustainable, and socially inclusive economies and jobs. To guarantee that skills needs are satisfied and climate pledges are effectively executed, action planning on skills development must be integrated with important climate and environmental policies and regulations, including the nationally determined contributions.

Furthermore, specific disadvantaged and vulnerable groups, such as young people, particularly those who are not in education, employment, or training. Moreover, women, older workers, people with disabilities, people living with HIV/AIDS, migrant workers, refugees, unemployed people, informal workers, low-skilled workers, indigenous and tribal peoples, and those living in rural areas, as well as owners and workers of Micro, Small and Medium Enterprises (MSMEs), must be included in skill development programmes, allowing a greater level of participation.

Skills development is a critical component of a just and inclusive transition, but other measures are necessary. A comprehensive approach should include bipartite and tripartite social dialogue, active labour market programmes (ALMPs), social protection, compliance with international labour standards, occupational safety and health, green enterprise development, counselling, and effective labour market institutions to provide job-matching and career counselling services, as well as to create and facilitate the transition to decent green jobs.

Coordination with macroeconomic, sustainable investment, industrial, sectoral, social, and enterprise policies will also be critical in enabling businesses to develop and implement greener and more resource-efficient production practises, to align skill supply with growing demand, and to facilitate smooth and efficient worker reallocation to newly created green jobs.

A just transition needs that education and training be regarded as vital for all individuals at all times of their lives, with a view to maximising the advantages of employment creation while minimising the difficulties of the transition to carbon neutrality. Although approaches to skills may differ depending on the national context and priorities in pursuit of a just transition, let us give a look at some key principles and concrete steps that countries can take in collaboration with social partners to advance a just transition toward environmentally sustainable economies and societies.

2 SKILLS POLICY IMPLICATIONS FOR A FAIR AND GREEN TRANSITION

Although substantial progress has been made in the last decade, there are critical skill difficulties that must be overcome in order to achieve a just transition to ecologically sustainable societies. National commitments and sectoral goals to execute the Paris Agreement, to name a few, have not included a significant skills development component to facilitate their implementation. Many countries lack comprehensive and systematic methods for green transition skills and active participation of stakeholders in debates about the greening agenda. While increasing skill gaps and shortages pose a challenge to the green transition, effective mechanisms for anticipating and monitoring those skill needs are uncommon. The special requirements of vulnerable and disadvantaged populations in responding to change during the green transition are not being addressed properly.[2]

A lack of policy coordination among tripartite constituents, training providers, and other stakeholders continues to be a major impediment to an effective and sustainable transition to greener production and consumption. For example, responsibility for policy areas important to green employment skills is still split across multiple ministries at the federal level. While ministries in charge of environmental policy are in charge of policies such as climate change, disaster risk management, and biodiversity, as well as the use of renewable energy sources and technologies, the transition to more inclusive and green economies can involve ministries in charge of the economy, employment/labour, education, agriculture, energy, industry, and trade. Labour, education, and training ministries are often the least involved in decisions and consultations on climate change and the environment. Inadequate inter-ministerial coordination is an obstacle to the effective design, planning, implementation, and assessment of policies on green jobs and climate action.

2.1 Skill Shortages Persist

Massive investments in reskilling and upskilling are required to equip workers with the technical (occupation-specific) and core (soft) skills required for the green transition. When a new product or service is introduced, skill gaps and shortages are almost unavoidable, and the green economy is no different. To this end, there has been progress in identifying and anticipating skill gaps, but it remains inadequately systematic to give comprehensive information on demand and supply of green jobs skills.[3]

Developing countries are particularly challenged by a scarcity of professionals and university graduates. Even in advanced countries with well-developed skills anticipation systems, employers face major recruitment challenges due to a dearth of both technical and transferrable core skills. Inadequately established skill anticipation

2. ILO, *Skills for a Greener Future: Challenges and Enabling Factors to Achieve a Just Transition*, Geneva, 2019.
3. ILO, *Global Commission on the Future of Work, Work for a Brighter Future*, Geneva, 2019.

systems impede countries' ability to identify skill gaps and analyse future training demands and shortages in a systematic and comprehensive manner.

Increased worker mobility is one emerging driver of change. Labour migration provides opportunities for many people, especially the unskilled. However, it may contribute to 'brain drain' and talent shortages in sending countries. In fact, climate-driven migration among impoverished communities needs the acquisition of new skill sets (including core skills) for workers entering new labour markets or seeking alternative employment.

Another significant global trend that emphasises the need to promote information and communication technology for the green economy and to build skills for green transitions to promote sustainable development is digitalization.[4]

3 RECENT DEVELOPMENT AT SECTORAL LEVEL

The green transition continues to have an impact on established occupations, necessitating reskilling, upskilling, and – less commonly – the formation of new green occupations. Higher skill levels are often where new occupations emerge, whereas lower skill levels typically merely require basic process improvements or more environmental awareness. Because these processes take time and frequently include minor stages, it is unknown how many professions have been 'greened' until now.

Environmental goods and services, as well as renewable energy, have made substantial progress at the sectoral level. For example, the majority of construction-related occupations have been affected. Despite the fact that agriculture faces considerable environmental challenges, it does not appear that skill sets have evolved considerably to date. The demand for green manufacturing capabilities varies substantially. Green employment requires both technical (occupationally specialised) and general (core) abilities. There are most likely multiple skill shortages and job openings in the workforce. While wealthier economies face gaps and shortages in both technical and soft skills, emerging countries face higher-level talent shortages in particular.[5]

Specific national settings and varying levels of development across sectors have shaped green structural change. Green structural change is more likely to harm fossil fuel-based industries and high-carbon-emitting sectors. Although the emergence of green jobs is commonly predicted, countries have made varying degrees of progress.

In circumstances when new technology or processes are used, the green transition continues to affect existing employment while also creating new green occupations.

Two elements are driving the green transition in economic and employment policies in high-income countries. The first is a push to increase energy efficiency and renewable energy consumption while minimising negative environmental repercussions. The second is the growing trend in green goods marketplaces. The sector of environmental goods and services is presently well-developed in those countries.

4. ILO, *World Employment and Social Outlook 2018: Greening with Jobs*, Geneva, 2018.
5. ILO, *Skills for a Greener Future: Key Findings*, Geneva, 2019.

Green markets, in general, have been key sources of employment development in industrialised nations in recent years; they are also emerging, albeit slowly, in developing ones.

The environment has a greater direct impact on people's lives in low-income countries. Climate change and environmental deterioration are most likely to have an impact on these countries' growth prospects, especially in sectors such as agriculture and extractive industries.

The most significant changes in skills and vocations for the green economy are occurring at higher skill levels, necessitating vocational training or university education. This is a key difficulty for many low-income countries, where access to education and training is limited, dropout rates are common, and essential skills are scarce.

Renewable energy has experienced the largest increase in job possibilities. Where government laws and actions support it, the environmental goods and services sector, which encompasses waste, energy, and water management, has grown tremendously. The employment implications of construction vary depending on the degree to which the existing built environment is 'greened' through retrofitting (primarily in high-income nations) and the emergence of the green building sector and 'smart cities'.

Other sectors' employment consequences of the green transition are likely to be complex. Manufacturing, particularly the automotive sector, is steadily shifting its production to make more energy-efficient goods, resulting in small net job growth but major changes in skill demand. However, it is also manufacturing green products and creating jobs in supply chains with large indirect employment benefits, such as the creation of parts for use in renewable energy, such as wind turbine production.

Agriculture, despite being subject to serious environmental issues and a major source of employment in most developing nations, does not appear to have undergone significant skill changes.

Green jobs in transportation and tourism have yet to be fully realised, although they have created considerable interest in countries seeking sustainable development.[6]

The COVID-19 pandemic-induced economic crisis and associated employment crisis decreased job options, including green jobs. Due to limited fiscal room for crisis management strategies, developing nations are disproportionately impacted; nonetheless, reskilling and upskilling initiatives will be crucial for economic recovery across the board. Employers, employees, and job seekers all realised the importance of investing in training for the green transition during the worldwide pandemic in order to either keep their current positions or take advantage of new employment opportunities created by the recovery of the economy. In order to ensure a human-centred, inclusive, resilient, and sustainable recovery from the current global crisis, the Global Call to Action, adopted at the 2021 International Labour Conference, outlined the promotion of skills development opportunities that are responsive to labour market needs and support for effective transitions as required policy measures.[7]

6. Cedefop, *Understanding Technological Change and Skill Needs: Skills Surveys and Skills Forecasting*, Cedefop practical guide 1, Luxembourg, 2021.
7. ILO, *Global Call to Action for a Human-centred Recovery from the COVID-19 Crisis that is Inclusive, Sustainable and Resilient*, ILC 109th session, Geneva, 2021.

Programs for developing skills do not put enough emphasis on gender issues or the needs of disadvantaged populations.

There are still not many programmes specifically geared toward the needs of vulnerable groups. The jobless and people in insecure employment situations are typically the focus of ALMPs relating to skills for green jobs. One of the few instances of national policies or specific public employment services (PES) efforts that concentrate on skills for green jobs is ALMPs to support populations made vulnerable by the transition and to foresee potential skills shortages. Low-skilled workers and individuals who are either currently jobless or in danger of becoming unemployed as a result of some activities being phased out as part of the greening process are frequently included in these groupings. PES projects frequently target youth, indigenous peoples, people with impairments, or migrant workers who are unemployed.

4 SKILLS PREDICTION AND MONITORING

In recent years, efforts to detect and forecast skills needs have grown, but systems to offer full information on green job skills demand and supply are still lacking. Some countries have an institution or monitoring mechanism to identify green employment skills. Most developing countries do not track skills needs for green occupations or otherwise, thus they are identified ad hoc.

Skills anticipation systems that involve the private sector are rare. This makes it hard to create specialised skills policies, adapt skills training and ALMPs to present and future need, and influence technical and vocational education and training institutions (TVET) (often by adding green components to existing curriculum, qualifications or education programmes). Few countries have procedures to create green work skills.

5 JUST TRANSITION PRINCIPLES AND STEPS

Current and future workers can become responsible producers and consumers with the proper technical and core skills for a just transformation. They may effectively promote a just transition in their workplaces and society. This requires governments (by creating the conditions and investing in education and training), employers (by training their employees), and individual workers (by developing their competencies and careers through active engagement in lifelong learning opportunities), with education and training institutions delivering demand-led training and social partners playing an active role.

6 POLICY COHERENCE, SOCIAL DISCOURSE, AND PARTNERSHIP CAN ACCELERATE THE GREEN TRANSFORMATION

The 109th session of the International Labour Conference of 2021 recognised that education and training is a right for all and stated that, taking into account national circumstances, governments should work in cooperation with social partners to ensure lifelong learning for all. The International Labour Organization (ILO) should support governments in coordinating education and training policies with other public policies. Sectoral or subnational policies and strategies can partially fill the national policy coordination 'gap' in the skills for green jobs landscape. Weak social partner's participation can harm green job skills policy coordination and relevance. Thus, top-down coordinated policymaking and bottom-up actions could support the green transition better and longer.

Policies and programmes at sectoral or subnational governmental levels can fill the policy coordination 'gap' that is so prevalent in the skills for green jobs landscape.

The coordination and relevance of policies regarding skills for green occupations can suffer where social partner's engagement is low. Therefore, a mix of bottom-up efforts and top-down coordinated policymaking could offer more efficient and long-lasting support for the green transition.

A crucial requirement of a just transition is providing workers with the appropriate training. Trade unions and employers' associations can significantly increase the responsiveness of education and training and spark a more widespread green transformation by actively participating in social dialogue and partnerships related to the planning, design, implementation, and evaluation of skills development. Additionally, all major stakeholders, including governments, social partners, and training institutions at all levels, will need to review and (re)formulate policies for skill development, including ways to validate and recognise skills and all forms of past learning. Through collaborative methods, skills development in formal TVET can be informed by knowledge of greening advancements from the front lines of industry, agriculture, and services. Public-private partnerships (PPPs) can combine public and private resources and draw on the practical expertise of businesses on the quality and usefulness of skills.[8]

7 WELL-DEVELOPED, SOUND NATIONAL AND SECTORAL POLICIES ENABLE THE JUST TRANSITION

Government policy is crucial to the effort to make the transition to a green economy. There are two major ways that policies pertaining to skills for green occupations come about: they are formed either specifically or as a component of larger environmental and economic policies. Economic and employment strategies usually have a sectoral or regional component, which offers an easy means of including a green component. At the sectoral, regional, and project levels, integrating skills for green occupations can be done as part of national strategy, independently in response to sectoral, regional, or local demands, or as a combination of the two. Sometimes national policy gaps are really filled by activity at the local level.

Sectoral programmes for green job skills, funded by government levies and incentives, are particularly prevalent in industries immediately impacted by climate

8. ILO, *Shaping Skills and Lifelong Learning for the Future of Work*, International Labour Conference 109th session, Geneva, 2021.

change and environmental degradation, such as waste management, energy, transportation, and construction. The shift to sustainable economies depends heavily on the involvement of both private and governmental enterprises as well as trade unions.

8 CORE AND TRANSFERABLE SKILLS

To support the shift to a greener economy, a variety of fundamental and technical skills is required. Regardless of the general level of competence required for their job, all workers require a certain set of core competencies.

In order to bridge the skills gap and facilitate the green transition, a more rigorous approach to the study and forecasting of demand for green work skills is urgently required, along with better information and statistics on skills and occupational demands. Effective and targeted planning of skills development for just transition and skills matching is challenging to achieve without good quality, systematic, and reliable data on supply and demand connected to green occupations and labour market information. In order to meet the need for skilled workers for green occupations, countries should provide themselves with the anticipating, forecasting, and monitoring tools they require.

Where systems for predicting skill requirements already exist, they can be modified to include additional specifications and elements. In less developed countries where such frameworks are lacking, there is an opportunity to establish structures like a national human resources development council (NHRC) that involve the government, employers, workers, and providers of training and education in order to promote information exchange and to establish industry groupings that could later be formally recognised as sectoral skills bodies. An inclusive, human-centred approach to the green transition is facilitated and supported through systematic anticipating of skills needs, career assistance, and counselling programmes through sectoral skills bodies.

9 TARGETED AND INCLUSIVE TRAINING BY WELL-EQUIPPED TEACHERS IS ESSENTIAL

The availability of teachers and trainers who are up to date on sustainable land and ecosystem management, energy efficiency, and green technology is essential for effective training. They play a crucial role in encouraging young people to be environmentally conscious and in extending climate education and environmental training outside of the traditional educational system to the adult population. Any skills response strategy at the national, sub-national, and sectoral levels should therefore give top emphasis to the education and training of such instructors and trainers.

Even if many countries try to incorporate less represented groups in their programmes for developing skills for green professions, these groups still don't get adequate access to useful training possibilities. Youth, older workers, women, people with disabilities, indigenous people, migrant workers, unemployed people, informal workers, people with HIV/AIDS, refugees, low-skilled workers, indigenous and tribal peoples, and those living in rural areas are among the groups in need of urgently developing systematic reskilling and upskilling initiatives on green jobs. To close gender gaps in the labour market and address skill shortages in certain occupations, women must be included in apprenticeship programmes and skill training for jobs in the environmentally friendly sector. Through technical training programmes in particular, incentives to increase women's participation in industries with the potential for green growth will accomplish the dual goals of addressing the skills shortage issues in this field and boosting women's employment in technologically oriented occupations. Additionally, MSMEs frequently lack the resources to conduct training on their own, therefore supportive policies for them to encourage workforce training in response to climate change are crucial for a just transition.

TVET must become more structurally involved in the transition to low-carbon and resource-efficient economies and societies in order to adapt to shifting job possibilities and skill requirements. They have the potential to guarantee that the transition to a greener economy is fair and just through their capacity to equip the existing and future workforce with the necessary knowledge and abilities to alter workplaces, communities, and society as a whole. Therefore, it is crucial to strengthen the governance and management frameworks needed to mainstream green transition in TVET systems as well as to include skills for green transition in the creation or renewal of competency standards, curricula, training, and assessment packages in both initial and ongoing TVET.

By fostering and empowering a PPP for green jobs, the private sector, multinational corporations, and the public sector can work together to address the demands for skills development and training. A sustainable and effective TVET system must be established in order to build skills within industries and businesses. Small and medium enterprises, as well as cooperatives and workers' organisations, must be included. PPPs can encourage collaborative peer learning and knowledge sharing among businesses, workers, and education and training institutions on the application of green technologies and good green practices. PPPs can also catalyse and boost diversified, innovative, and new approaches to financing lifelong learning. Additionally, they can serve as a platform for group efforts to promote systematically the TVET system.[9]

Financial incentives play a crucial role in how green markets function and support other factors that influence the development of skills for green professions. Some nations provide special financial incentives, such as tax exemptions, training vouchers, levy-grant programmes, and individual training accounts to promote training. Strong and inclusive PPPs may play a key role in easing budgetary restrictions on the efficient provision of high-quality training and in creating additional opportunities to establish novel, creative, and data-driven skills development policies.

A good number of countries have been implementing recovery plans and budgetary stimulus measures in the wake of the COVID-19 outbreak. An increasing number of requests are asking for the economic recovery from the pandemic to be more environmentally friendly, inclusive, and resilient after seeing how unprepared global systems were to handle the catastrophe and safeguard the environment, health, and

9. ILO, *Greening TVET and Skills Development: A Practical Guidance Tool*, Geneva, 2022.

economy. In order to recover from the crisis, governments are incorporating green initiatives into their economic stimulus plans.

The effectiveness of green fiscal stimulus and recovery measures depends critically on the availability of workers with the necessary skills for jobs in the green sector. Therefore, it is essential to allocate significant resources to upskilling and reskilling employees. This will improve countries' capacity to capitalise on new green job possibilities and increase transferability across industries and occupations. Green fiscal stimulus and recovery measures should include support for employers and workers in sectors adversely affected by the green transition and the present global crisis as well as skills development and training for green jobs.

10 CONCLUSIONS

The green transition has the potential to create millions of jobs, but only if the necessary knowledge and abilities are widely disseminated. The Just Transition Guidelines emphasise the importance of anticipating skill needs and gaining insight into the labour market to understand how the green transition will affect the demand for specific types of workers. Skills for green jobs need to be mainstreamed and standardised across countries.

Climate and environmental policies should also incorporate proactive labour market and career guidance measures and social protection mechanisms, in addition to a forward-looking skills strategy. In addition, it is essential to consider the requirements of marginalised and defenceless communities in order to accomplish a fair and inclusive transition. It will also need tripartite social dialogue between government, employer, and worker representatives, as well as involvement from civil society actors, educators and trainers at all levels, and the international community. By coordinating line ministries and agencies, actively involving social partners with a stake in the green agenda, and increasing the coherence of skills policies and environmental policies, governments can play a crucial role in advancing the green agenda.

Training can be made more relevant and effective if employers' organisations share data on the dynamics of the labour market and how the demand for different skills is evolving. They play a crucial part in both the dissemination of learning opportunities and the continued application of acquired skills in the workplace.

Workers' organisations are crucial in facilitating the acquisition of green-sector job-related skills and promoting the recognition of prior learning and experience. Their importance cannot be overstated when it comes to just transition measures like training and green clauses in collective bargaining agreements.

In order to make a just transition toward environmentally sustainable economies and societies for all, educational institutions must increase the responsiveness of their curricula to the needs of the labour market and equip their students, faculty, and staff with the knowledge and skills necessary to become change agents.

CHAPTER 6

The Labor Instruments of Internal Flexibility at the Service of the Just Ecological Transition in the Context of the Next Generation EU

Margarita Miñarro Yanini

1 INTRODUCTION: THE CHANGES IN THE INDUSTRY IMPOSED BY THE CLIMATE EMERGENCY AND BY THE CRISIS OF DIRTY ENERGY SOURCES

The situation of "climate emergency" was institutionally declared by Resolution of November 28, 2019, of the European Parliament, involving actions that affect climate change as a threat to life on the planet. On the reality level, the torrid summer of 2022, with temperatures in Spain up to 4°C above average and heat waves extended for weeks,[1] confirmed that the forecasts are not catastrophic messages of the future, but rather evidence of what is already difficult to evade and that is unfolding totally perceptible consequences.[2]

Scientific reports have long pointed out this "global social risk"[3] of destruction of the planet of Anthropocene[4] origin, and the need to act urgently and intensely to stop it. The emission of greenhouse gases (GHG) has been in exponential progression since the Industrial Revolution, rampant in recent decades. Industrial activity is the priority

1. https://www.aemet.es/es/noticias/2022/09/resumen_clima_agosto_2022.
2. The number of people who died in Spain from causes related to heat amounts to 4,700 people, tripling the figure for the previous year, vid https://www.rtve.es/noticias/20220907/muertes-atribuidas-calor-espana/2397831.shtml.
3. Vid. U. Beck, *Word Risk society*, Polity Press-Blackwell Publishers, 1999, p. 12.
4. Vid. UNESCO "Antropoceno: la problemática vital de un debate científico," https://tg24.sky.it/salute-e-benessere/2023/07/10/morti-per-il-caldo.

source of these emissions, so it is essential to reduce them by changing energy sources to cleaner ones and adopting energy-saving measures. These measures, which are obvious to achieve the result of reducing GHG, do not seem so obvious to the authorities. Regarding the second, although it is the most logical and simple to apply, it has not been seriously considered in the context of the fight against climate change. However, opportunely, energy saving measures have been implemented in the framework of the current energy crisis caused by the cut in Russian gas supply, but even though this has not been their priority objective, they forget to also link it with the reduction of emissions, focusing exclusively on the goal of maintaining production.

There is no doubt that the necessary global action adds complexity to the approach to climate change, as it lacks a "planetary constitutionalism"[5] and a global institutional authority that guarantees the protection of the environment. With regard to the states considered independently, generally, prevailing in this area are cosmetic measures, weak commitments and plans so flexible that they are useless in curbing climate change. Unlimited economic growth seems to be the only watchword to follow,[6] with cosmetic measures, weak commitments and plans so flexible that they are useless to stop climate change prevailing in this area.

2 THE NECESSARY GREEN TRANSITION IN INDUSTRY: LEGAL BASES AND TECHNIQUES IN KEY TO FLEXIBILITY

2.1 The Concurrent Green and Digital Transition Processes and Their Necessary Interconnection

The new community legal order regulating the green transition process is promoting reforms in labor and Social Security systems in order to introduce channels that improve the sustainability of employment as well as the resilience of legal systems and institutions.[7] As far as Spain is concerned, the processes of economic and technological transition—green and digital—in the workplace are reflected in the Spanish labor reform introduced by Royal Decree-Law (RDL) 32/2021, of December 28, on urgent measures for labor reform, the guaranteed stability in employment and the transformation of the labor market. This standard reflects from its preamble the evolution that is taking place in the workplace, alluding to the need to address the transformations

5. Vid. L. Ferrajoli, *Por una Constitución de la Tierra*, Madrid, Trotta, 2022, p. 47.
6. In Spain, there seems to be more concern about the reduction in income from tourism that rising temperatures will bring, than the effect that this will have on the health and living conditions of Spanish people, https://cincodias.elpais.com/cincodias/2022/08/29/companias/1661784356_656971.html.
7. Interesting global analysis of the impact of the sustainability approach in Labor Law in B. Caruso, R. Del Punta, T. Treu, T., 2020, *Il Manifesto per un diritto del lavoro sostenibile*, http://csdle.lex.unict.it/Archive/AC/Webliography/Blogs/20200521-032536_Manifesto_Caruso_Del_Punta_Treupdf.pdf. A critical vision, from the trade union point of view, P.P. Bombardier, *Il Manifesto per un diritto del lavoro sostenibile*, en "Il Diritto del lavoro del futuro. Opinione a confronto sul "Manifesto di Caruso, Del Punta, Treu, *Lavoro, Dritti, Europa* n. 2, octubre 2020. Also on the subject, M.E. CASAS BAAMONDE, 2021, *El derecho del trabajo en la emergencia de la pandemia de la covid-19. ¿Y después?*, Real Academia de Ciencias Morales y Políticas.

and challenges of the future, the changing circumstantial situations, or the necessary adaptation to changes in productive transitions.

Regarding the specification of the causes of this transit, he repeatedly refers to the digital transition as a trigger for the changes that will affect companies, and also, but less frequently, to the ecological transformation. Although the green transition is implicit in the reform law, it is objectionable that it is not referred to the same extent as the digital one, since both transitions are interrelated, so they must be treated together. It is also missing that no regulatory mechanism has been introduced that involves workers in environmental sustainability, such as environmental alert rights[8]—which are included in the proposal for a due diligence Directive on sustainability.

The Council Conclusions of December 17, 2020,[9] establish the connection between the two transitions, showing that it is not univocal, but rather has positive and negative effects. Thus, from the first dimension, it highlights that digitization creates opportunities for environmental protection and climate action. From the second, it promotes channels to limit the emissions produced by high energy consumption, or the "rebound effect" that digitization can cause in the environment.

The Next Generation funds also have an impact on the ecological and digital transitions, which they place on an equal footing,[10] since both involve the transformation in the way of producing, consuming and working, which will mean short-term staff adjustments for working people and/or need to be trained in new skills to carry out their tasks or to carry out different ones in the event that their positions disappear.

2.2 The Impact of the Green Transition on Employment

It has been pointed out that the current ecological transition is a new industrial revolution since it involves a change in energy sources that also has a "drag effect" on all productive sectors.[11] This transition to a model without or with low emissions, or more broadly to "green" processes, requires redesigning the way of producing and consuming, but also the way of working, for which profound reforms will be necessary for all sectors, which will have important labor consequences.[12]

However, this transition will not affect all sectors to the same extent, because although it will have the most intense effect on the fossil fuel and "dirty energy" industries, which must necessarily be transformed or disappear, in other cases, it will require lesser transformations entity or mere adjustments.[13]

8. Vid. M. Miñarro Yanini, *Libertad de crítica de la persona trabajadora como derecho de alerta: de la lucha contra la corrupción a la protección medioambiental*, 2020, Revista de Trabajo y Seguridad Social CEF, n°453, p. 207 ss.
9. https://data.consilium.europa.eu/doc/document/ST-13957-2020-INIT/es/pdf.
10. Next Generation EU, https://nexteugeneration.com.
11. B. Estrada, (coord), 2009, "Reflexiones y propuestas para el cambio de modelo productivo en España," Fundación 1° de Mayo, p. 37.
12. The green modernization of the industrial model must involve an energy-efficient organization of work and the redefinition of the relationship between workers and the company in productive activity, vid. *Ibid* p. 33.
13. OIT *Directrices de política para una transición justa hacia economías y sociedades ambientalmente sostenibles para todos*, 2015, p. 6.

This process can have a traumatic effect on employment in the short term, requiring adjustments to the workforce, entity and variable duration, and thereby generating a scenario of some "instability," However, in the medium and long term, the implementation of a green, or at least sustainable, industrial model can have a positive balance in terms of employment, and even be a source of decent jobs.[14] In any case, this impact will be less if "just labor transition plans" have been established that balance the needs for flexibility and security.[15]

3 INSTRUMENTS FOR THE ECOLOGICAL TRANSITION

3.1 The Tools for the Green Transition: Brief Reference to Its Background and Rationale

The cost in labor terms of the green transition must be alleviated by legal-labor regulations and institutions through instruments that facilitate the "just ecological transition." These must give companies flexibility and protect workers during the transition process and prepare them for the new stage. In this sense, it is an essential condition for the transition of the model to be successful, the training of workers in the new skills, in relation to the work that was being developed or to the one that will be developed in the future, as well as in internships companies and technologies from the standards of sustainability and respect for the environment, including, where appropriate, requalification.[16]

To this end, two instruments have been introduced into the legal system, the new ERTES and the RED mechanism for Employment Flexibilization and Stabilization. Its design—more than that of the first, but also in the second—is based on a flexibility mechanism that has been included in the Spanish legal system for decades in Article 47 Worker's Statute—ET—and which was later redefined during the COVID pandemic in order to protect economic activity and employment,[17] the "ERTE covid."[18] It is a tool that gives prevalence to the management of internal flexibility of employment against the rupture of the employment relationship.

14. S. Foster y D. Elzinga *El papel de los combustibles fósiles en un sistema energético sostenible*, ONU, https://www.un.org/es/chronicle/article/el-papel-de-los-combustibles-fosiles-en-un-sistema-energetico-sostenible.
15. Vid. https://www.lavanguardia.com/economia/20220204/8021155/coche-electrico-empleo-trabajo-destruir-crear.html.
16. OIT *Directrices de política para una transición justa hacia economías y sociedades ambientalmente sostenibles para todos*, 2015, p. 14.
17. Regulation (EU) 2021/241, of February 12, which establishes the Recovery and Resilience Mechanism, which has a stable and standardized vocation, although the execution period is temporary, responds to this orientation. For its part, Regulation (EU) 2021/1056, which creates the Just Transition Fund, in its Recital 4, states that it must contribute to addressing the social, economic and environmental consequences for the workers affected in the process. transition to climate neutrality of the Union by 2050.
18. On these, can *see* C. Molina Navarrete, *El COVID-19 y el arte de lo (jurídicamente) posible: del estrés legislativo al colapso interpretativo*, 2020, Revista de Trabajo y Seguridad Social CEF, n°446, p. 5 ss. y *Del dulce sueño de los ERTE al (abrupto) despertar del concurso*, 2021, Revista de Trabajo y Seguridad Social CEF, n°455, p. 167 ss.

3.2 ERTEs for the Green Transition

The ERTEs regulated in Article 47 ET have been modified by RDL 32/2021 to adapt them to the green (and digital) transition processes. This is a temporary employment regulation measure that can be applied for economic, technical, organizational, production or force majeure reasons.

After the rediscovery of their usefulness in the crisis caused by COVID-19, the government has maintained them in the context of the ecological and digital transition but introduced some changes to adapt them to the specific demands that they pose, with the aim that may constitute a useful transitional channel.[19] With them, the company is allowed to reduce the working day or suspend contracts—with legal preference of the first—from 10% to 70%, configuring a flexible application measure that offers some benefits—recognition of exemptions or reductions in business fees ...—(Article 153 *bis* General Social Security Law—LGSS). Although this instrument does not require that training be provided, it should be noted that it entails greater advantages when training actions are carried out (Additional Provision—DA—25ª ET and Article 9 Law 30/2015). At the same time, it gives working people occupational stability and social protection during the transition—unemployment coverage, ease of reconciling reduced working hours and effective work ... (Article 267 LGSS).

Regarding the adoption procedure, ERTEs due to economic, organizational and production techniques can be applied by the company after negotiation with the labor representative, without the need to reach an agreement, while those due to force majeure require administrative authorization from the labor authority (Article 47 ET).

3.3 The RED Mechanism for Flexibilization and Stabilization of Employment at the Service of the Fair Green Transition

RDL 32/2021 has introduced in Article 47, *bis* ET the "RED Mechanism for Flexibilization and Stabilization of Employment"—RED mechanism. This is a new measure that is designed to deal with periods of instability, such as the productive transition phase to a model of environmental sustainability, as it is an instrument that gives flexibility to companies and stability to workers.

The RED mechanism, unlike the ERTEs ex Article 47 ET, requires a government's political decision to be activated—Order of the Council of Ministers—which will activate its financing through a fund created and provided ad hoc. In addition, in this mechanism, the training of workers is a mandatory element, which makes it even more useful for the transitional effects examined.

This mechanism has been developed by RD-Law 4/2022, by which support measures are adopted for the agricultural sector due to drought—also linked to climate change. The objective of this development is to speed up the application of this instrument in the sectors most threatened by the new emergency derived from the

19. On the potential of ERTEs in the ecological transition, vid. C. MOLINA NAVARRETE, *Angelus novus, del futuro de los ERTE a los ERTE del futuro*, 2021, Revista de Trabajo y Seguridad Social CEF, nº464, p. 5 ss.

inflation crisis—especially due to uncontrolled energy prices, also unrelated to the digital transition—aggravated by the war in Ukraine.

Like the ERTE, the RED mechanism allows the company to reduce the working day or suspend contracts—with legal preference for the first—from 10% to 70%. This is a measure that, once activated, must be authorized in each case by the labor authority, and that is accompanied by social protection for workers through a special benefit analogous to unemployment but with ad hoc and different regulation (DA 41 LGSS, and Temporary Provision—DT—3 RD-Law 4/2022), since they are not listed as unemployed, and benefits in contributions and exemptions for the company (Article 153 *bis* and DA 44 RD-Law 4/2022).

There are two modes of RED mechanism. The first is designed for "cyclical" crises, in order to deal with emergency situations or recurrent difficulties that affect all sectors of activity—such as a new pandemic, or a new global economic crisis—and its maximum duration is of a year The second is of a "sectoral" nature and its purpose is to facilitate balanced management of the transformations of specific sectors, when permanent changes occur in them that cause requalification needs and transition processes of the workers, being its duration of a year with the possibility of two six-month extensions. In this way, this second instrument has the specific purpose of dealing with the green and digital transitions, mitigating their impact on employment. Consequently, it can be said that it is a tool at the service of a just ecological social transition.

An example of the orientation of the sectoral RED mechanism to these transitions is that the training of affected workers plays a fundamental role in it, since the regulation requires that a plan be presented that meets the needs of retraining and professional transition processes, so that training constitutes an essential element of the temporary employment regulation mechanism. The DA 25ª ET corroborates the relevance of occupational guarantees linked to requalification in the RED mechanism, although again it only makes express reference to training in technological skills, although it is clear that it must also be integrated with ecological skills required by the green transition. Thus, within the framework of the green—and digital—transition processes, it is essential to reinforce continuous professional training, and even requalification, to meet the demands of environmental sustainability—and technological transformation. In this way, training in/for sustainable employment is configured as an obligation, and also as a duty, within the framework of what would be a new fundamental human social right.[20] In Spain, this specific training for the new professional skills is guaranteed in Organic Law—LO—3/2022, of March 31, on the organization and integration of Vocational Training, through the so-called dual system of vocational training.

For the rest, the mechanism foreseen for the financing of the RED mechanism also shows its connection with green recovery policies. Thus, Article 47, *bis*, 6, includes the Next Generation EU Funds among its sources of financing, and it should be noted that 37% of the almost EUR 2 billion of the Next Generation Funds and the

20. For training as a "universal social right" vid. B. Caruso, R. Del Punta, T. Treu, *Il Manifesto per un Diritto del lavoro sostenibile,* cit. p. 33 y ss.

Budget will be allocated to the Green Deal in the long term of the EU. The RED Fund, created to finance the measure, will be made up of these amounts plus the excess income that finances unemployment benefits and the contributions that are consigned in the General Budgets (Article 47, *bis*, 6 ET and DA 5ª RD—Law 4/2022).

4 CONCLUSIONS

To conclude this brief analysis, we must focus on the reality of industrial change in which we are immersed, which is going to produce very notable effects on employment. In this way, the ecological transition that the industry must undergo will necessarily be projected in labor relations. The new sustainable model of producing and working that must be implemented constitutes an opportunity to create decent employment. However, for this, it is necessary to establish a regulatory framework that ensures decent working conditions and guarantees compliance for workers.

However, before reaching that situation there will be a period that is especially complicated and can cause an employment crisis. Therefore, this transit time must be well managed, in order to avoid the vulnerability of workers or even their expulsion from the labor market. It is the task of governments and social agents to establish measures aimed at mitigating the effects of these changes on workers so that they are not left unprotected and to ensure adequate labor to develop new production processes. This must be done through the adoption of measures that guarantee the maintenance of the contractual bond, a livelihood that allows them to lead a decent life and adequate training in the new green production processes. Although it seems obvious, it must be emphasized that this training is essential not only for workers to be able to return to work once the transit process is over but also for companies, since otherwise they will not have staff adequately instructed in the new production processes. In this way, it is essential that instruments are established for a just ecological social transition that meets these demands. In Spain, this need has been covered by RDL 32/2021, which has introduced two appropriate mechanisms in the ET to deal with this transition, the new ERTEs and the RED mechanism, the latter measure of great relevance given that it is specifically designed to deal with these processes of change.

CHAPTER 7

Challenges When Combining Labour and Environmental Objectives: Trade and Sustainable Development Chapters and Beyond

Tonia Novitz[*]

1 INTRODUCTION

'Sustainable development' is the catchphrase for the design (and re-design) of social policy across the globe. This chapter explores the potential implications for labour law of this policy-based approach in the context of European Union (EU) efforts to combine trade and sustainable development (TSD) and their global impact. In particular, the chapter examines challenges that arise when combining labour and environmental objectives, considering the relationship between substantive sustainable development norms (economic, environmental and social), as well as their connection to procedural sustainable development norms concerned with 'good governance'.

There might seem to be a tension between the longer-term aims of sustainable development, which have become associated with the achievement of concrete and durable goals, and the process-based orientation of good governance. My argument is that this would be a false dichotomy. The actual shape and content of Sustainable

* Professor of Labour Law, University of Bristol. Earlier versions of this paper were presented at the 8th Seminar on International and Comparative Labour Law and Climate Change: towards just transition' at Ca' Foscari University of Venice in May 2022, and as an invited lecture at the University of Luxembourg hosted by Professor Luca Ratti as the Jean Monnet Chair on a Sustainable European SociAl ModEl (SESAME). I am grateful to my hosts and for the comments from those who attended. Any errors in this final version of the chapter are my own.

Development Goals (SDGs),[1] which can only be stated in general terms within a guiding framework at the international level, are going to be determined by the processes through which they are interpreted and implemented at the global, regional, transnational, national and local levels. So it is not only the substantive norms associated with sustainability but also how sustainable processes (or good governance systems) operate which matters. It is here that the importance of what is 'good' in governance needs to be interrogated.

We can identify certain substantive values understood as intrinsic to sustainable development: such as equality within and between states, between persons (gender equality but also between various categories of workers – precarious, migrant, young and old for example), as well as procedural norms of transparency, participatory access, inclusiveness and influence. My suggestion is that we need to think about freedom of association and collective worker voice as part of that process, seeking representation of all those in the world of work and across the globe, when crafting TSD policies which pursue environmental and labour objectives.

The EU has for some time now made a connection between sustainable development and good governance explicit in the language used in its external trade instruments, for example, in the Generalized System of Preferences (especially GSP +) and in TSD chapters included in free trade agreements (FTAs).[2] So, rather than demanding an external relations policy which reflects and is consistent with internal EU policy norms,[3] as is often the case when looking for policy social coherence,[4] there is an interesting role reversal here. We could ask instead: how can the internal social policy of the EU also be recrafted along sustainable development lines, and which norms (economic, environmental and social) could be applied and, as importantly, *how* should that be done?

The EU is facing a number of challenges when crafting social policy today – to 'build back' from COVID and counter the impact of war in Ukraine, but also to

1. As set out by United Nations (UN), Transforming our World: The 2030 Agenda for Sustainable Development, General Assembly, 70th Session, A/Res/70/1, New York, 2015 (UN 2030 Agenda) available at: https://sustainabledevelopment.un.org/post2015/transformingourworld.
2. Regulation (EU) No 978/2012 of the European Parliament and of the Council of 25 October 2012 applying a scheme of generalised tariff preferences and repealing Council Regulation (EC) No 732/2008 OJ L 303/1 31 October 2012 which applies until 31 December 2023. For the Commission's most recent proposal for a new GSP Regulation, *see* COM(2021) 579 22 September 2021 available at: https://eur-lex.europa.eu/resource.html?uri = cellar:0fe49a24-1c94-11ec-b4fe-01aa 75ed71a1.0024.02/DOC_1&format = PDF. *See also* Commission Communication, 'The power of trade partnerships: together for green and just economic growth' COM(2022) 409 final, 22 June 2022.
3. European Commission Communication, 'Europe in the world – some practical proposals for greater coherence, effectiveness and visibility' COM(2006)278, 8 June 2006 at 4: 'There is an inextricable link between the EU's internal and external policies. From the very beginning the Treaty recognized that there could be no internal market without the common customs regime and a common trade policy … Similar reasoning applies in a range of other policies – for example, … employment and social policy … – where the development of internal policies has naturally led to a more active external role for the EU.'
4. Tonia Novitz, 'In Search of a Coherent Social Policy: EU Import and Export of ILO Labour Standards?' in Jan Orbie and Lisa Tortell (eds), *The European Union and the Social Dimension of Globalization: How the EU Influences the World* (London, Routledge, 2009), 27-44.

operationalise the new Green Deal and Just Transitions (both green and digital) within EU Member States and beyond EU borders. The von der Leyen Commission has been extremely active on all these fronts. This chapter will examine how sustainable development has been treated by this Commission as foundational to its external and internal policy objectives regarding environmental and labour protections but also interrogate the extent to which collective worker voice has been contemplated as desirable for the adoption and implementation of these measures.

My suggestion is that this engagement with workers and their representatives is of particular importance in relation to what I term 'hybrid' internal market measures. These pursue policies motivated by sustainable development objectives, which will have significant implications for the trade, environmental and social aspirations of third countries, especially for those who work there. My argument is that attention to freedom of association is vital, as are norms regarding equality and representative participation set out in the SDGs. The experience of workers both within and outside Europe, including those engaged in a wider 'world of work', which encompasses precarious and so-called atypical work,[5] is vital to the reconciliation of environmental and social objectives which the European Commission espouses.

2 THE SDGs: WHAT CAN THEY DO FOR THOSE 'AT WORK'?

Sustainable development has gradually emerged as a powerful and influential concept on the global stage. Without necessarily wholly subscribing to all the assumptions that underlie this notion or advocating its current dominance in policy debates, it is important to acknowledge that its significance is indisputable. Labour lawyers and social policymakers cannot afford to let this issue pass us by. Instead, we need to interrogate the relevance of sustainable development for those at work.

Sustainability is usually understood in terms of the construction of durable policies for the three so-called pillars of economic, social and environmental development.[6] Famously, it has been said that development is 'sustainable' that 'meets the needs of the present without compromising the ability of future generations to meet their own needs', which requires consideration 'of the long term as well as the short-term advantages and disadvantages of alternative actions'.[7] In this context, '*intra-generational justice*' can be understood as the fair distribution of resources between countries and people within a current generation, while the term '*inter-generational justice*' refers to the need to balance what is fair for present *and* future generations.[8]

5. Jeff Kenner, Izabela Florczak and Marta Otto (eds), *Precarious Work: The Challenge for Labour Law in Europe* (Edward Elgar 2019). *See* regarding use of the term 'world of work', the 2008 ILO Declaration on Social Justice for a Fair Globalization and most recently ILO Convention No. 190 on Violence and Harassment.
6. Ben Purvis, Yong Mao, & Darren Robinson, 'Three Pillars of Sustainability: In Search of Conceptual Origins' (2019) 14(3) *Sustainability Science* 681 DOI: 10.1007/s11625-018-0627-5.
7. World Commission on Environment and Development, *Our Common Future* (Oxford, Oxford University Press. 1987), at 51.
8. Discussed in Tonia Novitz, 'Gig Work as a Manifestation of Short: Termism – Crafting a Sustainable Regulatory Agenda' (2021) 50(4) *Industrial Law Journal* 636, at 640 onwards DOI: 10.1093/indlaw/dwab027.

The latter can have implications for a trade-off between the current generation's social needs (including those of workers) and the longer-term future of the planet.

Seventeen SDGs and associated targets were elaborated in the 2030 Agenda adopted by a United Nations (UN) General Assembly Resolution in 2015.[9] Further 'indicators' for assessment of whether the targets have been realised were created in 2017.[10] These UN policies can be viewed as the culmination of a series of international initiatives adopted by the international community from 1972 onwards.[11] Arguably, there has been some see-sawing between the priorities given to economic and environmental development, with social development receiving more limited attention over the years. Some legal academic commentators like Klaus Bosselmann[12] and Virginie Barral[13] view sustainability as predominantly an ecological principle; while others consider that economic development and aspirations for a 'green economy' lie at its core.[14] However, it is most helpful for the purpose of this chapter to focus on the actual terms of the 2030 Agenda and its significance for potential regulation of work.

This first part of the chapter seeks to analyse how the 2030 Agenda and the SDGs can have relevance for labour. This will involve examination of what we can learn from the preamble and other statements made in the UNGA Resolution. This part then goes on to consider the importance of the substantive norms (whether environmental or social) set out in the SDGs (as well as their associated targets and indicators), together with the processes for their realisation. There are both substantive and procedural norms at play here.

2.1 The Aims of the 2030 Agenda

The preamble to the 2030 Agenda stated that the economic, environmental and social aspects of sustainable development are to be regarded as 'integrated and indivisible'. The aim is to 'balance' these 'three dimensions'.[15] Moreover, '[t]he interlinkages and integrated nature of the Sustainable Development Goals are of crucial importance in

9. The 2030 Agenda n. 1 above.
10. *See* International Institute for Sustainable Development, *Policy Brief: Getting to 2030: Tracking SDG Indicators for Evidence of Implementation Progress* (2018) available at: http://sdg.iisd.org/commentary/policy-briefs/getting-to-2030-tracking-sdg-indicators-for-evidence-of-implementation-progress/; and *Decent Work and the Sustainable Development Goals: A Guidebook on SDG Labour Market Indicators* (Geneva, ILO, 2018).
11. *See* the analysis in Margherita Pieraccini and Tonia Novitz, *Sustainability and Law: A Historical and Theoretical Overview* in Margherita Pieraccini and Tonia Novitz (eds), *Legal Perspectives on Sustainability* (Bristol, Bristol University Press, 2020).
12. Klaus Bosselmann, *The Principle of Sustainability: Transforming Law and Governance*, 2nd ed. (London, Routledge, 2016).
13. Virginie Barral, 'Sustainable Development in International Law: Nature and Operation of an Evolutive Legal Norm' (2012) 23(2) *European Journal of International Law* 377 DOI: 10.1093/ejil/chs016.
14. For a critical view of this trend, *see* Lucien Georgeson, Mark Maslin, and Martyn Poessinouw, 'The Global Green Economy: A Review of Concepts, Definitions, Measurement Methodologies and Their Interactions' (2017) 4(1) *Geo: Geography and Environment* e00036 DOI: 10.1002/geo2.36.
15. *See* UN 2030 Agenda n. 1, preamble and Introduction to the Declaration, para. 2.

ensuring that the purpose of the new Agenda is realized'.[16] This suggests that the social dimension of sustainability (which could include labour-related issues) will be placed on a par with economic and environmental dimensions[17] and that an overall 'holistic' approach is envisaged. Social policy including labour standards, cannot be crafted without attention to its environmental and economic effects; but by the same token, the design of ecological and economic measures must also take into account the impact on people in the labour market.

The preamble says that the SDGs 'seek to realize the human rights of all', while the Introduction to the Declaration states that the aim is to 'respect, protect and promote' universal human rights established under international law,[18] with particular reference to gender equality, principles of non-discrimination and the treatment of migrants. This makes sense, given the extensive evidence that social and environmental harms can be linked to systemic inequality and a failure to promote capabilities.[19] The current 'environmental crisis' has been widely attributed to 'a crisis of inequalities'.[20] Perhaps most powerfully the preamble to the 2030 Agenda states that 'no one will be left behind'.[21]

Achievement of the SDGs is to be an inclusive collective process. According to the preamble, 'all stakeholders, acting in collaborative partnership, will implement this plan'.[22] Realisation of the SDGs is said to require, not only 'respect for human rights', but the 'effective rule of law and good governance at all levels', including 'transparent, effective and accountable institutions'.[23] This is the element of procedural justice which accompanies the substantive norms in the 2030 Agenda. It is evident that implementation and follow-up processes are to be determined primarily by national governments, but with input from civil society at local, national, regional and international levels and in diverse fora, and can be linked to finance, trade and other modes of delivery.[24] It is said to be: 'an Agenda of the people, by the people and for the people'.[25]

16. *Ibid. See also* discussion in Sara Seck, 'Transnational Labour Law and the Environment: Beyond the Bounded Autonomous Worker' (2018) 33(2) *Canadian Journal of Law and Society* 137, 135 DOI: 10.1017/cls.2018.15.
17. This non-hierarchical approach has been advocated, for example, by William M. Lafferty and Oluf Langhelle, 'Sustainable Development as Concept and Norm' in William M. Lafferty and Oluf Langhelle (eds) *Towards Sustainable Development* (London, Palgrave Macmillan 1999), 13.
18. UN 2030 Agenda n. 1, Declaration, paras 3, 8, 10, 19, 29 and 35.
19. Martha Nussbaum, *Creating Capabilities: The Human Development Approach* (Cambridge, Harvard University Press, 2011), 18-19; Anna Grear, 'Towards "Climate Justice"? A Critical Reflection on Legal Subjectivity and Climate Injustice: Warning Signals, Patterned Hierarchies, Directions for Future Law and Policy' (2014) 5 *Journal of Human Rights and the Environment* 103, 111 and 127 DOI: 10.4337/jhre.2014.02.08.
20. Paolo Tomassetti, 'From Treadmill of Production to Just Transition and Beyond' (2020) 26(4) *European Journal of Industrial Relations* 439, at 441 and 452 DOI: 10.1177/0959680120951701.
21. UN 2030 Agenda n. 1, preamble; and Declaration, para. 4.
22. *Ibid.*, preamble.
23. *Ibid.*, Declaration, para. 35.
24. *Ibid.*, Declaration, paras 21-22, and paras 39-48.
25. *Ibid.*, Declaration, para. 52.

2.2 The Substantive Norms Embedded in the SDGs

Specifically, when considering the implications for work, SDG 8 becomes relevant alongside the associated targets and indicators.[26] Of course, the title of SDG 8 involves a nod to the International Labour Organization (LO) and its promotion of a 'Decent Work Agenda' in the broader world of work,[27] encompassing job creation, social protection, social dialogue, and protection of 'fundamental principles and rights at work' (also known as 'core labour standards').[28] Four of the *now five* 'fundamental rights at work' are expressly set out in SDG 8 targets. Elimination of forced labour and prevention of the worst forms of child labour are addressed in target 8.7, alongside trafficking and modern slavery. Target 8.8 makes provision for 'all workers' to claim 'labour rights' (recognising a principle of non-discrimination) which notably includes promotion of 'safe and secure working environments'. This principle of non-discrimination notably extends to migrant workers, including migrant female workers and those engaged in 'precarious employment'.

Only freedom of association and collective bargaining do not receive explicit recognition in the SDG 8 targets. However, since 2017, SDG indicator 8.8.2 requires attention to any 'increase in national compliance of labour rights (freedom of association and collective bargaining) based on ILO textual sources and national legislation', with reference to 'sex and migrant status'.[29] That indicator would seem to suggest that freedom of association and collective bargaining are to be understood as 'labour rights' under SDG indicator 8.8. Also, in 2018, the then Special Rapporteur on the rights to freedom of peaceful assembly and association argued that these collective labour rights (including a right to strike) could also be understood to be protected as 'fundamental rights' in SDG target 16.10.[30]

26. *See* the UN 2030 Agenda n. 1, 'Means of implementation and the Global Partnership', paras 61, 75 and 83; and the website at: https://sdgs.un.org/goals/goal17.
27. *See* the ILO Declaration on the Social Dimension of Globalisation 2008; and for a contemporary summary: https://www.ilo.org/global/topics/decent-work/lang--en/index.htm.
28. Originally, the ILO Declaration on Fundamental Principles and Rights at Work 1998, Art. 2 set out four 'core labour standards' or fundamental freedoms: (a) freedom of association and the effective recognition of the right to collective bargaining; (b) the elimination of all forms of forced or compulsory labour; (c) the effective abolition of child labour; and (d) the elimination of discrimination in respect of employment and occupation. In June 2022, the International Labour Conference added to Art. 2 an entitlement to 'a safe and healthy working environment'. *See* Resolution on the inclusion of a safe and healthy working environment in the ILO's framework of fundamental principles and rights at work, ILC.110/Resolution1, 10 June 2022 available at: https://www.ilo.org/wcmsp5/groups/public/---ed_norm/---relconf/documents/meetingdocument/wcms_848632.pdf. For background, *see* Zahra Yusifli and Colin Fenwick, 'Workers' Rights and Human Rights: Toward a New Fundamental Principle?' in Kimberley Elliott (ed.), *Handbook on Globalisation and Labour Standards* (Cheltenham, Edward Elgar, 2022).
29. IISD, *Policy Brief: Getting to 2030: Tracking SDG Indicators for Evidence of Implementation Progress* (2018): http://sdg.iisd.org/commentary/policy-briefs/getting-to-2030-tracking-sdg-indicators-for-evidence-of-implementation-progress/. For other current SDG indicators, *see*: https://unstats.un.org/sdgs/indicators/Global%20Indicator%20Framework%20after%202022%20refinement_Eng.pdf.
30. Report of the Special Rapporteur on the rights to freedom of peaceful assembly and association, 7 August 2018, A/73/279, paras 6 and 58, also paras 87-89.

However, it would be a mistake only to focus on the norms explicitly related to 'work' and not to acknowledge the potency of other social objectives (alongside those associated with ecological and economic ambitions).[31] For example, SDG 1 endeavours to 'end poverty in all its forms everywhere', akin to Millennium Development Goal 1 on poverty to which a 'decent work' target was attached on the basis that work is a way of preventing poverty.[32] It is therefore perhaps not surprising that the ILO is a custodian required to assist in collection of information, not just for SDG 8 but also for various other work-related indicators under other SDGs, including indicators 1.3.1 and 1.a.2 relating to poverty.[33]

Also significant is SDG 10, which seeks to 'reduce inequality within and among countries', offering a framework for addressing material forms of discrimination. Targets 10.7 and 10.c make provision for the welfare of migrant workers in a way that is complementary to target 8.8. The International Labour Office report titled *Time to Act for SDG 8* in 2019 recognised how SDG 8 could be linked with, not only SDGs 1 and 10 but also *inter alia* SDG 3 (on health), SDG 4 (education) and SDG 5 (gender equality).[34] These synergies (or 'dynamic interlinkages') between SDG 8 targets and others engaging with economic and social issues[35] could place limits on 'sustainable consumption', having economic and environmental effects.[36]

In terms of 'how environmental, social and economic targets can be balanced',[37] the Office Report advocated attention to the precepts of 'social justice' established at the ILO,[38] and concluded by saying that there should be a return to Article II(c) of the Declaration of Philadelphia in 1944 in that: 'Where there are trade-offs and conflicting interests among SDG targets, social justice, in accordance with the ILO mandate, should be applied as the guiding principle in developing new technologies, institutions and policies that can help strike a balance between the various targets.'[39] This may be a problematic claim since ILO expertise arguably lies in intra-generational rather than inter-generational justice; in other words, many environmentalists may question whether social rather than ecological imperatives should take priority. More compelling is the case that the Report makes for 'a consensus' to be 'forged through social

31. Tonia Novitz, 'Sustainable Development Goal 8: Promote Sustained, Inclusive, and Sustainable Economic Growth, Full and Productive Employment, and Decent Work for All' in Jonas Ebbesson and Ellen Hey (eds), *Cambridge Handbook on the United Nations Sustainable Development Goals and International Law* (Cambridge, Cambridge University Press, 2022), forthcoming.
32. Diane F. Frey and Gillian MacNaughton, 'A Human Rights Lens on Full Employment and Decent Work in the 2030 Sustainable Development Agenda' (2016) 6(2) *Journal of Workplace Rights* 1, 6 DOI: 10.1177/2158244016649580.
33. *Ibid.*, 5.
34. ILO International Labour Office, *Time to Act for SDG 8: Integrating decent work, sustained growth and environmental integrity* (Geneva, ILO, 2019), Report issued 10 July 2019 available at: https://www.ilo.org/global/publications/books/WCMS_712685/lang--en/index.htm, Executive Summary, x, 2, 29 and 32.
35. *Ibid.*, Executive Summary, x.
36. *Ibid.*, 35-37.
37. *Ibid.*, 38.
38. *Ibid.*, 39.
39. *Ibid.*, 79.

dialogue between the main stakeholders – especially employers, workers and governments, but also civil society organizations'.[40]

2.3 Processes for Good Governance Envisaged by the SDGs

The value of participatory engagement in the achievement of the goals is emphasised in SDG 16, concerned with the promotion of 'just, peaceful and inclusive societies'. The importance of 'global partnerships' for their realisation (including engagement of civil society) is stressed in SDG 17. As noted above, the term 'good governance' is referred to in the 2030 Agenda Declaration[41] as one of the necessary prerequisites for sustainable development; but what indications do we have of what this might mean in practice? And to what extent might this be recognised as requiring engagement with collective worker voice?

Trade unions are only mentioned expressly in SDG indicator 16.10.1, insofar as the 'killing, kidnapping, enforced disappearance, arbitrary detention and torture of [inter alia] trade unionists' would negate the assertion of the protection of fundamental freedoms in SDG target 16.10.[42] However, one may safely assume that trade unions are covered by reference throughout the 2030 Agenda to 'civil society' and 'stakeholders'. For example, the Declaration states that: 'The Goals and targets are the result of over two years of intensive public consultation and engagement with civil society and other stakeholders around the world, which paid particular attention to the voices of the poorest and most vulnerable.'[43] It is hard to believe that trade unions or other forms of worker representation are intended to be excluded from such a statement or in subsequent references to civil society and stakeholders, including SDG indicator 17.17 which seeks to: 'Encourage and promote effective public, public-private and civil society partnerships, building on the experience and resourcing strategies of partnerships.'

Claire Kilpatrick, for example, argues that the global financial crisis exposed how any sharp divide between NGOs and trade unions 'is overstated'.[44] She observes that trade unions were among the principal civil society actors mobilising to oppose austerity measures in Europe (and using the ILO to do so),[45] an account also endorsed by Margot Solomon's investigation of the assertion of social rights within the Council of Europe and internationally.[46] It should then be possible for trade unions to be understood as included in the wider frame of civil society.

40. *Ibid.*, 39.
41. *See* UN 2030 Agenda n. 1 above, preamble and Declaration, para. 9.
42. The indicator 16.10.1 requires gathering the following information: 'Number of verified cases of killing, kidnapping, enforced disappearance, arbitrary detention and torture of journalists, associated media personnel, trade unionists and human rights advocates in the previous 12 months.'
43. UN 2030 Agenda n. 1 above, Declaration, para. 6.
44. Claire Kilpatrick, 'Taking the Measure of Changing Labour Mobilization at the International Labour Organisation in the wake of the EU Sovereign Debt Crisis' (2019) 68 *International & Comparative Law Quarterly* 665, at 688 DOI: 10.1017/s0020589319000113.
45. *Ibid.*, at 689.
46. Margot Salomon, 'Of Austerity, Human Rights and International Institutions' (2015) 21(4) *European Law Journal* 521 DOI: 10.1111/eulj.12138.

It might also be observed that vast numbers of those at work are in the informal economy without official trade union support, represented by NGOs or 'independent unions' (not affiliated to larger trade union confederations), in part because there are legal constraints on precarious workers joining and being represented by a trade union.[47] A generous view of civil society takes more account of this diversity while accepting the need to represent those at work and enable their meaningful participatory engagement with their broader working environment.

Here we might also want to acknowledge the explicit reference to 'the imperatives of a just transition of the workforce and the creation of decent work' in the preamble to the Paris Agreement on Climate Change also in 2015.[48] This reference to 'decent work' resonates with SDG 8 and seems to have been intended to give force to the ILO Guidelines on Just Transition 2015,[49] which insist that social dialogue and collective bargaining with trade unions should be part of the transitional process to address climate change and other environmental objectives, such as biodiversity.[50]

I have argued elsewhere that SDG targets 16.6 and 16.7 are indicative of the need for 'good governance' to incorporate representation of collective voice at work.[51] In particular, 16.6 refers to the need to: 'Develop effective, accountable and transparent institutions at all levels'; while 16.7 aims to: 'Ensure responsive, inclusive, participatory and representative decision-making at all levels.' This reference to 'at all levels' indicates that the institutions that are of concern include those at international, regional, transnational, national and regional levels. To be 'responsive, inclusive, participatory and representative' requires engagement with those affected by policy decisions and arguably sets some parameters for the legitimacy of that engagement. For example, those included in the decision-making process cannot be unrepresentative, the participation should be genuine such that the representatives cannot be without influence, and inclusivity suggests that those likely to be 'left behind' should have a voice at the table. Moreover, SDG target 16.3 indicates that any such engagement must

47. This is, for example, a live issue in the 'gig economy' and platform work at present in the UK and elsewhere. *See* discussion in Sanjukta Paul, Shae McCrystal and Ewan McGaughey (eds), *The Cambridge Handbook of Labor in Competition Law* (Cambridge, Cambridge University Press, 2022).

48. *See* N. Singh Ghaleigh, *Just Transitions for Workers: When Climate Change Met Labour Justice.* Edinburgh School of Law Research Paper No. 2019/30 (Edinburgh: University of Edinburgh, 2019).

49. ILO Guidelines for a just transition towards environmentally sustainable economies and societies for all (Geneva, ILO, 2015).

50. *See* more generally on the emergence of policy relating to 'just transitions' and its influence, *see* David Doorey, 'Just Transitions Law: Putting Labour Law to Work on Climate Change' (2017) 30(2) *Journal of Environmental Law and Practice* 201; and Dimitris Stevis, Edouard Morena and Dunja Krause, 'Introduction: The Genealogy and Contemporary Politics of Just Transitions' in Edouard Morena, Dunja Krause and Dimitris Stevis (eds), *Just Transitions: Social Justice in the Shift Towards a Low-carbon World* (London, Pluto Press, 2020), 9.

51. Tonia Novitz, 'Engagement with Sustainability at the International Labour Organization and Wider Implications for Collective Worker Voice' (2020) 159(4) *International Labour Review* 463 DOI: 10.1111/ilr.12181; and Tonia Novitz, 'Tripartism as Sustainable Governance' in George P. Politakis, Tomi Kohiyama and Thomas Lieby (eds), *ILO 100: Law for social justice* (Geneva, ILO, 2019).

be subject to the rule of law at the national and international levels and ensure 'equal access to justice for all'.

The remainder of this chapter considers how SDGs are transposed into EU external and internal social policy, and whether these parameters for engagement with collective worker voice are respected. Inclusivity, participation, representation and attention to gender and other bases of inequality, for example, can all be considered vital facets of 'good governance' both in the internal market and EU external relations. Further, as there is to be a global partnership for realising the 2030 Agenda, it is argued that the voices of those in the 'world of work' from other parts of the globe need to be represented and heard when they are to be affected by internal market measures.

3 TRANSPOSITION OF THE SDGs INTO 'A STRONG SOCIAL EUROPE FOR JUST TRANSITION'

There are at least two ways in which the SDGs can be transposed at the EU level which have implications for labour laws. The first that we are familiar with is the inclusion of ILO standards into the terms of trade on the basis that to do so promotes 'sustainable development'. The second, which is actually more recent, is the attempt to meaningfully promote the 'sustainable development of Europe' through regulation of the internal market. Moreover, the two may meet and interact when EU internal market measures are designed to have external effects, which I shall term 'hybrid measures'. It is argued here that in relation to both external and internal EU social policy, it is not only substantive sustainable development standards that matter but also whether their implementation coheres with 'good governance' incorporating the freedom of association and engagement with those affected at work. This is of particular importance regarding the proposed 'hybrid' measures now being contemplated by the European Commission regarding corporate 'due diligence' and products relating to 'forced labour'.

3.1 EU External Relations

EU policy can be understood as a trailblazer for the recognition of a labour dimension to the notion of sustainable development. Long before the attention given to 'decent work' as an indicator for MDG1 and then its inclusion in SDG 8, the European Commission was committed to the notion that adherence to international labour standards should be regarded as a fundamental aspect of the aspiration of sustainable development. Inclusion of internationally agreed labour standards (as well as environmental norms) in EU GSP and FTAs seem consistent with the EU's conception of sustainable development, which has since been endorsed on the world stage, particularly in the SDGs and by the ILO. Subsequently, that endorsement has been written back again into EU external relations instruments. In these ways, the EU wields both tangible trade power and more intangible ideological influence.[52]

52. *See* Anu Bradford, 'The Brussels Effect' (2012) 107(1) *Northwestern University Law Review* 1, 9 and Anu Bradford, *The Brussels Effect: How the European Union Rules the World* (Oxford

3.1.1 *GSP and GSP+: 'Sustainable Development and Good Governance'*

The Council Regulation of 2005 'applying a scheme of generalised tariff preferences' introduced for the first time tariff conditionality for developing countries based on 'the promotion of sustainable development and good governance'.[53] The 2005 Regulation made provision for withdrawal of GSP preferences on the basis of breach of certain core labour standards, but more importantly included ratification of ILO Conventions as a basis for the 'special incentive arrangement' which came to be known as 'GSP+'. A further 'special arrangement for least developed countries' (the Everything But Arms scheme) was also adopted, to which such conditionality did not attach. This is a three-pronged model which has been applied and adapted by the EU subsequently and there is little sign of significant change to the ways in which the EU folds labour standards into a social and environmental sustainability paradigm in 2022.[54]

This appeal to sustainable development as a basis for GSP conditionality was a response to the findings of the World Trade Organisation (WTO) Appellate Body in the 'Drug Arrangements' case brought by India against EC trade preferences.[55] The EC's response and subsequent EU GSP policy have been criticised by scholars as not wholly compliant with its findings regarding, for example, requirements of equal treatment and transparency arising under the Enabling Clause appended to the General Agreement on Tariffs and Trade (the GATT). There have been plausible challenges made by academics to the effect that the requirements of good governance are not fully met.[56] And, yet, the 2005 GSP Regulation and its successors have not been challenged in practice on this basis, perhaps in part due to the appeal made by the EU to the popular but contested notion of 'sustainable development'. This three-pronged formula for EU GSP was retained in subsequent GSP Regulations of 2008 and 2012 and is anticipated to be continued in the proposed Regulation to be adopted in 2022.[57]

University Press 2020), Chapter 3, which highlights the limitations of application of this theory to preferential trade agreements or, as described here 'FTAs'. Cf. Chad Damro, 'Market Power Europe' (2012) 19(5) *Journal of European Public Policy* 682, 689-696 DOI: 10.1080/13501763.2011.646779.

53. Council Regulation No. 980/2005 of 27 June 2005, OJ L169/1, especially Arts 9 and 16.
54. COM(2022) 409 final, at 4.
55. *European Communities – Conditions for the granting of Tariff Preferences to Developing Countries*, WT/DS246/AB/R, 7 April 2004.
56. Bruce Wardhaugh, 'GSP+ and Human Rights: Is the EU's Approach the Right One?' (2013) 16 *Journal of International Economic Law* 827 DOI: 10.1093/jiel/jgt031; and Lorand Bartels, 'The WTO Legality of the EU's GSP+ Arrangement' (2007) 10 *Journal of International Economic Law* 869 DOI: 10.1093/jiel/jgm035.
57. Regulation (EU) No. 978/2012 of the European Parliament and of the Council of 25 October 2012 applying a scheme of generalised tariff preferences and repealing Council Regulation (EC) No. 732/2008 OJ L 303/1 31 October 2012 which applies until 31 December 2023. For the Commission's most recent proposal for a new GSP Regulation, *see* COM(2021) 579 22 September 2021 available at: https://eur-lex.europa.eu/legal-content/EN/TXT/PDF/?uri=CELEX:52021PC0579&from=EN. *See also* Commission Communication, 'The power of trade partnerships: together for green and just economic growth' COM(2022) 409 final, 22 June 2022.

3.1.2 FTAs: Trade and Sustainable Development Chapters

Inclusion of labour standards as a crucial aspect of sustainable development, with an appeal to ILO Conventions and 'core labour standards' alongside environmental protections, have also become a familiar facet of TSD chapters in EU free trade agreements (FTAs).[58] That model was initiated in the EU-Korea FTA,[59] and provisions standardly included in TSD chapters have since been enhanced, for example, with express reference to the ILO's 'Decent Work Agenda' and more recently the 2030 Agenda and SDGs. Examples include the recent EU-Vietnam FTA[60] and the EU-UK Trade and Cooperation Agreement (TCA).[61] The latter is of particular interest, because of the potential scope for 'rebalancing' under Article 411 of the TCA where a breach of EU and more specifically UK international commitments, including under the TCA, relating to, *inter alia,* 'labour and social, environmental or climate protection' lead to 'material impacts on trade or investment between the Parties'. That provision enables much more far-reaching corrective action (that is, 'enforcement') than has previously been contemplated under previous TSD chapters.[62] This is partially indicative of an increasing determination by the EU to take stronger action on TSD chapters, for example by enforcing existing TSD obligations in the EU-Korea FTA and even enhancing dispute settlement in future FTAs.[63] But the TCA was also a special case given the UK's particular capacity, as a close neighbour to the EU, to engage in negative competition with the EU on the basis of low labour standards.[64] Most recently, the Commission has stated its intention to maintain a sustainable and just transitions

58. Lore Van den Putte and Jan Orbie, 'EU Bilateral Trade Agreements and the Surprising Rise of Labour Provisions' (2015) 31(3) *International Journal of Comparative Labour Law and Industrial Relations* (IJCLLIR) 263 DOI: 10.54648/ijcl2015015.
59. *See* Ludo Cuyvers, 'The Sustainable Development Clauses in Free Trade Agreements of the EU with Asian Countries: Perspectives for ASEAN' (2014) 22(4) *Journal of Contemporary European Studies* 427, 433-436 DOI: 10.1080/14782804.2014.923752; and Hoang Ha Hai, 'The Social Dimension in EU Free Trade Agreements: ASEAN perspectives' (2017) 25(4) *European Review* 532.
60. Free Trade Agreement Between the European Union and the Socialist Republic of Viet Nam 12 June 2020 OJ L 186/3, Chapter 13, especially *see* Arts 13.1, 13.2 and 13.4, as well as Arts 13.10 and 13.14.
61. Trade and Cooperation Agreement (TCA) between the European Union and the European Atomic Energy Community, of the one part, and the United Kingdom of Great Britain and Northern Ireland, of the other part OJ L 149/10 30 April 2021, version approved by European Parliament (following provisional application of the TCA from 1 January 2021). *See* Title XI 'Level Playing Field for Open and Fair Competition and Sustainable Development', especially Chapters 1, 6 and 8 (and Arts 355, 386, 387, 397 and 399).
62. Phil Syrpis, 'The Influence of the EU on UK Labour Law – Before and After Brexit' (2022) *Industrial Law Journal* DOI: 10.1093/indlaw/dwac016; cf. James Harrison et al., 'Labour Standards Provisions in EU Free Trade Agreements: Reflections on the European Commission's Reform Agenda' (2019) 18(4) *World Trade Review* 635.
63. *See* the determination to engaging in 'mainstreaming sustainability throughout the entire trade agreement' and to extend general state-to state dispute settlement to the TSD chapter, discussed in COM(2022) 409 final, 7-12.
64. Discussed by K.D. Ewing, 'The EU-UK Trade and Cooperation Agreement: Implications for ILO Standards and the European Social Charter in the United Kingdom' (2021) 32(2) *King's Law Journal* 306 DOI: 10.1080/09615768.2021.1969757.

framework, but in doing so to be more responsive to 'the country-based implementation priorities' of EU trade partners,[65] although how this will be operationalised is less clear.

A further feature of these TSD chapters more generally has been the creation of consultative bodies. These typically include 'domestic advisory groups' (DAGs) which reflect civil society interests, including trade union representation; and a common feature is a wider 'Civil Society Forum'. Arguably, these bodies, by virtue of the representatives they include, can act as a check on implementation of the FTA and raise economic, environmental and social concerns. These bodies have been criticised for being ineffectual and even potentially obscuring trade union voice and influence. However, in what became the EU-Korea FTA dispute, they acted in concert with the International Trade Union Confederation and European Trade Union Confederation, as well as the Korean Confederation of Trade Unions pushing for active reform and pressure to be exercised by the EU. They may be more effective than at first thought.[66] Moreover, these established patterns of engagement with civil society and the enhancement of trade union ability to engage with the implementation of labour standards in the EU context do assist good governance, even though there may not be complete parity of influence. The EU DAG may be more efficacious in representing EU civil society (including trade unions) than their trade partners. An example perhaps is the difference in the time it took for the UK to establish a DAG under the TCA compared to the EU, which also had the advantage of the 'single entry point' for complaints.[67] While this fault can safely be laid at the doorstep of a so-called first world country like the UK, this may not be the case for other trade partners like Vietnam – and SDGs 16 and 17 offer a reminder that inequality of capabilities and bargaining power of third countries should be borne in mind by EU institutions.[68]

The EU claim that eventuated in relation to the TSD chapter of the EU-Korea FTA raised several issues.[69] One was whether Korea was in breach of 'best efforts'

65. COM(2022) 409 final, 6.
66. *See* for more detailed discussion Tonia Novitz, 'Sustainable Labour Conditionality in EU Free Trade Agreements? Implications of the EU-Korea Expert Panel Report' (2022) 1 *European Law Review* 3, 10-11.
67. *See* the EU-TCA complaint form available at: https://ec.europa.eu/assets/sg/complaint_eu_uk_tca/complaints_en/; regarding the 'increased efforts' of the Commission to reach civil society in EU Member States and the operation of the single entry point, *see* COM(2022) 409 final, 8-9. For the EU DAG for the EU-UK TCA, *see*: https://ec.europa.eu/info/strategy/relations-non-eu-countries/relations-united-kingdom/eu-uk-trade-and-cooperation-agreement_en; on the recent establishment of the UK DAG, *see*: https://assets.publishing.service.gov.uk/government/uploads/system/uploads/attachment_data/file/1091936/2022-04-28_DAG_Minutes.pdf. As at September 2022, the UK was still seeking to appoint members to the TCA DAG and Civil Society Forum: https://www.gov.uk/government/publications/uk-domestic-advisory-group-membership-and-civil-society-forum-participation-under-the-uk-eu-trade-and-cooperation-agreement-expressions-of-interest.
68. *See* acknowledgement of the need for capacity building in third countries in COM (2022) 409 final, at 10.
69. Report of the Panel of Experts (2020) Proceeding constituted under Art. 13.15 of the EU-Korea Free Trade Agreement, 25 January 2021, Panel: Dr J. Murray (Chairperson), Professor L. Boisson de Chazournes and Professor J. Lee; available at: https://ec.europa.eu/commission/presscorner/detail/en/ip_21_203.

obligations to ratify core ILO Conventions, which was found by the expert panel not to be the case.[70] That said, the expert report was delivered, Korea did in fact ratify ILO Conventions Nos 29, 87 and 98,[71] although ratification of ILO Convention No. 105 remains outstanding.

A more fundamental preliminary question was a jurisdictional issue as to whether the part of the TSD chapter on which the EU relied could be enforceable in the absence of any proven impact on trade. Korea had sought to rely on an earlier arbitral decision where breach of freedom of association by Guatemala was not actionable in the absence of sufficient effect on trade.[72] The EU-Korea FTA expert panel found that the wording of the relevant provision of the TSD chapter did not require an effect on trade,[73] but even if it had, the outcome could be very different in the present case.[74] The reason was the 'dynamic interactions between economic, social and environmental objectives as interdependent and mutually reinforcing components of sustainable development'.[75] The earlier case did 'not have the same contextual setting of sustainable development'.[76] In this way, the holistic nature of sustainability, and its combination of economic, environmental and social (or labour) objectives was not viewed so much as a challenge but as beneficial to the protection of collective labour rights. Ultimately, various aspects of the Korean Trade Union and Labour Relations Act 1997 were found to be in breach of the ILO principles of freedom of association, that had been given binding force by virtue of their incorporation into the FTA. They notably included the right of self-employed atypical workers, for example, in the platform economy, to be trade union members represented in collective bargaining.[77] In this way, the panel's decision not only recognised the remarkable multifaceted and entwined objectives of sustainable development but the significance of collective bargaining for their realisation.

3.2 Internal Measures Relating to Labour and Sustainable Development

The notion of sustainable development has since 2018 gained profile in the content and implementation of the European Pillar of Social Rights and the European Green Deal initiative. In this context, there would seem to be some significant new protections of collective bargaining which would seem to serve precepts of good governance, even if

70. *Ibid.*, paras 287-289.
71. *See* the ILO report at: https://www.ilo.org/global/standards/WCMS_785448/lang--en/index.htm accessed 2 January 2022.
72. CAFTA-DR Arbitral Panel Established Pursuant to Chapter Twenty in the Matter of Guatemala – Issues Relating to the Obligations Under Art. 16.2.1(a) of the CAFTA-DR Final Report of the Panel 14 June 2017. Discussed in Lance Compa, Jeffrey Vogt and Eric Gottwald, *Wrong Turn for Workers' Rights: The US-Guatemala CAFTA Labor Arbitration Ruling – and What to Do About It* (Washington, International Labor Rights Forum, 2018).
73. EU-Korea FTA, Art. 13.4.3.
74. EU-Korea Report n. 69 above, paras 42-53 and 61-73.
75. *Ibid.*, para. 74.
76. *Ibid.*, paras 93-94.
77. *Ibid.*, para 148 on the status of self-employed workers and their rights to engage in collective bargaining.

they have their limitations. However, difficulties can arise where apparently internal market regulatory measures have connections to EU investment in and trade with third countries. There may be a need to further develop the nascent participatory elements of the measures currently being proposed regarding corporate due diligence and products of prison labour.

3.2.1 *The European Pillar of Social Rights: 'The Sustainable Development of Europe'?*

EU policy documents relating to the internal market increasingly refer to 'sustainable development' as a normative base. One prominent example is the preamble to the European Pillar of Social Rights adopted in 2017,[78] referring to Article 3 of the Treaty on the European Union (TEU), which in turn states that 'the aims of the Union are inter alia to promote the well-being of its peoples and to work for *the sustainable development of Europe* (my emphasis) based on balanced economic growth and price stability, a highly competitive social market economy, aiming at full employment and social progress, and a high level of protection and improvement of the quality of the environment' (in other words, all three pillars which are recognised as key facets of sustainable development in the 2030 Agenda).[79]

Principle 3 of the Pillar on 'equal opportunities' is relevant to SDGs 5, 8 and 10, stating that: 'Regardless of gender, racial or ethnic origin, religion or belief, disability, age or sexual orientation, everyone has the right to equal treatment and opportunities regarding employment, social protection, education, and access to goods and services available to the public. Equal opportunities of under-represented groups shall be fostered.' The aim it seems is not only equality but inclusivity.

Further, Principle 5 of the Pillar places emphasis on protection of the most precarious workers, stating that, 'Regardless of the type and duration of the employment relationship, workers have the right to fair and equal treatment regarding working conditions, access to social protection and training.' The Pillar also envisages collective voice and action, both in the preamble and Principle 8, which recognises 'social dialogue and involvement of workers', seeking to promote access to information and consultation of collective representatives at the European and national levels, as well as enabling collective bargaining and collective action.[80] This initiative is of particular significance, given restrictions placed on collective bargaining and the right

78. Interinstitutional Proclamation on the European Pillar of Social Rights 2017/C 428/09, 13.12.2017: https://eur-lex.europa.eu/legal-content/EN/TXT/PDF/?uri=CELEX:32017C1213(01)&from=EN.
79. The term 'sustainable' is repeated in paras 7 and 11 of the preamble.
80. Discussed further in Tonia Novitz, 'Addressing 'Social Dumping' and 'Unfair Competition': An analysis of EU pillar initiatives from a sustainability perspective' in Ann-Christine Hartzén, Andrea Iossa, and Eleni Karageorgiou (eds.), *Law, Solidarity and the Limits of Social Europe: Constitutional Tensions for EU Integration* (Cheltenham, Edward Elgar, 2022), 2-21, at 9-10.

to strike in Court of Justice judgments of 2007,[81] but there has yet to be further case law to test the significance of Principle 8.

3.2.2 *The European Green Deal and 'A Strong Social Europe for Just Transitions'?*

'The European Green Deal' proposed by Ursula von der Leyen's Commission in 2019 is primarily concerned with ecological sustainability.[82] However, despite initial concerns that insufficient attention would be paid to the principle of 'just transition' involving collective worker voice,[83] its announcement was followed by the 2020 Commission Communication on 'A Strong Social Europe for Just Transitions'.[84] That document begins with explicit reliance on the SDGs and their application to EU social policy in the context of green and digital transitions.[85] Reference is also made to how the European Semester will not only monitor progress on the European Pillar of Social Rights but from 2020 will 'integrate the United Nations' Sustainable Development Goals so that sustainability and the citizens' well-being will be at the centre of economic policy and governance'.[86] There are some bold measures in the Communication which not only reinforce the 2030 Agenda, such as the proposal for the Gender Equality Strategy, which can be linked to SDG 5,[87] but also go beyond the UN Resolution in terms of strengthening rights for persons with disabilities.[88] The Communication might appear sparse in its treatment of social dialogue and collective bargaining,[89] but commitments to both have since been repeated and elaborated in the European Pillar of Social Rights Action Plan issued on 4 March 2021[90] and the Porto Commitment of 7 May 2021.[91]

The 2021 Action Plan is notable also because it seems to go further than previous policy instruments in acknowledging the precarity of migrant workers and spells out measures that may be taken for their benefit. For example, it is noted that: 'Migrants'

81. Case C-438/05 *International Transport Workers' Federation (ITF) and Finnish Seamen's Union (FSU) v. Viking Line* [2007] ECR I-10779; Case C-341/05 *Laval un Partneri v. Svenska Byggnadsarbetareförbundet* [2007] ECR I-11767.
82. Commission Communication, 'The European Green Deal' COM (2019) 640 final 11 December 2019, 16 and 23.
83. Sebastian Sabato and Boris Fronteddu, *A Socially Just Transition Through the European Green Deal?* (Brussels, European Trade Union Institute, 2020).
84. Commission Communication, 'A Strong Social Europe for Just Transitions' COM (2020) 14 final 14 January 2020.
85. *Ibid.*, 3.
86. *Ibid.*
87. *See*: https://ec.europa.eu/info/policies/justice-and-fundamental-rights/gender-equality/gender-equality-strategy_en.
88. *See also* the Strategy for the rights of persons with disabilities 2021-2030 adopted in 2021 available at: https://ec.europa.eu/social/main.jsp?catId = 1484&langId = en.
89. COM (2020) 14 final, 9.
90. European Commission Employment and Social Affairs DG, 'European Pillar of Social Rights Action Plan', 4 March 2021, 5–10, 36–37, 42 and 44-45.
91. Porto Social Summit, Porto Social Commitment, 7 May 2021 available at: www.2021portugal.eu/en/porto-social-summit/porto-social-commitment/.

participation in the labour market was also disproportionally affected by the pandemic.'[92] It is also clear that migrants are to be regarded as an 'under-represented group' to be more included in the labour market in future, in line with Principle 3 of the Pillar.[93] An Asylum, Migration and Integration Fund 'will support the integration and inclusion of migrants'.[94] Such an approach could include enabling migrant workers to participate effectively in collective bargaining, but this is not explicitly stated, although one would hope it is presumed.

3.2.3 *Measures to Promote Collective Bargaining: Trade Union Engagement*

There have, arguably, been two significant policy proposals identified in the 2020 Communication, which have since been acted upon in ways likely to promote the 'sustainable development of Europe' from a collective labour law perspective. One has been the Directive on adequate minimum wages, the proposal being published in October 2020,[95] and the instrument receiving approval from the Council and Parliament in June 2022.[96] The Directive aims not merely to set statutory minimum wage levels but to encourage 'constructive, meaningful and informed negotiations'. Where collective bargaining coverage is less than 80%, the Member State is to establish an 'action plan' to encourage collective bargaining (either by law after consultation with the social partners or by agreement with them). This instrument thereby reverts to Principle 8 of the European Pillar of Social Rights, stressing the important regulatory role that collective bargaining can play in the labour market, and improves on the initial Commission Communication on the 'New Industrial Strategy for Europe', which elaborated on environmental aims but failed to mention social dialogue, collective bargaining or trade unions.[97]

Also significant are likely to be measures taken to promote the rights of platform workers (including those relating to collective bargaining), as part of the wider Digital Services Act Package.[98] On 9 December 2021, the Commission published a *Proposal for a Directive on improving working conditions in platform work*.[99] 'Guidelines on the application of Union competition law to collective agreements regarding the working conditions of self-employed persons' were adopted on 29 September 2022.[100] These

92. EPSR Action Plan 2021, n. 90, 9.
93. *Ibid.*, 10.
94. *Ibid*, 34.
95. Commission Proposal for a Directive of the European Parliament and of the Council on adequate minimum wages in the EU COM (2020) 682 final, 28 October 2020.
96. We are now awaiting publication in the Official Journal. *See*: https://ec.europa.eu/social/main.jsp?langId=en&catId=1539&furtherNews=yes&newsId=10290.
97. Commission Communication, 'A New Industrial Strategy for Europe' COM (2020) 102 final, 10 March 2020.
98. *See*: https://ec.europa.eu/commission/presscorner/detail/en/ip_20_1237.
99. *Proposal for a Directive on improving working conditions in platform work* COM(2021) 762 final, 9 December 2021 available at: https://eur-lex.europa.eu/legal-content/EN/TXT/PDF/?uri=CELEX:52021PC0762&from=EN.
100. Commission Communication, Guidelines on the application of Union competition law to collective agreements regarding the working conditions of solo self-employed persons C(2022) 6846 final, 29 September 2022. Cf. European Commission 'Draft Guidelines on the application

offer the possibility not only of promoting collective voice but also of doing so for the most vulnerable and precarious workers who are 'solo-self-employed' and who experience a demonstrable imbalance of bargaining power. They may not be 'left behind' after all. Moreover, the obligations that the European Commission sought to impose on Korea regarding trade union representation of the most precarious workers may now potentially be applied within the EU.

What is missing in these measures is any reference to the prospect of lawful industrial action, which should be present for meaningful negotiations (as opposed to 'collective begging'). It is possible that excessive caution at the ILO at present, regarding promotion of a right to strike, after the employers' protests in 2012,[101] has also impacted the EU, leading to reticence on this subject. Another factor may be the exclusion of 'the right of association' and 'the right to strike' from EU social policy competence under Article 153(5) of the Treaty on the Functioning of the European Union (TFEU); and the legacy of the *Laval* and *Viking* litigation.[102] Nevertheless, collective action remains protected in Principle 8 of the Pillar. Also, at least at the International Labour Conference, the EU has been robust so far in its defence of ILO supervisory mechanisms which recognise the right to strike.[103]

Another omission is that collective bargaining across national borders, and related solidarity action, is not contemplated. Given that the 2030 Agenda recognises that ecological, social and economic concerns are not bounded according to national borders, but operate globally and require transnational responses, this may need to be addressed.[104] However, the ways in which the Commission now proposes to address this cross-border facet of sustainability in 2022 also have their difficulties.

3.3 Hybrid Solution: Internal Market Measures with External Effects

It was evident in the 2019 Commission Communication on a European Green Deal that there was an interest in pursuing corporate governance measures applicable to European companies, which could have implications further afield: 'Sustainability should be further embedded into the corporate governance framework, as many companies still focus too much on short-term financial performance compared to their

of EU competition law to collective agreements regarding the working conditions of self-employed persons' available at: https://competition-policy.ec.europa.eu/public-consultations/2021-collective-bargaining-2_en.

101. Claire La Hovary, 'Employers' Group 2012 Challenge to the Right to Strike' (2013) 42(4) *Industrial Law Journal* 338; Janice Bellace, 'The ILO and the Right to Strike' (2014) *ILRev* 29 DOI: 10.1111/j.1564-913x.2014.00196.x; and Jeffrey Vogt et al., *The Right to Strike in International Law* (Oxford: Hart, 2020).
102. *See* n. 81 above.
103. International Labour Conference 109th session: EU Statement – Committee on Application of Standards, Geneva, 3 June 2021; available at: https://eeas.europa.eu/delegations/un-geneva_en/99523/International%20Labour%20Conference%20109th%20session:%20EU%20Statement%20-%20Committee%20on%20Application%20of%20Standards.
104. *See* Agenda 2030 n. 1 above, preamble.

long-term development and sustainability aspects.'[105] In February 2022, the Commission's ambitions were extended in a Communication 'on decent work worldwide for a global just transition and a sustainable recovery'.[106] The Commission proposals in this document go beyond mere regulation of the corporate governance of European companies and instead seek to ensure global delivery of the ILO's 'Decent Work Agenda', although the aim seems to be to use EU internal market regulatory measures to achieve these ambitions. This is said to be a response to the COVID-19 pandemic, in terms of the ways in which it exposed violation of international labour standards and 'has highlighted the urgency of promoting decent work including in global supply chains'.[107]

That overarching determination 'to champion decent work both at home and around the world, in line with the UN 2030 Agenda for Sustainable Development'[108] is connected to two detailed Commission proposals:

- an accompanying proposal for a Directive 'on Corporate Sustainability Due Diligence';[109] and
- a later proposal for a Regulation 'on prohibiting products made with forced labour on the Union market'.[110]

In both cases, the EU is careful not to go beyond the substantive standards adopted by the wider international community. This is not only an appeal to the more general aspirations set out in the SDGs (and the substantive values they represent) but a careful tie-in with established widely ratified international instruments. In the case of the proposed 'Due Diligence' Directive, the annex to the proposal sets out in detail in Part I 'the violations of rights and prohibitions included in international human rights agreements', together with a list of the 'human rights and fundamental freedoms conventions' to which that itemised set of potential violations relates. Part II does the same with respect to 'violations of internationally recognised objectives and prohibitions included in environmental conventions', also listing those instruments.[111] This arguably satisfies transparency requirements, while also being extensive in terms of its explanations. From a collective labour rights perspective, it is significant that the right to strike is explicitly protected;[112] although it is interesting that this can be expressly required of corporate conduct in third countries when internally to the EU industrial

105. Commission Communication, 'The European Green Deal' COM(2019) 640 11.12.2019, 17.
106. Commission Communication 'on decent work worldwide for a global just transition and a sustainable recovery' COM(2022) 66 final, 23 February 2022.
107. *Ibid.*, 2.
108. *Ibid.*, 1.
109. *Proposal for a Directive of the European Parliament and of the Council on Corporate Sustainability Due Diligence and amending Directive* (EU) 2019/1937 COM(2022) 71 final, 23 February 2022.
110. *Proposal for a Regulation of the European Parliament and of the Council on prohibiting products made with forced labour on the Union market* COM(2022) 453 final, 14 September 2022.
111. *ANNEX to the proposal for a Directive of the European Parliament and of the Council on Corporate Sustainability Due Diligence and amending Directive (EU) 2019/1937* (COM)2022) 71 final, 23 February 2022.
112. *Ibid.*, 3.

action and its regulation is such a sensitive subject that its explicit recognition seems to be left out of the new Directive on an adequate minimum wage.[113]

Similarly, the Commission's proposal for a Regulation on products made with forced labour refers explicitly to SDG 8.7, but goes beyond this to link its remit to the Annex to the proposed 'Due Diligence Directive'.[114] The draft Regulation itself defines 'forced labour' in Article 1(1) as meaning 'forced or compulsory labour as defined in Article 2 of the Convention on Forced Labour, 1930 (No. 29) of the International Labour Organization, including forced child labour'. Again, the plan seems to be that internationally agreed norms will prevail.

So, the substantive standards and aims can be legitimate from these terms of reference, but there may remain a question as to whether 'good governance' will really be achieved on the EU side. This matters because, if adopted, these will be unilateral EU measures which could have a significant effect on third countries. SDG 17 advocates a global partnership for sustainable development, whereas both measures proposed by the European Commission are arguably one-sided.

Good governance could enter here potentially in two ways. The first is the extent to which those likely to be affected, those at work in third countries (or at least their representatives) have had some say and influence over the EU instruments to be adopted, namely the standards and procedures they require. The second is the way in which these workers and their representatives will have a voice in the subsequent processes contemplated for enforcement of the Directive and Regulation, as applied by EU Member States. To be fair, it is apparent that the EU has made efforts on both fronts. But there remain questions as to whether they are sufficient.

In terms of the proposed Due Diligence Directive, there was extensive EU-wide consultation with members of the public, social partners and NGOs, company law experts and various kinds of business representatives.[115] There was not however evidence of consultation with worker representatives or other entities in third countries in terms of the standards or scrutiny to be applied.

There does seem to be some scope for the voices of those at work in third countries to be included in the implementation of the draft Directive, which contemplates in Article 7(2) the design of a 'prevention action plan' to be conducted with 'affected stakeholders' in terms of violations and in Article 8(3)(b) the potential for a 'corrective action plan' again to be 'developed in consultation with stakeholders'. It is evident that such stakeholders will include (under Article 3) 'the company's employees, the employees of its subsidiaries, and other individuals, groups, communities or entities whose rights or interests are or could be affected by the products, services and operations of that company, its subsidiaries and its business relationships'; so is to be broadly understood to include workers and the wider community of labour, potentially even in third countries.

However, the actual mechanics of what will be regarded as the appropriate process for such planning will be left to implementation by EU Member States, which

113. *See* n. 96 above.
114. COM(2022) 453 final, 1.
115. *Ibid.*, 18-19.

may not necessarily involve consultative engagement with the interests of those at work in third countries. Recital (49) does indicate that Member States and the Commission should be acting 'in partnership' with the governments and 'stakeholders' in the affected countries, but again the mechanisms by which this will be achieved are unclear.

In terms of the Regulation on products made with forced labour, there has been extensive consultation, this time both within and beyond the EU. The ILO and the OECD were also involved.[116] However, this may be because the measure is innately much more controversial since it involves blocking access to goods at the EU border and arguably, in so doing, goes beyond the explicit permission to prevent goods made by prison labour entering (as set out in Article XX of the General Agreement on Trade and Services at the WTO).[117]

There is no action plan, it would seem, associated with the proposed Directive on prison labour products which would ameliorate the situation for those at work in third countries dependent for their livelihoods on the export of certain goods. This matters because the allegations regarding forced labour could be untrue and EU actions disproportionate. The record of consultations in the Commission proposal observes that: 'There were disagreements between what evidence is needed by authorities to withhold a consignment at the point of entry.'[118] There is scope for cooperation between the Commission and relevant authorities in third countries (under Article 26) but the extent to which the voices of those at work from third countries can feed into this process will be crucial.

Investigations under Article 4 are to accord with 'due diligence guidelines or recommendations of the UN, ILO, OECD or other relevant international organisations' and 'any other due diligence in relation to forced labour'; but we know that at present concerns have been raised regarding the extent to which local workers (and their representatives) feed into extant due diligence processes.[119] There is promise here regarding potential for enhanced good governance, but it is too early to say it can and will be realised.

4 CONCLUSION

This chapter has introduced the substantive norms that underlie a sustainable development approach (encompassing both environmental and labour objectives) but has sought to marry these to the procedural conception of 'good governance' which can

116. COM(2022) 453 final, 5-8; with the summary reflecting differences of opinion.
117. For debates over the 'product-process' distinction usually applied regarding 'public morals' and problems of extra-territoriality, *see* Olivier De Schutter, *Trade in the Service of Sustainable Development: Linking Trade to Labour Rights and Environmental Standards* (Hart Publishing 2015), Ch. 4; and Kofi Addo, *Core Labour Standards and International Trade: Lessons from the regional context* (Springer 2015) Ch. 5.
118. COM(2022) 453 final, 6.
119. Christophe Clerc, The French 'Duty of Vigilance' Law: Lessons for an EU Directive on Due Diligence in Multinational Supply Chains (13 January 2021). ETUI Research Paper - Policy Brief 1/2021, Available at SSRN: https://ssrn.com/abstract=3765288 or http://dx.doi.org/10.2139/ssrn.3765288.

also be detected in the 2030 Agenda. It is argued that issues of decent work as well as ecological protections, aligned with inclusivity and equality, evident in the SDGs deserve attention in EU regulation. Indeed, much-needed attention has increasingly been given to both the realms of external relations and internal market regulation. What has been less evident, perhaps, is the acknowledgement of the procedural norms set out in the 2030 Agenda, namely transparent, inclusive and participatory institutions, which include those most affected and reflect the need for a *global* partnership to remedy social and environmental harms.

This chapter has presented the argument that freedom of association, collective bargaining and a right to strike can be regarded as both part of the substantive values that underlie the SDGs and a feature of procedural good governance. Inclusion of the representatives of those in the 'world of work' (broadly understood) can then be viewed as vital to EU social policy endeavours which seek to promote sustainable development. The EU-Korea expert panel report provided recognition, in the context of a trade dispute, that sustainable development may be an important interpretative device in the context of TSD chapters and that trade union rights can be derived from protections of freedom of association set out in FTAs. There are signs that the von der Leyen Commission in its introduction of a European Green Deal, replete with just transitions for workers, has understood the need for greater protection of collective bargaining internal to Europe. The result is that regulation of the EU internal market is beginning to reflect the understandings of social sustainability that the Commission has promoted through trade conditionality for some time on the world stage.

However, there is still a need for attention to the ways in which the procedural mechanisms of good governance could respond to the challenges of combining labour and environmental objectives. Certainly, in the new 'hybrid' instruments designed to impact the EU internal market, but which will affect workers in third countries, there remains reason for caution. 'Global partnership' does not only include identification and application of transparent internationally agreed standards (as a foundation for sustainable development) but also inclusion of the representation of the concerns and voices of those most affected, those at work outside Europe, including the most precarious (and atypical) workers. Identifying this need is perhaps the first stage towards seeing it met.

CHAPTER 8

The Role of Public Administration in Italy's Integrated National Energy and Climate Plan

Elena Buoso

1 THE DISASTROUS GLOBAL CLIMATE CHANGE

Climate change and the upcoming related risks for societies are at the top of the political agenda all over the world.

The last "State of the Global Climate Report," published by the World Meteorological Organization in 2022, confirmed the septennium 2016-2021 as the warmest on record[1] and the current year sadly shows that the situation is getting worse.

The Italian strategy against climate change is summarized in the "Integrated National Energy and Climate Plan" (Piano Nazionale Integrato per l'Energia e il Clima - PNIEC). The Plan has very wide-ranging and diversified content, but the paper concentrates on the role of public administrations to implement it.

2 EUROPEAN TARGETS AND NATIONAL ACTION PLANS

As is well known, in 2019 the European Green Deal set ambitious short and long-term emissions reduction targets.[2] The European Union (EU) aims to be climate-neutral by 2050 with the interim target of reducing CO_2 emissions by 55 % in 2030 compared to the emissions in 1990.[3]

1. *See* the full Report at https://library.wmo.int/index.php?lvl=notice_display&id=22080#.Y8QMtRXMI2w.
2. About the disruptive impact of the EU Green Deal, *see* E. CHITI, *Managing the Ecological Transition of the EU: The European Green Deal as a Regulatory Process, Common Market Law Review*, vol. 59, 1 (2022), pp. 19 ff DOI: 10.54648/cola2022003.
3. Find the whole package at https://www.consilium.europa.eu/en/policies/green-deal/.

In this regard National Energy and Climate Plans (NECPs) were introduced by the Regulation on the governance of the energy union and climate action (EU) 2018/1999), agreed as part of the Clean Energy for all Europeans package adopted with the Green Deal.[4]

The national plans shall outline how the EU countries intend to address five "prime dimensions":[5] (1) energy efficiency, (2) renewable energy sources, (3) emissions reductions, (4) interconnections, and (5) research and innovation.

According to the Regulation, by the end of 2018, each Member State had to submit a first draft NECP for the period 2021-2030 to the Commission. In June 2019, after considering the proposed plans, the Commission gave an overall assessment and country-specific recommendations. The Member States had subsequently to submit their final NECPs by December 2019. An important point is the continuous monitoring, to achieve which each country must submit to the Commission a Progress Report every two years.

Italy presented a first draft of National Climate Change Plan (Piano nazionale di adattamento ai cambiamenti climatici—PNAC) in 2018. The Commission did not have many recommendations, but one point is worth mentioning because it has become dramatically relevant due to the current armed conflict in Ukraine: Italy planned to reduce import dependence via the increase of renewable sources and energy efficiency efforts as well as further diversification of sources of supply and the promotion of a more secure, flexible and resilient gas sector. Nevertheless, regarding energy security Italy was not ambitious enough. The Commission observed that the centrality of gas in the future energy mix was too high and seemed to be in contradiction with the stated decarbonization objectives. The first draft lacked measurable indicators in the 2030 perspective and was unclear on the future development of key natural gas infrastructures.[6]

Eventually, the Plan became an "Integrated" National Energy and Climate Plan (PNIEC) and was presented, just in time, by December 2019.[7]

Lastly, it is also worth mentioning that one "mission" of the National Recovery and Resilience Plan (Piano Nazionale di Ripresa e Resilienza—PNRR) is about "green revolution and ecological transition."[8] This is the second out of six main targets and the richest in the entire Plan, gathering more than 30% of the allocated resources, amounting to nearly EUR 60 billion. Relevant is also the third mission "infrastructure and sustainable mobility," which includes 13.26% of the total resources with almost

4. Further details in https://commission.europa.eu/energy-climate-change-environment/implementation-eu-countries/energy-and-climate-governance-and-reporting/national-energy-and-climate-plans_en.
5. *See* Part I, § 1.1 PNIEC.
6. Draft Plans and Commission assessment are available at https://energy.ec.europa.eu/topics/energy-strategy/national-energy-and-climate-plans-necps_en#commission-assessment-of-the-final-necps.
7. *See* the full text https://www.mise.gov.it/images/stories/documenti/PNIEC_finale_17012020.pdf; in English https://energy.ec.europa.eu/system/files/2020-02/it_final_necp_main_en_0.pdf.
8. The PNRR could be downloaded at https://www.italiadomani.gov.it/content/sogei-ng/it/en/home.html.

EUR 30 billion. Italy has already issued several measures and regulations to implement the National Recovery Plan.[9]

3 MAIN GOALS OF ITALY'S PNIEC AND IMPLEMENTATION POLICIES

Italy has committed itself to pursue following main goals:[10] (a) accelerating the decarbonization process by setting an interim milestone in 2030 for achieving full decarbonization by 2050, which requires to integrate environmental factors in (all) other public policies (Part I, §§ 2.1 and 3.1 PNIEC); (b) evolving the energy system, improving renewable energy sources but also ensuring adequate supplies from conventional sources although in progressive decline (Part I, §§ 2.1 and 3.1. PNIEC); (c) promoting energy efficiency across all sectors, improving energy security and reducing energy costs for administrations, families and businesses (Part I, §§ 2.2 and 3.2 PNIEC); (d) renewing the internal energy market and infrastructure, particularly for the electricity sector, going from a centralized structure to distribution predominantly reliant on renewable sources in de-centralized manner (Part I, §§ 2.4 and 3.4. PNIEC); (e) maintaining the process for integrating the national energy system with the energy union.

These general objectives correspond to five "dimensions" of the European frame for 2021-2030,[11] decarbonization, energy efficiency, energy security, internal energy market and research, innovation and competitiveness.

Such aims are to be reached with the aid of research and innovation but also by involving citizens and businesses (in particular SMEs) for them to take a key role in the energy transition process, for example, by promotion of self-consumption and renewable energy communities.[12]

Moreover, the national system should minimize the negative impact of energy transition on other equally relevant public interests, such as the preservation of the quality of air and bodies of water, as well as landscape protection and limitation of land take.

Every dimension is provided with detailed policies and sector-specific measures (Part I, § 3 PNIEC) but some activities are cross-cutting and cover all sectors. Among these "horizontal" measures the Plan mentions two general strategies (Part I, § 1.1, ii, PNIEC): first careful governance that required the monitoring of the outcomes in terms of reorientation of the production system, and of costs and benefits; second the involvement of various Ministries and, in accordance with their constitutional attributions, Regions, municipalities, the Regulatory Authority for Energy, Networks and

9. Progress in the implementation of the Plan are reported at https://www.italiadomani.gov.it/content/sogei-ng/it/en/strumenti/andamento-sull-attuazione-del-piano.html?orderby=%40jcr%3Acontent%2FyearAndSemesterLabel&sort=desc.
10. *See* full and extended list https://www.mise.gov.it/images/stories/documenti/it_final_necp_main_en.pdf.
11. *See* Part I, § 1.1 of the document https://energy.ec.europa.eu/system/files/2020-06/ro_final_necp_main_en_0.pdf.
12. Part I, § 1.1 PNIEC, p. 6.

Environment (ARERA), representatives from the research sector and business associations as well as workers' organizations.

From a methodological focus, it is possible to relate all planned specific measures to three basic policies: (1) "improve measures," regarding efficiency and emissions reduction; (2) "avoid measures," reducing energy and resources consuming needs; and (3) shift measures, mainly referring to the efficiency of transfers (of goods and persons) and routes.[13]

An important and indispensable aspect of current environmental and energy policies is that objectives must be widely shared and agreed upon among different public bodies, economic operators and the public, as emerged during the consultation procedures for the Strategic Environmental Assessment of the Plan.[14]

4 A TASK FOR ALL LEVELS OF THE PUBLIC ADMINISTRATION

Such goals place before the entire Italian public administration important and challenging tasks. This involves not only central and state levels but also regional and municipal levels. Italy's constitutional framework designs a regional state (Articles 5 and 113 ff. Const.). Therefore, regions are assigned a key role in achieving all the purposes of the Republic, not least environmental protection and energy and climate targets (Articles 9 and 117 ff. Const.). The role of the local authorities is equally significant (Articles 114 and 118 Const.). This constitutionally guaranteed role requires mechanisms for coordination with the central government, which also operates on a preventive basis. One of these is the Unified State-Regions-Cities Conference that has been involved in an advisory function on the draft PNIEC.[15]

Central and local governments are thus active in all five dimensions of intervention. The following sections will explore the most significant aspects in this regard.

5 SPECIFIC CHALLENGES FOR THE PUBLIC ADMINISTRATION: DECARBONIZATION

The public sector should support renewable energy sources with regulations but also with administrative choices and by purchase of sustainable products.

To achieve the target of 30% of gross final consumption of energy from renewable sources in 2030 Italy has defined a lane of sustainable growth for them and must provide their full integration into the system (Part I, § 2.1.2 PNIEC), allocating renewables share in all sectors (55.0% in the electricity sector; 34% in the heating/cooling sector; 22.0% in the transport sector).

13. Part I, § 1.1 PNIEC, p. 9, where the policies are mainly referred to the transport sector.
14. *See* the final assessment published by Decree of the Ministry of the Environment in agreement with the Minister of Cultural Heritage and Activities and Tourism No. 367 of 31/12/2019 https://va.mite.gov.it/it-IT/Oggetti/Documentazione/7040/10060?Testo=&RaggruppamentoID=1031#form-cercaDocumentazione.
15. The Conference expressed a mainly positive opinion on the PNIEC in Document No. 137/CU of December 18, 2019 https://www.statoregioni.it/media/2298/p-8-doc-regioni-cu-18-dicembre-2019.pdf.

These ambitious targets regarding the electrical goals require first to stimulate new production of renewable energy. In parallel it is also necessary to preserve and modernize existing production by promoting the revamping and repowering of existing installations.[16]

The impact of new energy plants on landscape and environment has become a critical issue,[17] therefore to prevent further land take, installation of photovoltaics should be favored primarily in urbanized areas, such as existing buildings, car parks, service areas and similar. It is clear that these areas, however, cannot cover all the new needs for renewable energy and that large, new, ground-mounted photovoltaic installations will be required. Ideally, they must be set in unproductive areas, unsuitable for other uses (like agriculture) because contaminated or extremely polluted, like is the case of waste disposal sites and areas along the infrastructure system. In this regard, the contribution of municipalities and local communities to identify possible suitable sites can be crucial (Part I, § 2.3 PNIEC).

Regarding this dimension, the public administration could and should implement a framework for faster approval procedures. The authorization procedures relating to works connected to decarbonizations have been simplified and expedited in the last months, especially by the laws implementing the National Recovery and Resilience Plan.[18]

Second, it is possible to increase the efficiency of administrative decisions and procedures by promoting interaction between various authorities involved.[19]

Last, it is necessary to increase transparency and involvement in the approval process. Current legal systems favor with many tools a wide and more aware involvement of citizens in decisions relevant to the territory and the environment. Following the example of "débat public" in France, Italy has introduced a general

16. Part I, § 2.3 PNIEC, p. 68.
17. M. Meli, *Quando l'ambiente entra in conflitto con se stesso: fonti energetiche rinnovabili e tutela del paesaggio*, Rivista Giuridica AmbienteDiritto.it, 2/2021, pp. 1 ff.; R. Ferrara, *Il cambiamento climatico e il Piano Nazionale di Ripresa e Resilienza (PNRR): un'introduzione al tema*, Diritto e società, 2/2021, pp. 271 ff.; Id., Il PNRR e l'ambiente: verso quali scenari?, Rivista giuridica di urbanistica, 4/2021, pp. 767 ff.; S. Amorosino, *La "dialettica" tra tutela del paesaggio e produzione di energia da fonti rinnovabili a tutela dell'ambiente atmosferico*, Rivista Giuridica dell'Edilizia, 4/2022, pp. 261 ff.
18. R. Ferrara, *Politiche ambientali e sistema delle semplificazioni amministrative: verso quali scenari?*, Rivista giuridica di urbanistica, 3-4/2014, pp. 368 ff.; E. Scotti, *Semplificazioni ambientali tra politica e caos: la via e i procedimenti unificati*, Rivista Giuridica dell'Edilizia, 5/2018, pp. 353 ff.; P. Marzaro, *Semplificazione, coordinamento degli interessi pubblici e leale collaborazione come canone di legittimità dell'azione amministrativa*, Diritto e società, 3/2019, pp. 501 ff.; S. Lazzari, *Le energie rinnovabili: semplificazione amministrativa e compiti delle autonomie locali*, Giornale di diritto amministrativo, 5/2022, pp. 634 ff.; P. Piras, *Semplificazioni e buon andamento della Pubblica amministrazione. Tra Scilla e Cariddi: rispettare la complessità superando le complicazioni*, DPCE online, 2/2021, pp. 1923 ff.; M. Ramajoli, *I silenzi amministrativi nelle recenti 'semplificazioni'*, Rivista giuridica di urbanistica, 1/2022, pp. 38 ff.
19. E. Scotti, *La conferenza di servizi tra pluralismo e unilateralismo costituzionalmente orientato (a proposito di Corte cost. n. 9/2019)*, Federalismi.it, 17/2019, pp. 5 ff.; P. Corleto, *Verso una sostenibilità dell'ecosistema normativo: il caso della conferenza di servizi*, Diritto e processo amministrativo, 3/2021, pp. 805 ff.; F. Gambardella, *Il superamento della dimensione negoziale della conferenza di servizi decisoria: dalla riforma Madia alla recente legislazione emergenziale*, Federalismi.it, 6/2021, pp. 18 ff.

hypothesis of public debate[20] (Article 22 legislative decree No. 50/2016, Code of Public Contracts, and Article 40 Final outline of the new Code of Public Contracts[21]) in addition to the procedural participation options already present, for example, in urban planning law.[22] Wind and photovoltaic power plants are going to change the Italian landscape because a significant surface area will be occupied. This requires involving local communities and citizens considering that awareness and involvement could increase acceptance of public decisions, prevent litigation and avoid the onset of the so-called NIMBY syndrome.[23]

5.1 Transport Policies

The strategy about renewable energy sources could (and should) be profitably combined with a change in transport and civil (residential and tertiary) sectors and other fields where the role of local authorities is central because they have direct competence on them.[24]

The fleet of local public transport vehicles[25] is planned to be replaced since 2016 at a rate of 25% of new purchases planned on a triannual basis.[26] The rate of "green vehicles replacement"[27] has been now raised to 30% by 2022 and must become at least 50% by 2025 and 85% by 2030.[28] The effectiveness of this provision is assured by

20. V. Molaschi, *Il dibattito pubblico sulle grandi opere. Prime riflessioni sul d.P.C.M. n. 76 del 2018,* Rivista giuridica di urbanistica, 3/2018, pp. 386 ff.; G. Pepe, *Dibattito pubblico ed infrastrutture in una prospettiva comparata,* Federalismi.it, 5/2019, pp. 6 ff.; M. Timo, *Il dibattito pubblico sulle grandi infrastrutture fra codice italiano dei contratti e "code de l'environnement" francese,* DPCE online, 2/2019, pp. 1179 ff.; P. Vipiana, *La disciplina del dibattito pubblico nel regolamento attuativo del Codice degli appalti, tra anticipazioni regionali e suggestioni francesi,* Federalismi.it, 2/2019, pp. 5 ff.; I. Casillo, *Il "débat public" francese: difesa dell'ambiente o difesa della democrazia? Una lettura critica dell'offerta istituzionale di democrazia partecipativa in Francia in occasione dei venticinque anni del "débat public,"* Istituzioni del Federalismo, 3/2020, pp. 635 ff.; F. Cittadino, M. Trettel, *Il "dibattito pubblico" in prospettiva multilivello: tra mito partecipativo e prassi istituzionale,* Istituzioni del Federalismo, 3/2020, pp. 563 ff.; S. Donati, *La cultura della partecipazione in Francia fra 'Débat public' e 'Gran Débat National',* GiustAmm.it, 6/2021, pp. 7 ff.; D. Baldoni, *Praticare la democrazia partecipativa in ottica decentrata: il divergente percorso di Francia e Italia,* Italian Papers On Federalism, 1/2022, pp. 69 ff.
21. The new Code of Public Contracts has been issued ex Art. 1 Law No. 78 of 21/6/2022 and is expected to enter in force from April 1, 2023.
22. P.M. Rosa Salva, *Il principio di partecipazione nella sfida della sostenibilità territoriale: Italia e Francia a confronto,* DPCE online, 2/2021, pp. 1799 ff.
23. Acronym for "Not In My Backyard." On this topic: G. Manfredi, *Il regolamento sul dibattito pubblico: democrazia deliberativa e sindrome "nimby,"* Urbanistica e appalti, 5/2018, pp. 604 ff.; D. Foster, J. Warren, *The NIMBY Problem,* Journal of Theoretical Politics, 2022, vol. 34, pp. 145 ff.
24. For general but complete view on the topic: E. Scotti, *Servizi pubblici locali,* Digesto delle discipline pubblicistiche, Aggiornamento, 2012, pp. 629 ff.
25. That is, cars, buses and public utility vehicles, including those for collecting urban waste, owned by public administration, state and local providers of public utilities.
26. Article 18, 10, Legislative Decree No. 257/2016 (Transposition of the Development of Alternative Fuel Infrastructure Directive). The provision is referred to Municipalities with high levels of PM10 particle pollution.
27. This expression means: electric vehicles and hybrid vehicles with off-vehicle charging, powered by methane and hydrogen, and electricity and methane in the case of buses.
28. For the local public transport the rate is solely referred to urban services vehicles.

public procurement regulation, indeed tender procedures are void if they do not comply with it.[29]

A further point is the school transport service. Among the various measures to implement the obligations under the Air Quality Directive 2008/50/EC,[30] it is interesting to mention the promotion of sustainable school transport, through a number of pilot projects with hybrid and electric vehicles. Italy had an infringement proceeding for nonfulfillment of the Air Quality Directive obligations[31] and the project applied in the first phase for these areas, with populations of over 50,000. Interesting is the financing, because the measure was partially funded by CO_2 emission quota auctions.[32]

Pilot initiatives are not only intended as a trial to test the best solution, worth replicating on a larger scale; they also have a cultural function, promoting the use of electric or hybrid vehicles in general by the population.[33] This double purpose is particularly clear regarding vehicles used for surveillance in natural protected areas, visited every year by over 100 million people.[34]

5.2 Remote Working

So far the papers have briefly analyzed a strategy for achieving sustainability goals with "improve measures," that uses substitution of energy sources and reduction of emission-generating tools.

Another way to intervene is by reducing the demand for mobility and increasing collective mobility with "avoid measures."

Remote Working[35]—by the Italian legislator often referred to as "agile working"—could be perfectly framed in this perspective as it enables optimization of resources, infrastructure efficiency and implementation of the commuting transfers,

29. Article 18, section 10, Legislative Decree No. 257/2016.
30. Article 3 Law No. 141/2019, converting Law Decree No. 111/2019.
31. At the end of the proceedings the Court found that Italy had manifestly failed to adopt in good time the measures required: ECJ November 10, 2020, C-644/18, *Commission v. Italy*.
32. That gave a funding of EUR 20 million per year, *see* more details in Part I, § 3.2 PNIEC, p. 181.
33. So Part I, § 3.2 PNIEC, p. 185.
34. EUR 10 million has been allocated for the purchase of around 220 electric or hybrid cars for the military police (80%) and port authorities (20%): Part I, § 3.2 PNIEC, p. 185.
35. "Remote working" is the broadest concept. It describes the situations where workers perform their task and duties fully or partly from an alternative location of their own choosing instead of from the default place of work (employer's or client's premises, public space): *see* the definition by ILO, Defining and measuring remote work, telework, work at home and home-based work, Report of June 2020 https://www.ilo.org/global/statistics-and-databases/publications/WCMS_747075/lang--en/index.htm. Terminology is really various on this field, a definition of the different concepts could be find in M. Sostero et al., *Teleworkability and the COVID-19 Crisis: A New Digital Divide?*, 2020, European Commission, JRC121193, pp. 7 ff., available at https://joint-research-centre.ec.europa.eu/publications/teleworkability-and-covid-19-crisis-new-digital-divide_en; *see also* the study requested by the European Parliament's committee on Employment and Social Affairs: M. Samek Lodovici et al., *The Impact of Teleworking and Digital Work on Workers and Society*, European Union, 2021, pp. 18 ff., available at https://www.google.com/url?sa=i&rct=j&q=&esrc=s&source=web&cd=&ved=0CAIQw7AJahcKEwjI08rH_6SAAxUAAAAAHQAAAAAQAg&url=https%3A%2F%2Fwww.europarl.europa.eu%2FRegData%2Fetudes%2FATAG%2F2021%2F662907%2FIPOL_ATA(2021)662907_EN.pdf&psig=AOvVaw0m8NxphlAwCPlWlgBsS9Ec&ust=1690207447951201&opi=89978449.

and so does indeed the PNIEC.[36] Nevertheless, the Italian legal system seems not to consider it as an effective measure. The little space left for this form of work among those usually provided for public employees is quite objectionable, also regarding the integrative approach of environmental issues.

Remote work is still envisioned by our legislature mainly from a pandemic containment and worker protection perspective,[37] not as a tool for environmental sustainability and reduction of consumption and emissions. This is the approach of the so-called Reopening law decree (Decreto riaperture) n. 24 of 2022,[38] where this modality applies only to physically frail workers.[39] Also, the last guidelines published in 2022,[40] that will lead to reception of this formula in the National Collective Bargaining Agreements (NCBA) for employees of public administrations, refer to efficiency and work-life balance, not to environmental issues. However, it is likely that the fight against climate change will still gain from this way of work, which is slowly stabilizing in administrations.[41]

An "Organizational Plan for Agile Work" (Piano organizzativo del lavoro agile—POLA)[42] must be approved by every administration by January 31 of each year, after consultation with labor organizations, as a section of the mandatory Performance Plan. The POLA identifies the implementation modalities of agile work by providing that at least 15% of employees can make use of it, ensuring that they are not penalized for the purposes of recognition of professionalism and career progression.

The POLA defines organizational measures, technological requirements, training paths for staff, including managers, and tools for the detection and periodic verification of the results achieved, including the digitization of processes, and the quality of services provided. If POLA is not adopted, agile work applies to at least 15% of employees where they request it.

36. Part I, § 1.2 PNIEC, p. 25.
37. L. Zoppoli, *Lavoro agile, persone e amministrazioni: le sfide post-pandemia*, Rivista Italiana di Diritto del Lavoro, 2/2022, pp. 199 ff.
38. Converted with amendments by Law No. 52/2022.
39. M. Brollo, *Lavoro agile per i lavoratori fragili: lezioni dalla pandemia*, ADL Argomenti di diritto del lavoro, 3/2022, pp. 405 ff.
40. Available at https://www.funzionepubblica.gov.it/sites/funzionepubblica.gov.it/files/PA_Linee_guida_lavoro_agile.pdf.
41. *See* https://www.forumpa.it/riforma-pa/smart-working/smart-working-cose-come-funziona-la-normativa-e-i-vantaggi-per-le-pa/. *See also* R. Romei, *Il lavoro agile in Italia: prima, durante e dopo la pandemia*, Labor, 4/2020, pp. 423 ff.; A. Lupo, *Lavoro agile e pubblico impiego dopo la legge Madia: quali prospettive future?*, Istituzioni del Federalismo, 2/2021, pp. 553 ff.; C. Peiti, *Il lavoro agile nelle pubbliche amministrazioni come questione organizzativa, RU Risorse umane nella pubblica amministrazione*, 2/2022, pp. 13 ff.; A. Topo, G. Pensabene Lionti, *Smart working ai tempi del coronavirus: lavorare a distanza nella P.A. Un* focus *sull'Università*, Il lavoro nelle pubbliche amministrazioni 2/2021, pp. 296 ff.; P. Polliani, A. Coldesina, *Lo "smart working" in Italia tra rivoluzione culturale, normativa emergenziale e un futuro ancora da scrivere*, Rivista italiana di informatica e diritto, 1/2022, pp. 323 ff.; M. Brollo, *Il patto di lavoro agile nelle pp.aa. verso il post-emergenza*, Il lavoro nelle pubbliche amministrazioni, 3/2022, pp. 447 ff.
42. Article 14, section 1, Law No. 124/2015, as amended several times.

From the year 2022 onwards, these contents are integrated into the Integrated Plan of Activities and Organization (Piano Integrato di Attività e Organizzazione—PIAO), that is going to be the summary and comprehensive planning and governance document of public administrations.[43]

6 SPECIFIC CHALLENGES FOR THE PUBLIC ADMINISTRATION: ENERGY EFFICIENCY

The greatest potential for public administrations in terms of energy efficiency policies is provided by buildings projects.

The Energy Efficiency Directive 2012/27/EU requests each year a renovation of 3% of the floor area of the central public administration (Article 5). The current programme of measures included in the Energy Renovation Programme for the Central Public Administration (Programma di riqualificazione energetica degli edifici dell'amministrazione pubblica centrale—PREPAC)[44] is expected to meet this obligation.[45] To grant the achievement and accelerate it, the existing measure was reinforced with further resources, totaling EUR 40 million each year from 2020 to 2022. The overall floor area of buildings subject to the provisions of the Energy Efficiency Directive covers 15.2 million m^2 per 4.102 occupants and the Italian public administration will renovate 3.2 million m^2 by 2030.[46]

In addition to interventions on public buildings, energy efficiency measures will include public lighting, public housing and all public properties, supporting also municipalities and local administrations.[47] The funding can also be used by the municipalities for projects in the areas of sustainable local development and sustainable mobility.

7 SPECIFIC CHALLENGES FOR THE PUBLIC ADMINISTRATION: GREEN PUBLIC PROCUREMENT

Purchases of public administrations and public service concessionaires are an important tool of action against climate change. Both because the volume of business is able to affect the market and producers, and because the eco-sustainability of the items and services purchased is relevant to long-lasting effects.[48] Italy has a National Action Plan

43. Article 6 Law Decree No. 80/2021, converted with amendments by Law No. 113/2021. The PIAO for 2022-2024 is available at https://www.lavoro.gov.it/Amministrazione-Trasparente/Performance/Pagine/PIAO.aspx. *See also* F. Coruzzi, *Il regime transitorio del lavoro agile: le amministrazioni pubbliche ancora al bivio tra smart working emergenziale e PIAO*, RU Risorse umane nella pubblica amministrazione, 1/2022, pp. 25 ff.
44. Legislative Decree No. 102/2014.
45. *See* the Court of Auditors' monitoring report of 2021: https://www.corteconti.it/Download?id=d965782b-365d-4257-bafb-19b9c89bbe88.
46. Part I, § 2.2 PNIEC, p. 89.
47. In 2020 the Budget law assigned EUR 500 million for the purpose: Part I, § 3.1.2 PNIEC, p. 159.
48. F. Fracchia, S. Vernile, *I contratti pubblici come strumento dello sviluppo ambientale*, Rivista quadrimestrale di Diritto dell'Ambiente, 2/2020, pp. 4 ff.; G. Quinto, *Le variabili ambientali nella disciplina degli appalti pubblici. Storia di un difficile equilibrio tra tutela dell'ambiente e promozione dello sviluppo economico*, Ambientediritto.it, 1/2020, pp. 90 ff.; M. Cafagno,

on Green Public Procurement since 2008 (PAN GPP).[49] The plan sets three strategic environmental main goals: energy efficiency and reduction in greenhouse gas emissions; reduction in hazardous chemicals; and recycling and reuse of materials (Part I, § 3.5. PAN GPP). The strategies must respond to two principles of sustainable development: (1) the "dematerialization," meant as a process of gradual reduction of waste and optimization of the resources used (material and energy), for the fulfillment of the same functions to be achieved by favoring technological innovation technology in production cycles, the use of renewable raw materials or those with lower resource content, the use of renewable energy sources, and the replacement of the purchase of products with that of services that perform the same function; (2) the dissemination of green purchasing, by which the public administration aims to spread purchasing and consumption patterns that are mindful of environmental impacts and conscious use of resources. This involves strategies for information and proper management of products and waste.

The PAN GPP identifies 11 categories of products and services of priority interest in terms of spending volume and environmental impact[50] and defines for each of them "minimum environmental criteria," i.e., requirements of an environmental nature related to the different stages of the procurement process (subject matter of the contract, technical specifications, award criteria, conditions of contract execution) to be integrated into public procurement procedures.[51]

According to Article 34 Code of Public Contracts (and Article 57 of the Final outline of the new Code) the public administration contributes to the achievement of the environmental objectives set out in the PAN GPP through the use of those minimum environmental criteria in public tenders. Such "green clauses" justify higher spending on eco-friendly works and supplies and are one of the elements for identifying the most economically advantageous bid—which is a different concept from the cheapest bid—under Article 95 Code of Public Contracts (Article 108 new Code).

L'ambiente nei contratti pubblici: due angoli visuali e una morale, Diritto e processo amministrativo, 4/2021, pp. 859 ff.; E. Caruso, *I contratti pubblici tra obiettivi di sostenibilità e finalità concorrenziali: alla ricerca di nuovi equilibri,* P.A. Persona e Amministrazione, 1/2022, pp. 284 ff.; I. A. Nicotra, C. Sagone, *Green Public Procurement: a look into the past to meet future challenges,* Federalismi.it, 6/2022, pp. 259 ff.; S. Rossa, *Sviluppo sostenibile e appalti pubblici. Sul ruolo degli appalti innovativi come strumento di sostenibilità,* CERIDAP, 4/2022;

49. The "Piano d'Azione Nazionale per la sostenibilità ambientale dei consumi della pubblica amministrazione" was approved by Interministerial Decree No. 135/2008, https://www.acquistiverdi.it. *See* F. De Leonardis, *L'uso strategico della contrattazione pubblica: tra GPP ["Green Public Procurement"] e obbligatorietà dei CAM,* Rivista quadrimestrale di Diritto dell'Ambiente, 3/2020, pp. 62 ff.

50. Listed in Part I, § 3.6 PAN GPP: furniture; construction; waste management; urban and land services; energy services; electronics; textiles and footwear; stationery; catering; building management services; transport services.

51. E. Bellomo, *Appalti verdi in urbanistica ed edilizia: i criteri ambientali minimi,* Rivista giuridica di urbanistica, 1/2020, pp. 143 ff.

8 THE CONTRIBUTION OF DIGITAL ADMINISTRATION

Finally, with respect to resource-saving and sustainability, it is worth mentioning the contribution of digital public administration and online public services.[52]

The Next Generation EU Program, as well as the National Recovery and Resilience Plan, integrated the Green Revolution and Sustainability Dimension with the Digitalization Mission. Indeed the first mission of the National Recovery Plan is dedicated to Digitalization, Innovation, Competitiveness, Culture and Tourism,[53] which absorbs EUR 49 billion (21% of the total resources).

The tools are many, for example, the application of blockchain technology could be time- and resource-saving for certifications, public registers, data exchange and payments to the public sector.[54] At the European level in 2018 all EU Members States, plus Norway, Lichtenstein and the EU Commission created the European Blockchain Partnership (EBP).[55] It has been implemented in Italy as Italian Blockchain Service Infrastructure by several public bodies and research institutes such as the Italian Digital Agency, Politecnico di Milano, and Poste Italiane.[56] The project aims to test the mode of design and development of an ecosystem based on Distributed Ledger-Type Technologies, in line with the European Strategy of implementing a similar infrastructure within the EBP.

However, even if this technology as well as the digitization of paper documents saves time and paper resources, the environmental costs of exchanging and storing

52. A. Masucci, *Digitalizzazione dell'amministrazione e servizi pubblici on line. Lineamenti del disegno normativo,* Diritto Pubblico, 1/2019, pp. 117 ff.; R. Cavallo Perin, D.U. Galetta (eds), *Il diritto dell'amministrazione pubblica digitale,* Torino, 2020; D.U. Galetta, *Technological Transition in response to COVID. Scattered Thoughts on the possibility of a (Technological) transition to a Digitalized Public Administration in Italy, with the help of the Recovery and Resilience Plan,* CERIDAP, 4/2021.
53. The Italian PNRR an information on its implementation are available at https://www.italiadomani.gov.it/content/sogei-ng/it/it/home.html.
54. C. Iaione & S. Ranchordas, *Smart Public Law. Automation and Decentralization of Public Power: Smart Contracts and the Blockchain as Stepping Stones for a Digital and Polycentric Good Administration,* IJPL, 2/2021, pp. 416 ff.; M. Macchia, *Blockchain e pubblica amministrazione,* Federalismi.it, 2/2021, pp. 117 ff.; M. Matassa, *"Blockchain" e pubblica amministrazione: stato dell'arte e prospettive,* Istituzioni del Federalismo, 3/2021, pp. 803 ff.; O. Pollicino, G. De Gregorio, *Blockchain and Public Law: Global Challenges in the era of Decentralization,* Cheltenham, 2021; P. Rubechini, *"Blockchain" e pubblica amministrazione italiana: i primi passi di un cammino ancora lungo,* Giornale di diritto amministrativo, 3/2021, pp. 298 ff.; A. Saporito, *L'intelligenza artificiale nel procedimento amministrativo: il sistema della tecnologia "blockchain,"* ambientediritto.it, 4/2021, pp. 70 ff.; P. D'Onofrio, *La blockchain nell'azione pubblica e privata di governo,* Il Lavoro nelle pubbliche amministrazioni, 2/2022, pp. 275 ff.; P. La Selva, *"Blockchain" e "Smart Contracts" nella Pubblica Amministrazione: aspetti di un tentativo di digitalizzazione del settore pubblico,* Amministrativ@mente, 2/2022, pp. 279 ff.; M. Rhao, *Il paradosso di Nakamoto: utilità attese e pericoli potenziali di un impiego istituzionale della tecnologia "blockchain,"* Rivista italiana di informatica e diritto, 1/2022, 2, pp. 213 ff.; F. Votta, *L'amministrazione pubblica e la tecnologia "blockchain,"* Giornale di diritto amministrativo, 4/2022, pp. 450 ff.; G. Gallone, *"Blockchain" e "big data" nel settore pubblico: spunti in tema di G.D.P.R. "compliance,"* Federalismi.it, 14/2022, pp. 66 ff.
55. https://ec.europa.eu/digital-building-blocks/wikis/display/EBSI/Home.
56. *See* more at https://progettoibsi.org/.

data are high.[57] For this reason, rationalization of rules and simplification of procedures is a key factor in the efficiency of administration.[58]

The same can be said for the "single cloud project" for government information, data and procedures, which plans to unify in a single cloud all information and data of the Italian public administration.[59]

9 CONCLUDING REMARKS

Some trends and lines of action contrasting climate change in this chapter are not new in the Italian legal system. Today, however, they are set in a very different context than they were a few years ago.

The first difference is the huge amount of funding that has come to Italy as a result of the Next Generation EU program and the fact that they are to be used more or less under the control of the European institutions.

The second novelty is the amendment of Articles 9 and 41 of the Italian Constitution, that took place in February 2022.[60] The first part of the Constitution, containing the fundamental principles, has been amended for the first time introducing expressly that the Republic "shall protect environment, biodiversity and ecosystems, also in the interest of future generations" and that although "private economic initiative is free" it cannot be carried out contrary to social utility or in a way that harms health and the environment.[61]

This implies a new status for environmental protection in our system, by all components of the state and are important conditions for Italy's climate change strategy.

We are in the middle of a transition (a just transition), and we are about to see big changes. We should try to look to the future with confidence, also because we have everything to lose and no more time to waste.

57. M. Beraldi, *L'impatto della "blockchain" sull'ambiente. Il caso della "Crypto art"*, GiustAmm.it, 4/2022, pp. 1 ff.
58. *See* footnote No. 18.
59. *See* more at https://cloud.italia.it/.
60. Constitutional Law No. 1/2022.
61. On the new constitutional provisions, *see* R. Cabazzi, *Dalla "contrapposizione" alla "armonizzazione"? Ambiente ed iniziativa economica nella riforma (della assiologia) costituzionale*, Federalismi.it, 7/2022, pp. 31 ff.; A. D'Aloia, *La Costituzione e il dovere di pensare al futuro*, BioLaw Journal—Rivista di BioDiritto, 2/2022, pp. 1 ff.; M. Iannella, *L'"European Green Deal" e la tutela costituzionale dell'ambiente*, Federalismi.it, 24/2022, pp. 171 ff.; A. Lauro, *Dalla tutela ambientale in Costituzione alla responsabilità politica (anche) verso le future generazioni? Detti e non-detti di un principio di origine giurisprudenziale*, BioLaw Journal—Rivista di BioDiritto, 2/2022, pp. 115 ff.; R. Montaldo, *La tutela costituzionale dell'ambiente nella modifica degli artt. 9 e 41 Cost.: una riforma opportuna e necessaria?*, Federalismi.it, 13/2022, pp. 187 ff.; M. P. Poto, *La tutela costituzionale dell'ambiente, della biodiversità e degli ecosistemi, anche nell'interesse delle future generazioni*, Responsabilità civile e previdenza, 3/2022, pp. 1057 ff.; G. Sobrino, *Le generazioni future "entrano" nella Costituzione*, Quaderni costituzionali, 1/2022, pp. 139 ff.

Part III Climate Change and Its Implications on Labour Contract and Industrial Relations System

CHAPTER 9

Climate Change, Sustainability, Organisational Changes and Workers' Professionality

Elena Gramano

1 INTRODUCTION

The correlation between climate change and labour, and more specifically the potential and actual effects of climate change on labour law, are currently under debate by many scholars in different jurisdictions.[1] More recent studies focus their attention on the impact of climate change and the so-called green transition on the labour market and on the dynamics of migration and trajectories[2] – basically, the impact of climate change outside the perimeter of the employment relationship, as an external factor that drives or potentially distorts the labour market.[3]

Today, we face a different but equally challenging task: reasoning on the potential and actual effects of climate change and the green transition inside the

1. P. TOMASSETTI, *Labor Law and Environmental Sustainability*, in *Comp. Lab. Law Pol. Journ.*, 40(1), 2018, 61; P. TOMASSETTI, *From Treadmill of Production to Just Transition and Beyond*, in *Eu. Journ. Ind. Rel.*, 26(4), 2020, 439; D.J. DOOREY, *Just Transitions Law: Putting Labour Law to Work on Climate Change*, in *Journ. Envir. Law & Pract.*, 2017, 201; A. SUPIOT, *Labour is not a Commodity: The Content and Meaning of Work in the Twenty-first Century*, in *Intern. Lab. Rev.*, 1, 2021; A. LASSANDARI, *Il lavoro nella crisi ambientale*, in *Lav. Dir.*, 1, 2022, 7; G. CENTAMORE, *Una* just transition *per il diritto del lavoro*, in *Lav. Dir.*, 2022, 129; J. ESCRIBANO GUTIÉRREZ, *Lavoro e ambiente: le prospettive giuslavoristiche*, in *Dir. Rel. Ind.*, 3, 2016, 679.
2. W. CHIAROMONTE, *Migrazioni ambientali, protezione internazionale e inclusione lavorativa: la prospettiva nazionale*, in *Lav. Dir.*, 1, 2022, 53; V. BRINO, *Il raccordo tra lavoro e ambiente nello scenario internazionale*, in *Lav. Dir.*, 1, 2022, 97.
3. L. RUSTICO, M. TIRABOSCHI, *Employment Prospects in the Green Economy: Myth and Reality*, in *Intern. Journ. Comp. Lab. Law & Ind. Rel.*, 26 (4), 2010, 369; N. Sofroniou, P. Anderson, *The Green Factor: Unpacking Green Job Growth*, in *Intern. Lab. Rev.*, 1, 2021.

employment relationship, within the parties of such a relationship, and inside the individual dimension of the employment relationship.

We could ask a number of questions in this respect. Is the regulation of the employment relationship equipped to face the changes deriving from climate change? Shall we imagine new or specific solutions to address the specificities of the impact of climate change on the employment relationship? First and foremost, will climate change actually affect the inside of the employment relationship? Is it something that might affect what happens between the parties? If yes, why and how?

In order to answer these questions, we might start by considering, or reconsidering, the final goals of the enterprise in light of climate change. The prime goal of an enterprise, or rather an entrepreneur who conducts an economic activity, is to make profit. However, while still predominant, profit can no longer be the sole goal of an enterprise. It must be accompanied, on one hand, by the goal of producing a social impact on society,[4] as it offers employment, improving the economy of its community and of society in general. On the other hand, it must also have the goal of guaranteeing the full environmental sustainability of business activities in their impact on the environment and the planet.[5]

The third goal pertains to the broader social responsibility of the enterprise, not only directed to contemporary societies but also to future generations, to whom we owe the possibility of living on a planet where humans and nature can still coexist. It may also be a planet where we could overcome the anthropocentric perspective that mainly derives from a Western Christian view of the world, according to which human beings stay above the rest of the natural world.[6]

That said, we must acknowledge that there is a new goal that enterprises must pursue when conducting their business activities. We must acknowledge that such a goal also impacts the employment relationship at the individual level, between the single worker and the single employer. It redefines the content, the object of work activities and indirectly, the rules that govern the obligations of both parties within an employment relationship, or at least the traditional understanding of the perimeters of such obligations.

Protecting the environment by concretely conducting a fully sustainable, environmental business is possible not only by means of unilateral decisions by the employer in managing the business but also with the cooperation of the workers called to be active in this process. They shall be in the position of participating in the process,

4. S. Rodotà, *Funzione politica del diritto dell'economia e valutazione degli interessi realizzati dall'intervento pubblico*, in Barcellona (edited by), *L'uso alternativo del diritto*, Laterza, 1973, I, 249.
5. A. Perulli, V. Speziale, *Dieci tesi sul diritto del lavoro*, Il Mulino, 2022; B. Caruso, R. Del Punta, T. Treu, *Manifesto per un diritto del lavoro sostenibile*, Roma, 2020.
6. A. Zbyszewska, *Labor Law for Warming World: Exploring the InterSections of Work Regulation and Environmental Sustainability: An Introduction*, in *Comp. Lab. Law Pol. Journ.*, 2018, 40(1), 1; Ead., *Regulating Work with People and Nature in Mind: Feminist Reflections*, in *Comp. Lab. Law Pol. Journ.*, 2018, 40(1), 9; S. Routh, *Embedding Work in Nature: The Anthropocene and Legal Imagination of Work as Human Activity*, in *Comp. Lab. Law Pol. Journ.*, 40(1), 2018, 9.

meaning that they must be entitled to rights and prerogatives to make their role effective.[7]

With this article, I would like to open a line of research – with no expectations of being exhaustive – on the 'employee's right to be trained' by addressing the issue under the Italian legal system. I aim eventually to provide a possible answer to the given research question, which might be useful in extending the research to a more comparative level.

2 THE OBLIGATION TO TRAIN

The organizational choices aimed at sustainability will affect the employment relationship as they will lead to less impactful, different production processes at the organizational level, resulting in changes in workers' activities. Workers will therefore have to be empowered and trained.

In this context, we need to identify adequate tools especially to protect vulnerable workers within the transition period, providing them with the necessary tools to retrain their skills so that they may adapt their existing, acquired skills to the new needs of a sustainable economy.[8]

The necessity of adjusting the employee's skills to new, sustainable ways of organizing businesses and, more in general, to innovation, is nowadays considered essential. What distinguishes the current change from the previous ones, for example, the industrial revolution, is probably its rapid pace. Changes in the past happened from one generation to another, with the father not being able to perform the same job as his son. Today, the same employee in her professional life would face deep, even radical changes in the nature and content of the work she must perform to continue participating in the labour market.

This topic is of extreme interest to human resource managers and sociologists but also deserves specific attention from labour lawyers.

Scholars have recently pointed out that skill gaps and workforce shortages are almost inevitable; climate change and the connected consequences on labour demand higher skill levels from workers, and management often faces difficulty in filling new job requirements.[9]

The work of employees and their skills and competencies are at the core of the employment relationship. The exchange formalized in the employment contract can be described not as a simple exchange between a general working activity and a salary but rather as an exchange between a specific activity to be carried out with the proper competencies and the proportionate salary. Such a consideration is valid for every kind of job. All working activities require certain skills.

7. C. Chacartegui, *Workers' Participation and Green Governance*, in *Comp. Lab. Law Pol. Journ.*, 40(1), 2018, 89-108.
8. A. Occhino, *Diritto alla formazione e ricadute occupazionali in una prospettiva comparata*, in *Riv. It. Dir. Lav.*, 3, 2007, 91.
9. L. Casano, *Skills and Professions for a "Just Transition". Some Reflections for Legal Research*, in *E-Journal Intern. Comp. Lab. St.*, 8(3), 2019, 31; Ead., *Ripensare il "sistema" delle politiche attive: l'opportunità (e i rischi) della transizione ecologica*, in *Dir. Rel. Ind.*, 4, 2021, 99.

Therefore, the competencies that the employee owns, as well as the evolution of such competencies over time and the (legal) tools that incentivize such evolution are of extreme interest to lawyers who study the changes that climate change produces in the employment relationship and more in general in organizations.

For this reason, the relevance of training as an essential component of the employment relationship deserves specific attention from labour lawyers, especially in light of the deep changes currently affecting labour and labour law.[10]

Despite the current worldwide debate on climate change by labour scholars, very little has been said about the most visible effect of such a revolution: the deep change in the nature of work and the continuation of this process over time. One training programme, a course or a few classes is not enough for employees to keep pace with the innovations that their jobs require. The process of change is almost permanent, and the risk of not being able to adapt and perform properly hangs over workers like the Sword of Damocles.

To address the topic, labour lawyers traditionally focus on the side of the employer. Primarily, labour law scholars focus on the prerogative of the employer to amend the content of the contract unilaterally, adjusting it to organizational and business needs. This is often considered one of the typical powers of the employer and a specific feature of the employment contract. In this respect, labour lawyers ask the following fundamental questions: Can the employer require the employee to perform new duties not in the employment contract? If so, within which legal boundaries? What are the consequences for the survival of the contract if the employee's skills are outdated? Such questions are far from easy to answer. Indeed, the very concept of contract and obligation comes into question when one of the parties is entitled to amend the content of the contract unilaterally.

With a few exceptions,[11] a different perspective has often been neglected. Does an employee have the right to be trained and retrained during her working relationship with her employer? Does the employer have an obligation to cover the costs of the employee's training? In this perspective, the topic attracts the attention of labour lawyers when it involves the possible redundancy of the employee. In some countries, before making an employee redundant, the employer must make sure that no other position within the business structure is available for the employee to occupy. This duty involves an investigation into possible positions. Therefore, the nature and characteristics of work as well as the possibility of changing it determine whether the employer has considered all possible options before making an employee redundant.

In this article, I aim to address this research question by adopting a broad level of investigation: does the employee have a *right to be trained*? Can we rely on rigorous

10. M. Napoli, *Disciplina del mercato del lavoro e esigenze formative*, in *Riv. Giur. Lav.*, 1, 1997, 266.
11. M. Napoli, *Contratto e rapporti di lavoro oggi*, in Aa.Vv., *Le ragioni del diritto. Scritti in onore di Luigi Mengoni, Giuffrè*, 1996, II, p. 1191; C. Alessi, *Professionalità e contratto di lavoro*, Giuffrè, 2004; F. Guarriello, *Trasformazioni organizzative e contratto di lavoro*, Jovene, 2000; S. Ciucciovino, *Apprendimento e tutela del lavoro*, Giappichelli, 2013; G. Loy, *Formazione e rapporto di lavoro*, Franco Angeli, 1988; A. Loffredo, *Considerazioni sul diritto alla formazione e contratto di lavoro*, in Rusciano (edited by), *Problemi giuridici del mercato del lavoro*, Jovene, 2004, 136.

juridical arguments to sustain the existence of this right, or does it fall outside the *synallagma* of the employment contract? The answer is not easy to find and might largely change not only from common law to civil law legal systems but also within the two families of systems, in which the interpretation of the notion of a contract can be very different.

If we consider the Italian legal system, Article 2103 of the Italian Civil Code, as amended by Article 3, Legislative Decree No. 81 of 2015, provides that the change of the employee's duties decided by the employer shall be followed, when necessary, by the training of the employee. The rule certainly does not shine with clarity and imposes on its interpreters a careful exegesis of each of its terms.[12] The lawmaker classifies training as the employer's obligation only when she decides to amend the employee's duties, but *only if necessary*.

Before the 2015 reform, when the training obligation was not expressly provided by Article 2103 of the Civil Code, the doctrinal debate on training traditionally settled on two opposite poles. The prevailing doctrine had held that there could not be a real obligation for the employer to take care of the training of the employee so that she was able to perform the assigned work.[13] However, before the latest reform, some had already sustained the idea that professionality was a good that the parties of the employment relationship had to keep constantly updated. In particular, some had formulated a thesis in which the employer had a real obligation to elevate the professionality of the employee, under Article 35, paragraph two, of the Constitution[14]. Read in relation to Articles 2094 and 2103 of the Civil Code, this would be the regulatory vehicle for the inclusion of the right to training into employment, in light of the importance of professionality as an expression of the employee's person. This is also in light of the importance assumed in post-Fordist production organizations of the adaptability of the employee - and therefore of her training - to the changing needs of the company.[15]

This doctrine held that the employee's prerogative to be trained as a legal effect of the contract should be classified as a *right*.[16] The thesis was part of a broader

12. M. Brollo, *La disciplina delle mansioni dopo il* Jobs Act, in *Arg. Dir. Lav.*, 6, 2015, 1169; A. Avondola, *La riforma dell'art. 2103 c.c. dopo il* Jobs Act, in *Riv. It. Dir. Lav.*, 3, 2016, 369.
13. C. Pisani, *Formazione professionale «continua», equivalenza delle mansioni, giustificato motivo oggettivo di licenziamento*, in *Mass. Giur. Lav.*, 2004; L. Zoppoli, *Il lavoro di Aracne. Formazione e politiche attive dell'impiego nelle recenti dinamiche istituzionali*, in Realfonzo, Zoppoli (edited by), *Formazione e lavoro: l'efficacia dei nuovi strumenti giuridici e istituzionali. Atti del Convegno di Benevento 18 giugno 2002*, Franco Angeli, 2003, 13; M. Roccella, *Formazione, occupabilità, occupazione nell'Europa comunitaria*, in Aa.Vv., *Formazione e mercato del lavoro in Italia e in Europa, Atti del XV Congresso nazionale di diritto del lavoro, S. Margherita di Pula, 1-3 giugno 2006*, Giuffrè, 2007, 51; M. Magnani, *Organizzazione del lavoro e professionalità tra rapporti e mercato del lavoro*, in *Giorn. Dir. Lav. Rel. Ind.*, 1, 2004, 165; U. Carabelli, *Organizzazione del lavoro e professionalità: una riflessione su contratto di lavoro e post-taylorismo*, in *Giorn. Dir. Lav. Rel. Ind.*, 1, 2004, 20.
14. M. Napoli, *Commento all'art. 35, comma II*, in Branca (edited by), *Commentario alla Costituzione*, Zanichelli/Società editrice del Foro Italiano, 1979, I, 19; C. Alessi, *Professionalità e contratto di lavoro*, 2004, Giuffrè, 7; A. Loffredo, *Considerazioni sul diritto alla formazione e contratto di lavoro*, in M. Rusciano (edited by), *Problemi giuridici del mercato del lavoro*, Jovene, 2004, 136.
15. C. Alessi, *Professionalità e contratto di lavoro*, 2004, Giuffrè, 81.
16. C. Alessi, *Professionalità e contratto di lavoro*, 2004, Giuffrè, 102.

reflection on the professionality of the employee, according to which professionality was not simply an object of protection but instead the same object as the employment contract.[17] The exchange, in consideration of which the employee receives a salary, would not have as an object the agreed tasks but the professionality of the employee *tout court*.[18] From this perspective, the working activity would represent the descriptive synthesis of professionality, which is useful for defining the boundaries of the contractual debt of the employee within a *synallagma* in which the object of the exchange is professionality.[19]

While denying the configurability of a real obligation of training by the employer, Jurisprudence had sometimes admitted, on one hand, that the need for professional updating was not an obstacle to the legitimacy of exercising *jus variandi*. On the other hand, a training obligation could exist in the application of the principles of fairness and good faith, only in the presence of organizational and productive innovations occasioned by entrepreneurial choices in sectors subject to rapid technological evolution.[20]

All the theses certainly constituted an index for the process of growing the juridical relevance of the interest in – or, according to some, of the right to – training.

With the entry into force of the new Article 2103, the debate on training, regarding its purpose but mainly its legal role, has reopened.

In my opinion, to understand the meaning of the reference to training made by the current provision, it is necessary to clarify precisely the subjective legal positions of the parties to the employment contract. On this point, the reflections elaborated by a well-known doctrine pointed out the necessity, with reference to the *facere* obligations, of distinguishing between the subject on whom the obligation rests and 'that portion of the external world to which the activity itself must refer'. We can identify this 'in the same space or environment within which the promised activity is destined to be realised'.[21] More specifically, 'when the *facere* obligation consists in the performance of subordinate work, it is, however, evident to us that the supply of that objective substratum does not, in principle, fall within the object deducted in obligation and, therefore, is not incumbent on the debtor' (alias, the employee). The burden of placing the employee within a productive organization that allows him or her to carry out her obligation, therefore, falls on the employer. Now, considering the extension and the constant update of the possible tasks that can be demanded by the employer, the importance of that burden of cooperation on the employer can only be extended. In fact, the employer has the burden of ensuring that the employee is able to perform within the organization.

17. M. Napoli, *Disciplina del mercato del lavoro e esigenze formative*, in *Riv. Giur. Lav.*, 1, 1997; C. Alessi, *Professionalità e contratto di lavoro*, Giuffrè, 2004, 115; L. Galantino, *Lavoro atipico, formazione professionale e tutela dinamica della professionalità del lavoratore*, in *Dir. Rel. Ind.*, 3, 1998, 317; F. Guarriello, *Trasformazioni organizzative e contratto di lavoro*, Jovene, 2000, 191.
18. F. Guarriello, *Trasformazioni organizzative e contratto di lavoro*, Jovene, 2000, 191.
19. C. Alessi, *Professionalità e contratto di lavoro*, Giuffrè, 2004, 93.
20. Cass. 31 agosto 2011, n. 17849, in *Lav. Prev. Oggi*, 2012, 217; Cass. 1 settembre 2000, n. 11457, in *Not. Giur. Lav.*, 2001, 38; Cass. 7 maggio 2008, n. 11142, in *Riv. It. Dir. Lav.*, 2008, 2, 81.
21. G. Ghezzi, *La mora del creditore nel rapporto di lavoro*, Giuffrè, 1965.

It is essential in the very concept of contractual exchange (*synallagma*) that the answer to the research question on the existence of a right to be trained shall be found: such a right extends as far as the employer's power to determine unilaterally the working activities. The balance of the contract shall impose that if one party is entitled to expect certain activities to be carried out, the same party shall put the other party under the conditions to properly fulfil those activities.

3 CONCLUSION

Climate change intersects a context also characterized by rapid technological developments, the ageing population, the mechanization of working activities through new technologies, and the increased level of skills required of employees in the labour market. All these factors seem to have caused a crisis regarding the traditional legal parameters of labour.

However, the legal problems caused by environmental, technological and economic changes have often been viewed exclusively from an external perspective. Issues related to the need to move beyond the subordinate employment relationship, enlarge its scope of application and identify new contractual forms to regulate non-standard work have been addressed from different perspectives, and various solutions have been offered.

Nevertheless, the same factors are influencing the employment relationship itself. Even 'inside' the most regular and clearly subordinating employment contract, such factors are profoundly changing the ways in which employers and employees perform their relationship. Therefore, such phenomena create the necessity to adjust the employment contract to meet the needs of organizational flexibility, with reference to the duties that the employee is required to perform, the evaluation of such performance and the connection between the working activities and the employer's organizational prerogatives recognized under law, while ensuring the protection of the employee's rights and prerogatives.

We need to stress that employment is consistent with the changes that are deeply influencing our society and ways of living and working. The employment contract was originally conceived as and still is one of the most flexible legal tools for the regulation of work relationships. It has internalized organizational flexibility as a core feature of the employment relationship.

Pursuant to this view, reconsidering the employment contract and its relationship with the concepts of organization and of performance might be one of the keys to examining the new forms of work as well. In particular, in my opinion, the great flexibility granted to the employer should be counterbalanced by the recognition of the value in the employee's professionality. More specifically, the obligation of inserting the employee into a sustainable productive organization that allows her to fulfil her obligation fully falls on the employer. This being said, in consideration of the extension of the duties that an employee might be asked to perform, the importance of training can be extended to preserve professionality not only as a set of competencies but also as an extension of the employee's concrete chances to stay active in the labour market.

Only in this way can the changes we are observing be environmentally but also socially sustainable.

CHAPTER 10

Climate Change and Labour Law: Redefining the Collective Interest

Frank Hendrickx

1 INTRODUCTION

With climate change, we are facing a fundamental and unprecedented global challenge. There is hardly any field that escapes from climate change or its impact. Also, the world of work will, either directly or indirectly, experience major influences from climate change and the policy responses to it.

Climate policy (or 'climate action' in the words of the United Nations)[1] has been undertaken through international agreements and they have set governments on their way. With the 'conferences of the parties' (COPs) and the UN climate summits, there is indeed global and intergovernmental action, though still showing that it is a complex and difficult subject, also in political terms. The European Union (EU) is not staying behind with its 'Green Deal', a policy 'package', including legislation, in order to reach climate neutrality by 2050.

While intergovernmental initiatives are rather broadly known, the question is what it implies for labour law. The meaning of climate change for labour law is a rather 'recent' question. If we look back to just about a few years ago, the issue was not so prominent in the labour law scholarship toolbox. For some years, COVID-19 attracted a lot of attention, but even before, the issue of climate change was not broadly discussed, although some actors, such as the ILO, and scholars were pioneering. Doorey, for example, promoted the idea of bringing labour law and environmental law together, instead of seeing them as opponents and he suggested further theorising

1. https://unfccc.int/climate-action/introduction-climate-action.

about a new legal field called 'just transitions law'.[2] Novitz imagined the paradigm of sustainability in the context of labour law and industrial relations, pointing at the EU's commitment to sustainability. She forwarded the thought that sustainable development, including environmental and climate policies, requires broad-based participatory processes, including collective bargaining by trade unions, opening the suggestion that a sufficiently supportive (legal) environment is needed for this.[3]

The attention of scholarly labour law in the field of climate change and just transitions slowly grew, but it is still a 'young' area of study. The 'Venice conference', organised by the labour law scholars of Ca' Foscari University, under the auspices of the International Association of Labour and Social Security Law,[4] was most likely one of the first international academic conferences really focusing on this theme in such a broad manner.

At the same time, some specialised international institutions, such as the ILO, have been undertaking various initiatives in the area of just transition. The ILO is one of the forerunners in bringing attention to climate change policy in the world of work. In 2016, the ILO published its 'Guidelines for a just transition towards environmentally sustainable economies and societies for all', offering a framework and principles to guide policy through necessary transitions.[5]

The 'climate policy agenda' would present itself as rather inclusive and open. It includes a focus on the social dimension of climate change. The strategic concept may be broadly known as 'just transition', applied by international institutions while originating from the world of work and more precisely from the trade union movement.[6] This is how it also appears in the Paris Agreement of 12 December 2015 (COP21). At the same time, there are also other references to the interaction between the world of work and climate change. There is, for example, the reference to 'green jobs', which the ILO interprets as: 'decent jobs that contribute to preserve or restore the environment, be they in traditional sectors such as manufacturing and construction, or in new, emerging green sectors such as renewable energy and energy efficiency'.[7]

In the 'Green Deal', the European Union also insists on a fair and socially just transition. As such, this is a rather strong vision, including a focus on fairness in the world of work. In the European Green Deal, for example, it is stated that just transition

2. D.J. Doorey, 'A law of just transitions?: Putting labor law to work on climate change', Osgoode Legal Studies Research Paper Series, 2016, 49p.
3. T. Novitz, 'The paradigm of sustainability in a European Social context: collective participation in protection of future interests?', International Journal of Comparative Labour Law and Industrial Relations 2015, Vol. 31(3), 243-262 DOI: 10.54648/ijcl2015014.
4. ISLSSL 8th International Seminar 'Labour Law and Climate Change: towards a Just Transition' – Ca' Foscari Venice, 23-26 May 2022.
5. https://www.ilo.org/wcmsp5/groups/public/---ed_emp/---emp_ent/documents/publication/wcms_432859.pdf.
6. Cf. M. Mandelli, 'Mapping Eco-social Policy Mixes for a Just Transition in Europe', The European Trade Union Institute, ETUI, Brussels, 21 September 2022; https://www.etui.org/publications/mapping-eco-social-policy-mixes-just-transition-europe; Lene Olsen & Claire La Hovary, User's manual to the ILO's Guidelines for a just transition towards environmentally sustainable economies and societies for all, ILO, 2021, at pp. 11-12, https://www.ilo.org/wcmsp5/groups/public/---ed_dialogue/---actrav/documents/publication/wcms_826060.pdf.
7. https://www.ilo.org/global/topics/green-jobs/news/WCMS_220248/lang--en/index.htm.

implies that it must put people first,[8] that it should make consistent use of all policy levers, including dialogue with social partners, and that the European Pillar of Social Rights will guide action in ensuring that no one is left behind[9] so that it becomes a 'socially just transition' reflected in policies at EU and national level.[10] This political language looks stronger than the ultimate European Climate Law. This 'European Climate Law' entered into force on 29 July 2021.[11] Article 9 of the European Climate Law, provides for 'public participation', whereby the European Commission should engage with all parts of society 'to enable and empower them to take action towards a just and socially fair transition', to make sure that this is realised through 'an inclusive and accessible process at all levels', including social partners. It is, furthermore, provided that the European Commission shall use all appropriate instruments, including the European Climate Pact, to engage social partners and foster dialogue about climate change and its social and gender equality aspects.

Against this broader background of policy initiatives, the attention to climate change is accelerating in academic scholarship and labour law debate also gradually makes a connection with the climate issue. A challenge is to find ways to 'translate' this broad theme in a labour law discourse. In light of this, it must be noted that, while the meaning of climate change for labour law may be new, the concept of 'change' for labour law is not new. Labour law is familiar with broad and global challenges, with future-oriented questions. But the climate change issue may be of completely other nature. It may even lead to a redefinition of the field of study and the field of action. This is all the more important as climate awareness is much broader than government initiatives. Employment relations, HR practices and industrial relations will be equally important.

Labour law will thus play a role and/or be impacted. This is where the aims are of the present contribution. It deals with the question: what does the climate change phenomenon mean for labour law? Since this is still a developing domain, the idea of this contribution is to raise some thoughts and reflections, components for further thinking, rather than to give a full and exhaustive overview and synthesis. In this emerging field, the ambition of this contribution remains thus rather explorative, where the level of thought is seen as input for further debate. It assumes that major developments which affect labour law in an ever more complex world need also a 'language' for discussion, a 'narrative', rather than a rigidly defined state of play. It will be suggested that, within approaching climate change from a labour law perspective, it seems inevitable to pay attention to the collective interest dimension and how it is to be perceived.

8. Brussels, 11.12.2019 COM(2019) 640 final, p2.
9. Brussels, 11.12.2019 COM(2019) 640 final, p4.
10. Brussels, 11.12.2019 COM(2019) 640 final, p16.
11. Regulation (EU) 2021/1119 of the European Parliament and of the Council of 30 June 2021 establishing the framework for achieving climate neutrality and amending Regulations (EC) No 401/2009 and (EU) 2018/1999 ('European Climate Law'), PE/27/2021/REV/1, *OJ L 243, 9.7.2021.*

2 NEED FOR STRATEGIC LEGAL THINKING

The meaning of climate change for labour law raises a strategic question. Addressing climate change from a labour law perspective requires strategic thinking. In light of this, it should be noted that labour law is pre-eminently a strategic-legal field. This legal domain is essentially open to change. It may also explain why the climate theme shows itself to be inevitable for labour law, as it will most likely show itself to be receptive to it.

With the above in mind, it may become easier to accept a question for labour law in the following terms: what if the world changes?

A broad question like this is obviously challenging but is rather intrinsically connected with the dynamics and openness of labour law as a subject. Such broadness is not fully new. The 'modernisation' or 'future' debate once pushed labour law into a sort of 'regulatory crisis'. It is referred to as the crisis of the traditional socio-economic regulatory model, as described by Supiot.[12] Indeed, in its traditional formula, labour law worked well in an industrial setting. A classic approach of industrial relations - often labelled as 'Fordism' - bears elements such as a male full-time breadwinner, long-term service in the same firm, doing one or similar jobs, homogeneous and standardised working styles, clear-cut separation of working time from leisure or private time, relatively short terms of life expectancy, predominantly industrial unionism and collective bargaining.[13] This 'industrial' period of labour law has evolved and, in many areas or sectors of activity, has increasingly become something of the past. In 'post-industrial' globalised economies, with services and consumer-oriented markets, businesses (often employers) have been looking for means to adjust and readjust work and the workplace. The result has been a quest for flexible work patterns and the rise of contingent employment, non-standard forms of work (fixed-term, part-time), outsourcing operations, and the growth of triangular employment relationships, such as temporary work. In such a context, the traditional workplace would seem to have become weak. At the same time, the worker - and the concept of how work is done - has escaped a single model of understanding. The hierarchical and pyramidal enterprise structure is losing out. Small-scale units, teams and cooperation with individual expertise are becoming driving forces of business. Workers not only have to listen to their boss, but they now also have to take initiative themselves and create their own authority based on creativity, responsivity and expertise. Even in this post-industrial era, new challenges arise. In a further phase, called by some the 'second machine age',[14] digitalisation and robotisation determine new questions for the world of work and its regulation. This is also the issue with Industry 4.0. and its influence on labour law. The technological advancement of smart robots and AI is regarded as a cornerstone of 'Industry 4.0' and the intensive debate that it generates demonstrates the

12. A. Supiot, *Beyond Employment*, Oxford, Oxford University Press, 2001, 215.
13. T. Iwagami, 'The end of the classic model of labor law and Post-Fordism', Comparative Labor Law Journal, Vol. 31999, 691-692.
14. E. Brynjolfsson & A. Macafee, *The Second Machine Age: Work, Progress, and Prosperity in a Time of Brilliant Technologies*, London, Norton, 2015, 320 p.

potential impact of new technologies not only on society as a whole but also on the nature and the future of work.[15]

Labour law scholarship has thus been quite familiar with modernisation and adaptation issues. It mostly would give rise to strategic debates and thinking. It has related to the question of the impact of developments on labour law and to whether and how existing laws or legal strategies should be modified and adapted. Taking these perspectives into account, the labour law (modernisation) approaches and evaluation is often related to recommendations about future directions of labour law, or the impact that labour law rules have on our labour markets or even our lives.

In this situation, the changes in the (new) world of work are often been used as a benchmark for further reflection, but many of the developments are obviously linked with much larger developments in the world as such, following from the world in itself which is changing: one may think about demographic changes, ageing societies, the progress of medical science, the improvement of health care, and so on.

Climate change would also appear against this broader societal horizon about which the question arises what it means for labour law. It makes the reflection more complicated, and somewhat less evident. But it is still doable and also logical in a responsive labour law context.

3 EVOLVING LABOUR LAW DISCIPLINE

Dealing with major questions related to such a complex and global development as climate change also helps to appreciate the rich, and perhaps changing, character of labour law as a discipline.

Labour law has long since ceased to be a strictly 'monodisciplinary' block if it ever was one. Whereas in the past it was easy to divide it into individual and collective labour law, labour law always experienced interdisciplinary interaction, such as from civil law doctrines or from the practice of industrial relations. Through the years, labour law has further evolved. More than ever, it is an interdisciplinary cluster around labour or work. It leads to broadening and deepening. Thus, labour market law, with legal rules on employment mediation and employment, has established itself as a labour law component. The emergence of fundamental rights made anti-discrimination law part of labour law, but it grew as its own field of law. The right to privacy has become an integral part of labour law. Interdisciplinary connections are also prominent in European law, where labour law is viewed through the 'internal market law', partly from the perspective of economic objectives. The 'gig economy' opens up labour law to self-employment and economic law.

The openness of labour law to a broader social context reinforces all this. The world of work is subject to change, just like the world itself. Labour law tends to follow, whether hesitantly or not. All kinds of 'megatrends' are a source of change in labour law. Globalisation, technological evolution, demography, and economic efficiency are 'game changers' that have led to questions about how we can adapt or modernise legal

15. K. Schwab, *The Fourth Industrial Revolution*, Currency Publishing, 2017, 192 p.

rules. It, therefore, seems only a matter of time before the realisation dawns that the climate debate will also penetrate the labour law domain.

It brings the debate to responsive labour law. Climate change is, self-evidently, a major global issue. The role of regulation in the field of labour and industrial relations law, in relation to such a global phenomenon, should be engaged in the idea of responsive labour law. In earlier work, we have forwarded the idea of 'responsive labour law' referring to 'a sphere of labour law addressing major challenges that individuals and societies face, and could be seen as offering solutions which are adapted to the rights and needs of potential or actual individual labour market participants. Responsive labour law could then be seen as guaranteeing social justice for people in times of change'.[16]

The idea of 'responsive labour law' is useful to approach the relation of labour law towards major and global trends. While identifying game changers for labour law is rather complex, two developments usually stand out: globalisation and technological development.[17] These are phenomena, like climate change, that relate to developments from 'outside' the world of work, but with an evident huge impact on work, employment and industrial relations. Most of the major phenomena like these, that impact labour law, including demographic developments, such as diversity, and ageing societies, have brought discussions on the adaptation or the modernisation of labour law.

While many developments take place in the labour market itself, they may be part of a larger set of major developments.

4 APPROACHES OF SUBJECTS IN LABOUR LAW

The question is, of course, which concrete sections or topics of labour law will be affected by the climate issue. For that, a degree of creativity is important and it will be relevant to anticipate and engage in issue spotting. However, undoubtedly, there are many areas to be explored. For the purposes of the present contribution, three obvious employment law-oriented climate themes are emerging. They are inspired by what is possible in the practice and policy of personnel management. They are closely related to the formation of working conditions. The three areas, on which not only labour law but also industrial relations may be able to focus, relate to wages, well-being at work, and the new ways of working.

It would, most likely, be insufficient to just indicate intersections and areas where labour law will somehow play a role, or will be affected, in a climate change context. A critical approach also requires questioning as to whether old and existing approaches would still work and whether (or not) new ways of thinking, even new paradigms, are

16. F. Hendrickx, 'Regulating flexicurity and responsive labour law', in F. Hendrickx (ed.), *Flexicurity and the Lisbon Agenda, A cross-Disciplinary Reflection*, Intersentia, 2008, Social Europe Series; No. 17, pp. 123-161, 154.
17. F. Hendrickx & V. De Stefano, 'Introduction', in F. Hendrickx & V. De Stefano, *Game Changers in Labour Law. Shaping the Future of Work*, in Bulletin of Comparative Labour Relations, Vol. 100, 2018, Wolters Kluwer, 7.

needed to understand the role of labour law in light of global climate change. With this in mind, it may be relevant to point to a report on sustainable development and 'green jobs', made at the 2013 International Labour Conference, which ended with an interesting research question: 'What can be learned from previous transitions (such as those associated with the introduction of labour-saving technology and mechanization, information and communications technology or trade adjustments) and their impact on the world of work and what is new with the transition to sustainable development?'[18] This may suggest that major influences in the field of labour law from the past, and the responses to it, may also help to advance the labour law and climate change agenda. At the same time, climate change may be of such a nature that some approaches to existing labour law might need to be refreshed.

5 WAGES

A key component in the working conditions sphere concerns the worker's wages. Remuneration for work is not only core in the employment contract but also a crucial 'bread and butter' subject of collective bargaining. It now seems that this very classic working condition is becoming the subject of a new 'narrative', namely via strategies to influence the environmental impact on wages, creating a new dilemma.

The point to be made can be illustrated by a Belgian labour law example. In Belgian wage policy, the most obvious climate component is probably the 'eco-cheque' or 'eco-voucher'. The eco-voucher was introduced by National Collective Agreement no. 98, in implementation of a 2009-2010 national interprofessional agreement concluded by the national social partners. Employers can pay their staff part of their salary with an eco-voucher, which the employee then can spend on a limited number of goods and services. The products and services which an employee can buy with the voucher are agreed upon by the national social partners and are of an ecological nature, including items such as sustainable mobility or products that contribute to waste management. Of course, the eco-voucher is part of the employee's wage package, although it cannot replace the existing wage and is an additional element.

This measure is in theory an eco-friendly policy measure and could therefore be welcomed from a climate action point of view. Some important nuance, however, has to be made. First, it is difficult to separate the Belgian eco-cheque system from the discussion on purchasing power and labour costs.[19] From the Belgian (para-)fiscal perspective, the voucher is a 'cheaper' way to reward employees. Second, and perhaps more fundamental, is that behind the eco-voucher – and essentially behind every cheque – lies a deeper debate. The payment of wages in 'cheques' is, from a labour law

18. ILO, 'Sustainable development, decent work and green jobs', International Labour Conference, 102nd Session, 2013, https://www.ilo.org/wcmsp5/groups/public/---ed_norm/---relconf/documents/meetingdocument/wcms_207370.pdf.
19. It is part of the 'optimalisation' of wages, according to Y. Stevens & J. Put, 'Het laatste heilige huisje: professionele apartheid in de sociale zekerheid', in *Liber Amicorum Willy van Eeckhoutte. De taal is gans het recht*, Wolters Kluwer Belgium, Mechelen, 2018, 143.

perspective, not so obvious. It is at odds with the free disposal over wages, as laid down in (international) labour law.

The Belgian Wage Protection Act of 12 April 1965 implements ILO Convention No. 95 concerning the protection of wages. This convention implies that an employer cannot influence the way in which an employee spends his/her wage. The ILO Convention aims at complete freedom of disposition of employees and therefore favours free spending of 'cash' (or a money transfer). The ILO itself makes the historical link with 'benefits in kind'. In the past, for example, there was the so-called 'truck' system or the 'Tommy shop'. The employer paid out part of the wage in the form of a ticket or purchase voucher. This had to be spent in a shop of the employer, where one could buy all kinds of things like food, soap, clothes and household goods. Some vouchers were limited to certain goods, which were not always the best value for money. Thus, the newly earned salary immediately flowed back to the employer. A new form of dependency and abuse also arose.[20] When bringing this back to the eco-voucher, similar concerns arise. It concerns not a (freely disposable) benefit for employees. The question is, therefore, whether this system is in line with international labour standards.

The question is whether the pressure from the climate debate will not make us go beyond this history and lead to a different vision. Perhaps the individualistic perspective on pay is too narrow and there is room to build climate objectives into pay policies.

The 'cash-for-cars' ruling by the Belgian Constitutional Court[21] provides some support for this. The case before this court did not relate to eco-vouchers, but to what is known as the cash-for-cars arrangement, once introduced by the government. In the Belgian system, employers have the possibility to give staff members a company car, which employees can also use for private purposes. Also, this system is treated in a friendly (para-)fiscal manner. It is, therefore, again a way to reward employees in an alternative manner. Due to increasing criticism of this system, going along with climate concerns, the government aimed to decrease the number of company cars by allowing employees to return their company car and receive a tax-free cash benefit instead. The cash-for-cars idea was borne. The Belgian Constitutional Court, however, annulled this cash-for-cars scheme, as it gave rise to an unjustified difference in treatment between different categories of employees (those who previously had a company car versus those who did not). However, the Court did not seem to have any objection 'in principle' with regard to a restriction of the right to freely dispose of one's wages, with a view to developing a climate policy. According to the Court, a free disposal by the worker over a cash-benefit would precisely undermine the pertinence of the whole scheme (which was aimed at climate action).

This puts the discussion of individual freedom in another light. The question is how much individual free disposition is valued in labour law, seen in a new climate

20. International Labour Conference, 91st Session 2003, Report III (Part 1B), Information and reports on the application of Conventions and Recommendations General Survey of the reports concerning the Protection of Wages Convention (No. 95) and the Protection of Wages Recommendation (No. 85), 1949, par. 95.
21. Belgian Constitutional Court, judgment nr. 11/2020 of 23 January 2020.

change context, and whether it could be sacrificed for the sake of a higher collective interest, i.e., climate action.

6 WELL-BEING AT WORK

A 'climate' strategy cannot do without the domain of well-being at work. A healthy and safe environment (or climate) in the work organisation has become part of the universal labour guarantee.[22] Occupational safety and health (OSH) is a long-vested and well-developed (often technical) area in many jurisdictions. Gradually, the approach of health and safety at work has been complemented with a broader, more encompassing idea of 'well-being at work'. As the ILO itself explains, 'workplace wellbeing relates to all aspects of working life, from the quality and safety of the physical environment, to how workers feel about their work, their working environment, the climate at work and work organization'.[23]

The potentially broad and evolving interpretation of the well-being concept is recognised. The step to the broader climate topic is not so far-fetched. The experiences of COVID-19 – and in particular those of occupational medicine – show the relevance of a larger approach and connection of workplace well-being and societal safety, health and well-being. Corporate well-being is thus seen in conjunction with social well-being, confirming the inevitability of a wider contextual relationship.[24]

Well-being is physical, mental and contextual.[25] In a strict sense, one can understand the problem of well-being from the perspective of physical well-being. The climate issue is thus quickly linked to existing regulations and already-known risks. One can think of provisions relating to workplace equipment, temperature at work, air quality, ozone, and so on.[26]

But also psycho-social well-being will be an increasing point of attention. That too is what COVID-19 has taught us. Major changes bring stress. For example, technological evolutions bring, among other things, technostress. In the meantime, climate-related stress or 'solastalgia' is also known as a new phenomenon, a form of psychosocial strain that is not necessarily caused by work, but that people will bring to the workplace.[27]

22. Cf. V. Silva, 'The ILO and the future of work: The politics of global labour policy', Global Social Policy 2022, Vol. 22(2) 341-358.
23. https://www.ilo.org/safework/areasofwork/workplace-health-promotion-and-well-being/WCMS_118396/lang--en/index.htm.
24. Cf. D. Mangan, E. Gramano, M. Kullmann, 'An unprecedented social solidarity stress test', *European Labour Law Journal* 2020, Vol. 11(3), 247-275.
25. T. Mishiba, 'Workplace Mental Health Law: Perspectives Based on a Comparative Analysis of Legislation in Seven Countries,' *International Journal of Comparative Labour Law and Industrial Relations* 2022, Vol. 38, no. 1, 53-86 (in particular at 80) DOI: 10.54648/ijcl2022003.
26. P.A. Schulte & H. Chun, 'Climate Change and Occupational Safety and Health: Establishing a Preliminary Framework', Journal of Occupational and Environmental Hygiene 2009, Vol. 6/9, 542-554.
27. Cf. Lindsay P. Galway, Thomas Beery, Kelsey Jones-Casey & Kirsti Tasala, 'Mapping the Solastalgia Literature: A Scoping Review Study' International Journal of Environmental Research and Public Health 2019, Vol. 16, 2662 DOI: 10.3390/ijerph16152662.

There seems to be coherence in linking the well-being-at-work story with sustainability and climate change. This is not only linked to the 'OSH' agenda. It will also be part of human resources strategies and perhaps even become a form of 'corporate branding' for employers. It obviously will lead to new legal questions, related to job design, office life as well as work-life relations. Those questions will, again, relate to the relationship between the individual and the collective dimensions of rights, responsibilities and working conditions. Corporate policies on promoting 'healthy living', including exercise, sport, nutrition, sleep quality, etc., are not entirely unrelated. A broader climate policy-oriented position on working conditions will influence the value of individual freedom and limit that freedom with a view of preserving collective values, transcending the employment relationship. It also leads to questions about the scope of authority in the employment relationship, the extent to which control can be exercised over individual lifestyles and the choices of staff members. Similar questions have been raised already in light of the use of health-related wearables by workers, which also leads to blurring lines between the professional and the private domain.[28]

7 NEW WAYS OF WORKING

The 'new ways of working' – or the new 'WOW' – encompasses a broad domain.[29] It concerns working 'differently', with more autonomy, but also with more responsibility (sense). Teleworking is an example of new ways of working, but also working in more horizontal or self-managing teams, or working in less fixed structures.[30]

Presumably, the climate debate will force the new way of working to other horizons and to a new critical approach. Mobility, for example, is inextricably linked to how and when we move around, and thus also time- and location-independent working (part of the new way of working) is related to the climate question. Telework or remote work is often seen as the main example of these new ways of working, with the assumption that it generates less mobility, and less traffic, and may thus be good for the climate. But it is still under discussion as to how teleworking is good for our ecological footprint. Research suggests 'that teleworking has some potential to reduce energy consumption and associated emissions — both through reducing commuter travel and displacing office-related energy consumption'.[31] But the findings are dependent on many different factors, including the way how mobility is organised and used,

28. K. Maltseva, 'Wearables in the workplace: The brave new world of employee engagement', *Business Horizons* 2020, Vol. 63, 515 DOI: 10.1016/j.bushor.2020.03.007.
29. F. Hendrickx, 'Regulating new ways of working: From the new "wow" to the new "how", European Labour Law Journal 2018, Vol. 9(2), 195–205.
30. Cf. M. M. Bloka, L. Groenesteijn, R. Schelvisa and P. Vink, 'New Ways of Working: does flexibility in time and location of work change work behavior and affect business outcomes?', *Work* 2012, 2605-2610; M. Blok, L. Groenesteijn, C. van den Berg and P. Vink, 'New Ways of Working: A Proposed Framework and Literature Review' in M.M. Robertson (ed.), *Ergonomics and Health Aspects*, Berlin Heidelberg, Springer-Verlag, 2011, 3-12.
31. Andrew Hook, Victor Court, Benjamin K Sovacool and Steve Sorrell, 'A systematic review of the energy and climate impacts of teleworking', *Environ. Res. Lett.* 2020, Vol. 15, 27 DOI: 10.1016/j.bushor.2020.03.007.

what energy sources are involved, and so on. Teleworking will be able to contribute to climate change if accompanied by other measures and actions.[32]

This does not take away that the new way of working will also more explicitly include 'climate-conscious' working, both in the more traditional workplace as well as at home or on the road. From a personnel management point of view, and a corporate climate-goal perspective, a stricter policy is not unthinkable regarding matters such as the ecological footprint (also of staff members) in the way they work, the way energy is used, how mobility is handled, which work materials are used, how waste is managed, and so on. This will become even more important if economic efficiency also plays a role.

The legal questions will follow. If aspects of work (place, time, method) are modified for the sake of a climate policy by the employer, the issue will be whether it may lead to unilateral changes in working conditions. This issue plays inevitably a role in organisational transitions. If adjustments are to be made, the question will have to be asked whether, in concrete terms, they concern agreed working conditions or other aspects of the work. If, for example, one accepts that the employer has a right of direction and authority or an '*ius dominandi*', then there will still be limits, such as the principle of good faith. The question is whether the legal assessment for this takes into account the 'legitimate interests of the other party', or whether this acquires a more contextual - perhaps a more collective - meaning in light of the climate debate. The question will arise whether the employment relationship - and working conditions - are individual, mutual or collective responsibilities.

In the new world of work, the question is how autonomy and responsibility, or trust and control, relate to each other. This is also relevant in a climate context. The question is whether climate deals in the work organisation can also be the subject of control, even discipline in labour law. The law of authority provides a theoretical-legal basis for this, albeit dependent on labour regulations. However, the question of whether to motivate or coerce people is also linked to the finiteness and limits of this right of authority.

8 A NEW COLLECTIVE INTEREST

As the labour law discourse develops in relation to climate change, it seems that further reflection on the role of freedom and responsibility, in light of the individual versus the collective interest, seems inevitable.

It is clear that, in labour law, the collective dimension is crucial, and quite likely the most powerful one, as was also noted by Kahn-Freund.[33] The responsibility for climate action appears as individual but is pre-eminently collective. The individual and collective layers make it all the more challenging. These two dimensions, the individual and the collective, relate to basic components and structures of employment and labour relations. But the climate issue will trigger the question of how freedom and

32. M. Bisello, 'Is teleworking really a 'green' choice?', *Eurofound Blog*, 23 June 2022, https://www.eurofound.europa.eu/publications/blog/is-telework-really-a-green-choice.
33. O. Kahn-Freund, *Labour and the Law*, London, Stevens, 1972, 8.

responsibility (should) go together and how the individual, as well as the collective dimension of employment and labour relations, must be conceived or understood. The challenge with climate change is that reliance on existing pathways and knowledge based on existing practices may be too limited to conceive a new narrative for labour law. The 'collective' interest may not be similar to what was defined before.

The need of transcending old concepts may already be found in the approach of 'decent work', promoted by the ILO, with a human-centred agenda but also with attention to 'just transition'. The human-centred agenda will require a holistic understanding, in the framework of which a modernised view may need to be developed, perhaps going away from the (sole) idea of 'the individual at the centre'.[34] The human-centred agenda may have to be an agenda for mankind taking into account planetary interests, i.e., a planet-centred agenda.

Flanagan and Goods point out how industrial relations may need an adapted approach too, as 'the sense that the dimensions of current roles and responsibilities are not fit to deal with the societal challenge of climate change is widely shared, as is the sense that the primary agent of change should necessarily be larger than the workplace, union or occupation.'[35] In light of this, it is thus also necessary to look beyond the traditional assumption, that 'human resources management' would be responding to the individualisation of employment relations, while 'industrial relations' would take up the collective aspect and the idea of solidarity. The labour law examples, mentioned above, show that both within the collective bargaining field as well as within human resources management, themes, concerns and strategies are overlapping. The challenge is, again, to achieve an idea on the collective. Within a climate change context, the 'collective' is much bigger and larger than the parties and the interests involved in employment and labour relations. This comes within a broad spectrum where both from an employer as well as from a trade union perspective different strategies and responses towards the climate challenge are envisaged. There may thus be different views to receiving 'just transition', with varying ideas on the division of responsibilities.[36]

Even in a climate change discourse, the danger of self-interest will always be present. The question will be, though, whether all individual interests will be purely individual, as similarly, all collective interests may not be the sum of individual interests. Labour law and industrial relations, as a discipline but also as a practice, have been able to cope with a definition of a broader, societal 'collective interest' in the past. More philosophically, the idea of individual and collective action in labour law and industrial relations may need to turn into a 'global responsibility' related to climate action.[37] This will have an implication on how managerial viewpoints develop with

34. M. Biasi, 'An Essay on Liberty, Freedom and (Decent) Work', IJCLLIR 2022, Vol. 38, no. 3, 359-380 (in particular at 376).
35. F. Flanagan & C. Goods, 'Climate change and industrial relations: reflections on an emerging field', Journal of Industrial Relations 2022, Vol. 64(4), 493.
36. Cf. C. Goods, 'Climate change and employment relations', Journal of Industrial Relations 2017, Vol. 59(5), 673.
37. P. O'Mahony, 'Climate change: Responsibility, democracy and communication', European Journal of Social Theory 2015, Vol. 18(3) 308-326 (in particular at 325).

regard to individual employment relationships. It will also have an impact on how industrial relations will evolve. It will challenge the identification of the trade union movement with global collective concerns and, thus, with their identity itself of being a trade union.[38]

9 CONCLUSIONS

Climate change is a global phenomenon which cannot be ignored in the field of labour law. The academic scholarship in labour law in this theme is fastly evolving. It is still, however, at an early stage. Seen the complex nature and the enormous scale of climate change and climate action, there seems a need to find ways to approach labour law and to develop narratives to deal with the subject.

This contribution has made an attempt to offer a series of reflections. The question of how labour law receives an impact from climate change, or how it can contribute itself to climate action, does not seem to be so exceptional, though rather challenging. Labour law has been into major re-thinking exercises before, taking into account broader and global developments, such as demographic change, globalisation or technological development. The past shows that such major trends have delivered many interesting dynamics in and for the field of labour law, and this may even be welcomed, as labour law is a responsive legal area.

This contribution proposes that it is relevant not only to look, creatively, for legal areas and subjects of labour law that intersect with climate change issues but also to make the analysis sufficiently critical. That implies a reflection on the role of the individual and the collective, leaving a too-classical approach to the 'collective' interest. This may be a theoretical exercise, which could serve as an improved labour law narrative. However, concrete legal changes do not necessarily come from theory. As is often the case, practice will be a determining factor. What happens in companies, work organisations and industrial relations can be of major influence on climate action. The challenge there will be to define responsibilities in a way that may transcend the classical approach of individual and collective interests. Perhaps climate change will imply the need to consider all new labour law challenges as connected with a new collective interest: the interest of the planet. What individuals, groups and the HR environment have to offer in the future will therefore certainly also be 'planet'-related. Perhaps climate action will soon be a logical part of personnel policy and industrial relations. When that gets off to a start, the capability of change in labour law has proven itself sufficiently strong to accompany it all.

38. Cf. A. Thomas & N. Doerflinger, 'Trade union strategies on climate change mitigation: Between opposition, hedging and support', European Journal of Industrial Relations, 2020, Vol. 26(4), 383-399.

Chapter 11

'Seeking Coherence: Climate, Capability, and a Human-Centred Approach'

Brian Langille

1 A CONFESSION

I am rather certain that I do not know any more than the average Canadian citizen about the science of climate change or the economics or engineering of 'decarbonization'. I do know, as we all do, that we are confronted with a need to make a fundamental transition away from fossil fuels. I also know that the politics of the issue in my country, Canada, has a stylized and almost cartoon-like, shape. Canada has political parties, especially in the fossil fuel-producing provinces, that come at least close to denying the need for a transition. At the other extreme in Canada, there are parties that come at least close to saying that the time for transition is over – that we have at our disposal the means to transition now, or in the very near future. And in the middle ground, Canada has political parties that know we must transition, but believe that the idea of a transition entails a long and hard process of adjustment. The best recent book I have read about all of this is Vaclav Smil's *How the World Really Works.*[1] Smil has spent his life working on transitions in general,[2] and energy transitions in particular.[3] You might say he works in a tradition similar to that of the late Hans Rosling – with data and knowledge – in spaces where most debates have tended to have a more theological flavour.[4] The main lesson of Smil's new and very accessible

1. Vaclav Smil, *How the World Really Works: A Scientist's Guide to Our Past, Present, and Future* (Viking, 2022).
2. Vaclav Smil, *Grand Transitions: How the Modern World Was Made* (OUP, 2021).
3. Vaclav Smil, *Energy and Civilization: A History* (MIT, 2017) and *Energy Transitions* (Praeger, 2010).
4. Hans Rosling, Ola Rosling & Anna Rosling Rönnlund, *Factfulness: Ten Reasons We're Wrong about the World – and Why Things Are Better Than You Think* (Flatiron Books, 2018).

book is that very few of us have any idea how difficult the transition necessary to avoid climate disaster will be and, as a result, how long it might take. The basic idea is that fossil fuels are much more deeply embedded in our lives than we know.[5] Then there is the grim truth that the problem for most of the souls on this planet is not that they are using too much energy, it is that they have too little of it to use, and thus still yearn for the basics of a decent life that fossil fuels have made available to us who live in the global north – who are a small minority (20% or so) of the global 8 billion human occupants of planet earth. Smil seeks to address our ignorance about these issues, what he calls our 'comprehension deficit'.[6] In spite, or perhaps because, of my general ignorance, I have found Smil's contribution sobering and compelling.

With that confession of ignorance as the main issue, let me turn to a topic – the law of work – where my ignorance is slightly, but only slightly, less encyclopaedic. I seek to bring what I see as our best thinking about the law of work to bear upon our thinking about climate change and thus to reconsider the relationship between these two zones of contemplation. Note: the word 'thinking' carries a lot of freight here.

2 FIVE ASSERTIONS AND SOME IMPORTANT QUESTIONS

Here are five assertions about our thinking about labour law and a set of provocative questions about the relationship between labour law and climate change. The five *assertions* may be seen as an attempt to state very briefly some things I have been saying for some time about how we do, and should, think about the law of work.[7] The *questions* link these ideas to the issue of how we do and should think about climate change, and its relationship to labour law.

The five assertions:

1. 'Labour Law' – or as I am increasingly inclined to call it, 'The Law of Work', has long been shackled to a standard 'constituting narrative'[8] about its empirical domain, its legal structure, and its moral imperative. This accepted account holds that labour law is all about protecting the weaker partner (the employee) to the labour (employment) contract between employer and employee. Whether our goal is fair compensation, healthy workplaces, non-discrimination – the normative problem is lack of, or inequality in, bargaining power in the negotiation and administration of labour contracts (or, 'submission' and 'subordination' in such contracts.) On this standard view labour law is a form of consumer (or, in this case, producer) protection, and thus an interference in the 'normal operation' of the process of labour contracting. It is thus seen as a cost, a tax, upon our true ends of production, aggregate wealth, and overall economic prosperity – a tax which we impose in the name of, say, 'decency' (to use what I see as an unhelpful term popular at the ILO, and even elsewhere in recent times). The ideological dividing line which is thus

5. Especially in other elements of modern life – steel, plastic, fertilizer, cement.
6. Smil, *supra* n. 1 at 6.
7. *See*, for a summary, Langille, 'If Labour Law is a Subset of Employment Law, what is Employment Law a Subset of?' (2020), 43 Dalhousie Law Journal Issue 581.
8. On this idea *see* Langille, 'Labour Law's Back Pages' in Davidov and Langille (eds) *The Boundaries and Frontiers of Labour Law* (Hart, 2006).

constructed is that between those who think we should pay the tax, and those who, for various sorts of (often 'economic') reasons, think we should not.

2. This narrative is a very large, perhaps the largest, problem stalking the law of work in the world as we now find it. It is an 'internal'[9] problem. This idea of an 'internal' problem stands in contrast to most accounts of labour law's current dilemmas which focus upon external forces bearing upon labour law from the outside – forces such as globalization, 'fissuring', and so on.
3. The problem is that of sticking to our received explanatory and justificatory narrative in spite of the fact that the labour law so constructed has 'gone off the rails', and, gone off the rails precisely on all 3 dimensions that such narratives must and do express – empirical, legal/conceptual, and normative (as in 'moral'). First, while empirically the standard account (it's about employment) was always incomplete (think 'informality') it is now increasing not applicable in the world we see when we look out the window at real life (think 'gig economy'). As a result, our basic account of labour law has lost its empirical relevance, its grip on the real world. Second, the legal/conceptual apparatus deployed by our received wisdom is now obstructionist and a barrier to achieving labour law's purposes. Being an 'employee' is now the 'eye of the needle' which one must pass through to enter the heaven of labour law's protection.[10] Finally, on the standard moral justification of labour law it turns out, upon a moments reflection, that labour law has long had no positive normative account of itself. Certainly, 'labour is *not* a commodity'. Sure, workers need protection. Yes, inequality of bargaining power needs correcting. But why? What is labour law, as opposed to what is it 'not'? What is labour law for, as opposed to against? Why does it exist? It has become apparent that labour law's current moral underpinnings are thin gruel and have no answer to those rather painfully obvious questions
4. There is more. With our current dominant account of labour law in place, labour law is constantly under attack from forces it itself incentivizes and invites to go on the offensive against it: globalization, financialization, mobile capital, shareholder value theory, new transportation, monitoring and communications technologies, artificial intelligence, robotics, trade in goods and ideas, demographic change, immigration. The effects on the citadel of work law? Fissuring (or as Harry Arthurs correctly insists 'fracking'), vertical disintegration of firms, gig and platform work, offshoring, production/supply/commodity chains, deregulatory competition, more power to firms and less to states, dilution of worker power, the disconnection of productivity and wage gains, enfeebling of domestic work law, enfeebling of global labour governance, more inequality, more shifting of risk to workers, more agitation from the 'losers', in the new economic dispensation, the rise of right-wing populist, anti-state/ anti-science / and anti-education ideologies, and so on. And on. The road to all of this is greased by labour law's standard account of itself. In a sentence – only on a contract centred account is the corporate strategy of fissuring – which from a legal point of view is simply the strategy of 'decontractualization' – available, and incentivized.[11]

---

9. On the 'internal/external' distinction *see* Langille, 'The Political Economy of Decency' in *Law for Social Justice*, ILO, Geneva, 2019.
10. Langille, "Take These Chains from My Heart and Set Me Free": How Standard Labour Law Theory Drives Unnecessary Segmentation of Worker Rights' (2015), 36 Comparative Labour Law and Policy Journal.
11. Langille 'The Political Economy of Decency' *supra* n. 9.

5. There is a better view. A better constituting narrative. A better account with a broader domain, a better non-obstructionist legal grammar, and a positive, enlightening, and empowering normative mission. And on this third, normative dimension, the ideas of Sen and Nussbaum on ends and means, and substantive human freedom/capability, take centre stage. On this view, the truth is that the *tactic* (means) of addressing inequality of bargaining power in labour contracts is, and should be seen as, deployed in the service of a larger and positive idea – the *goal* of advancing real substantive human freedom/capability in so far as work has anything to do with it. And work has a lot to do with it, both intrinsically and instrumentally. Humans are not simply the *means* to production and prosperity. Human beings and their welfare, their lives, their freedoms, and their 'decent' work, are not an (expensive) tax on our goals. Rather, they are our goals - 'the ends of the exercise'.[12] Production and prosperity are the *means* to *those ends*. Further, inextricably linked to this new normative goal (as warp is to woof) is a new empirical domain (all work). And this reality is necessarily attended by the exit from centre stage of the legal grammar of contract – along with the central players – 'employee'. 'employer', 'independent contractor'. The scope of labour law is liberated from contract (and only contracts of a certain sort at that) – to all who labour. (Hence a new label – The Law of Work').

The central point is that labour law's current constituting narrative is an 'internal' obstacle of labour law's own making – one which labour law has placed in its own path. This is our most important current struggle – liberating labour law from its own account of itself.

Now, we turn to the resulting *provocative questions* about the law of work and climate change.

How will our ideas about climate change fit with these debates about how we do and should think about labour law? Are we now simply presented with yet another opportunity for yet more confusion of ends and means? That is, will climate change be framed as yet another external imperative, bearing down upon labour law and regarding which labour law's mission of seeking 'decency' will be seen, once again, as a costly barrier or limitation – i.e., a cost to be avoided? Or, will climate change help clarify our thinking? Will it be a catalyst for positive rethinking or yet another contribution to redirecting our thinking away from our true goals for work law? Will the law of work's engagement with climate change stall or advance our evolving thinking about labour law?

As I see it, there is a great risk that we will approach these questions in the way which we are, as I hope and have just explained, just learning to abandon when we law of work itself – but will not see this until it is 'too late' – or at least later than will be good for us.

That is, we will see climate change as simply the latest external force to arrive on labour law's doorstep after globalization, financialization, and all the rest– yet another horseman of the apocalypse – along with the pandemic, war, and much else. Labour law will yet again to be viewed as an expensive barrier to our real and necessary end of avoiding climate disaster, of a transition, of a sustainable future. So, this is the vital

12. Sen, *Development as Freedom* (Knopf, 1999) at 295.

question: are the words 'energy transition and sustainability" simply the new version of the words 'economic progress and prosperity' to which our labour law will be seen, again, as so much sand slowing the gears of progress? Or, does the climate crisis help us focus upon the truth that it is the lives of humans which are our core concern – our true end?

3 A MAP OF THESE QUESTIONS

My Canadian colleague David Doorey wrote, several years ago, a very perceptive article, 'The Law of Just Transitions', in which he discussed the rather fraught relationship between labour law and environmental law as follows:

> Labour law is the system of rules used to regulate work-related conflict between workers and employers. Its objectives are to strike an appropriate balance between employer efficiency interests (productivity and profitability) and worker interests in more decent jobs, within a system characterized by 'inequality of bargaining power'. The objective of environmental law is to strike a different sort of balance, between protection of the environment from harms caused by human activities, while also recognizing the economic and social need for decent jobs and a productive economy.
>
> Thus, both labour law and environmental law are concerned with balancing the need to promote jobs and economic activity with competing concerns about the impacts of that activity. Both legal fields are concerned in large measure with government-imposed legal restrictions on commerce and freedom of contract in the pursuit of broader public policy goals. Both impose a countervailing power on unbridled economic activity, but the countervailing interests involved are different and sometimes conflict.[13]

Not surprisingly, in light of my five assertions about labour law's standard account of itself, I see these remarks as very helpful. They assist us in drawing a map of the concerns of this chapter and thus, perhaps, a way of appreciating my provocative questions. As Doorey correctly observes, both labour and environmental laws are commonly seen, on the standard narratives constituting both subject matters, as 'justice against markets' types of endeavours. That is, both are commonly seen as brakes on 'unbridled economic activity' imposed in the name of something along the lines of 'decency' (labour) or 'sustainability' (environment). Then, as Doorey notes in the final line just quoted, the common picture is of a further fault line on the 'nonmarket' side of the line – the decency/sustainability fault line. The basic conflict can be seen in the following way – on the standard labour law view of the world, both sides to the discussion (labour and capital), whether they wish to pay the decency tax or not, are interested in 'more', i.e., a bigger pie. This is not so on the sustainability side – indeed quite the opposite. Unsustainable growth is seen by many as the problem to be solved, not the answer. This results our stand-off: from the labour side of the line, the 'environment' has usually been treated as just one of the various external systems

13. Doorey, 'Just Transitions Law: Putting Labour Law to Work on Climate Change' (2017), 30(2) Journal of Environmental Law and Practice 201 at 221.

that can affect labour law. Another external 'tectonic plate'[14] pushing against labour law – another addition to the list that includes 'globalization', financialization, fissuring, and so on. As Doorey puts it: 'the "environment" has usually been treated as just one of various external systems that can affect labour law'.[15]

This map, or structuring, or way of seeing, the essential conflicts in play is one into which labour law's traditional self-understanding fits very neatly. And that is the problem – the standard labour law view and the fact that the environmental narrative locks onto it in such a familiar way – to give us a very neat little view of the world. Not a neat solution. But a neat, simple, and familiar way of seeing the large difficulties we face.

So, our problem is that we need a new way of understanding our problems. We need to liberate ourselves from our familiar account of labour law itself and, as a result, be presented with a new way of seeing its relationship to climate change. We need to dismantle a barrier which we have constructed for ourselves.

4 A WAY FORWARD

Doorey's ambition in 'Just Transitions' was precisely to begin a conversation about a possible détente along the labour/environment decency/sustainability front. And for my purposes, it is significant that Doorey turns to Sen and the capability approach as one possible way forward. (He also mentions two other paths to possible progress[16]). Doorey's project has much in common with the views expressed here – beginning with the very basic idea that a lot of the action is to be found in the construction of legal fields – i.e., the construction of what I am calling their 'constituting narratives'. And while he understands a great deal of what I take to be significant in Sen's brief writings about the environment, Doorey passes directly from his discussion of Sen to a discussion of a new legal field of 'The Law of Just Transitions' – hence his title. But I think it is worth spending more time reflecting on what the consequences of Sen's thought are for the future of both labour and environmental law – as fields of law that exist now, but which stand in need of fundamental rethinking. And for the relationship between the two.

We can start with Sen, who has, at least briefly, deployed some of his basic ideas, about ends and means, in his interventions in the environmental sustainability debate. In a series of short and typically idea-altering essays, Sen has addressed in general the point I, in a specific labour law context, am after. Doorey very nicely summarizes some of Sen's ideas:

> Sen is critical of the definition of sustainable development developed initially in the influential 1987 Brundtland Report, which was: 'meeting the needs of the

14. On the idea of tectonic plates and labour law *see* Harry Arthurs, 'Charting the Boundaries of Labour Law: Innis Christie and the Search for an Integrated Law of Labour Market Regulation' (2011), 34 Dalhousie Law Journal 1 at p. 14.
15. Doorey *supra* n. 13 at 220.
16. One path following the work of Harry Arthurs (*see* Arthurs, *supra* n. 14) and a second path which becomes the title of his paper – what he (along with others) calls Just Transitions.

present without compromising the ability of future generations to meet their own needs'. He notes that the definition had been refined by thinkers like Robert Solow to mean the preservation or improvement of the 'standard of living' from one generation to the next. Sen notes that 'sustaining living standards is not the same thing as sustaining people's freedom to have – or safeguard – what they value and to which they have reason to attach importance.' Important human freedoms can be lost even though living standards are preserved.

Sen explains this point as follows:

In the ecological context, consider a deteriorating environment in which future generations are denied the opportunity to breathe fresh air (because of especially nasty emissions), but where those future generations are so very rich and so well served by other amenities that their overall standard of living may well be sustained. An approach to sustainable development on the Brundtland-Solow model may refuse to see any merit in protests against those emissions on the ground that the future generation will nevertheless have a standard of living at least as high as the present one. But that overlooks the need for anti-emission policies that could help future generations to have the freedom to enjoy the fresh air that earlier generations enjoyed.

Sen argues for a 'freedom-based view of sustainability', preserving or expanding 'substantive freedoms' without compromising the ability of future generations to have equal or more freedoms. Humans have good reason to value a clean environment and decent jobs, and therefore development policies should incorporate concern for the capacity of humans to enjoy both, now and in the future.

Doorey has it right and in 'The Ends and Means of Sustainability'[17] Sen's familiar and key ideas emerge – that in confronting climate change we, once again, are prone to confusing ends and means. For Sen, sustainability in the face of climate change is not first and foremost about the *needs* of our, and future, generations. Nor their *living standards*. Rather, it is about sustaining human freedom. That is what is valuable. This fundamental point is tied to another of the central themes of Sen's work (and which Smil has also emphasized[18]): the problem for the poor of the world is not that they are consuming too much energy – it is that they do not have access to enough energy to lead lives anything like lives which we, in well off countries would regard as minimally achieving an acceptable degree of substantive human freedom and capability.

These are two key themes which loom large, and which are to be expected in Sen's reflections. As Doorey noted above, keeping our eye on the prize of sustaining human freedom is not at all to deny or diminish the difficulties involved. It is rather to eliminate one large intellectual obstacle to progress – the picture we have painted that we are now in a world of necessary and tragic choices between incommensurable values – the values of labour law and the values now not simply of production and progress – but, and in addition, the 'existential' value of sustainability in the face of climate change and the need to decarbonize.

17. Amartya Sen, 'The Ends and Means of Sustainability' (2013) 14:1 J Human Development and Capabilities 6. *See also* Amartya Sen, 'Why We Should Preserve the Spotted Owl' (2004) 26:3 London Review of Books 10 DOI: 10.1080/19452829.2012.747492.
18. *Supra* n. 1.

That is, the point I (and I think Doorey) are making does not solve our problems. But it does remove one major obstacle to thinking clearly about them. It makes clear what we should focus upon as our goal and shows that what we now see as debilitating, zero-sum, incommensurable conflicts, about competing ends, are, rather pragmatic problems (very difficult pragmatic problems) about means to be publicly debated in light of a clear and compelling idea about what is important. As Sen puts it:

> The problem does not, of course, lie in the fact that the pursuit of economic prosperity [or, decarbonization] is typically taken to be a major goal of planning and policy-making. This need not be, in itself, unreasonable. The problem relates to the level at which this aim should be taken as a goal. Is it just an intermediate goal, the importance of which is contingent on what it ultimately contributes to human lives? Or is it the object of the entire exercise? It is in the acceptance – usually implicitly – of the latter view that the ends-means confusion becomes significant, indeed blatant.[19]

If these remarks are taken seriously then the achievement is to dismantle, at a fundamental level, the whole structure of the problem of labour, the environment, and market production mapped out above. It is to see a new fixed and common star by which to navigate these complex issues. This by seeing them as standing on common normative ground – which is a basic normative commitment to real substantive human freedom and capability.

That is, Sen offers the tools by which the required change in our thinking can be brought about. This change operates across all borders on the standard map of market activity/ labour law/ environmental law. This thinking underwrites a possible détente on the labour/market frontier which is in effect is a fundamental rewriting of our narrative of labour law. And the point here is that it also underwrites a reconciliation on the labour/environmental front. Both are made possible by a common change in our thinking – one which permits us to see common ground rather than contested terrain.

To this rather provocative and simple view, there will be objections.

It will be pointed out that the transition away from fossil fuels will involve transitions, i.e., job losses, for workers in, for example, fossil fuel and fossil fuel-related industries. This is certainly so – and it is where, as Doorey points out, many labour/climate discussions begin, and often end. But in response to this point, we need to make a rather fundamental distinction – between the direct and the indirect impacts of external pressures, whether involving something like free trade, robotics/artificial intelligence, or climate change. We must distinguish between the direct impact on the labour market (jobs) and the indirect impact on labour law.[20] The *direct* impact to which this first objection appeals is, simply, obvious. The *direct* impact of all the external forces – of globalization (think outsourcing), for example, is real. As are the well-rehearsed conversations about whether there will or will not be, all in, fewer jobs

19. Amartya Sen, 'Development as Capability Expansion' in Sakiko Fukuda-Parr & AK Shiva Kumar, eds, *Readings in Human Development: Concepts, Measures, and Policies for a Development Paradigm* (New Delhi: Oxford University Press, 2003) 3.
20. Langille, 'General Reflections on the Relationship of Trade and Labour (or: Fair Trade is Free Trade's Destiny)' in Bhagwati & Hudec (eds) Free Trade and Harmonization (M.I.T., 1996), 231-265 at 247.

as the result of these phenomena. But all that familiar territory is not the subject matter of this chapter. Discussions of such direct impacts are a problem of 'just transition' in a very direct sense – and one with which we have had a lot of experience in our recent era of what Dani Rodrik has called 'hyper globalization'.[21] This is something about which not only Smil, but my colleague Michael Trebilcock has had a lot of useful things to say. It is in part the basic issue of whether we should be in the business of 'compensating losers', to use some rather insensitive language.[22] As interesting and important as that discussion is (and I think the distributive justice issues involved are not that difficult to understand) it is not the subject matter of this chapter.

The point, which is not a completely new one, is that we also must come to grips with the indirect impact of climate change/transition on our labour laws, not only the direct impact on the labour market, i.e., jobs. Our main concern is the 'deregulatory' pressure such external forces unleash. That is the subject matter of this chapter. And a key idea is that this indirect impact is the result of and follows from how we think, in a fundamental way, about the problem in the first place. That is, whether we think in a Senian way about our true ends or, instead are focussed upon only possible means to those ends (increased trade, GDP and so on). The laws we put in place about free trade, international investment, taxation, compensation of 'losers', and all the rest all depend upon how we think about all of those issues – not just labour law and environmental/climate laws.

In prior moments of relatively recent history this conversation about indirect effects, certainly in connection with discussions of the pros and cons of free trade, was one about 'races to the bottom' and 'social dumping' brought about by the collective action problems individual nation states faced when attempting to maintain or improve 'labour standards' in the face of increasingly mobile capital and other non-labour factors of production. This was a result of a 'competition' problem among states who believed they were pursuing their self-interest (in seeking to attract or retain investment). In this regard, environmental law and standards faced the same problematic dynamic and indeed labour and environment were often bracketed together in the debates about such regulatory competition. These conversations established, to return to the 'map' of our problem set out above, how the battle was understood and structured on the market versus labour/environmental frontier. This was indeed a contested terrain. But all of that is, to repeat, a result of a view of labour and environmental laws costs, as barriers to, rather than constitutive of, our goals. It turns out that not only was this poor normative thinking but also based upon an empirical fallacy about the economic impacts involved.[23]

In this chapter, our concern is not this familiar 'market vs labour/environmental law' frontier but with the labour-environment side of that divide revealed by our mapping exercise above, that is, with labour/environment frontier itself. But, again,

21. Rodrik, *Straight Talk on Trade: Ideas for a Sane World Economy* (Princeton, 2017).
22. Trebilcock, Chandler and Howse, *Trade and Transitions* (Routledge, 1990) and Trebilcock, *Dealing With Losers* (OUP, 2014).
23. *See*, for example, sources cited in Langille, 'Re-reading the 1919 ILO Constitution in Light of Recent Evidence on Foreign Direct Investment and Workers' Rights' (2003), 42 Columbia Journal of Transnational Law 101-113.

our focus is not on how attending to our need for a transition affects jobs (the direct effect). Rather we are focused on the indirect impact on our labour laws. We can understand the basic problem by asking the question I posed above – 'will climate change be framed as yet another external imperative, bearing down upon labour law and regarding which labour law's mission of seeking 'decency' will be seen, once again, as a costly barrier or limitation – i.e., a cost to be avoided? Or, will climate change help clarify our thinking?'[24]

The idea advanced here is that we need the clarity of thought which Sen has brought to bear about ends and means to sort this out – just as we needed that clarity to sort out our understanding of labour law and its relationship to market ordering.

On this view the idea that ensuring workers have 'decent' conditions of work, a safe workplace, their human rights protected, an adequate provision for retirement, and so on, are or can be 'at odds' with, or a costly barrier to, what we mean by sustainability, is simply not possible. Rather, the goal of achieving and sustaining real human freedom at work underwrites all that we seek to do. Further, on this view the climate crisis can be and often is a promoter of decent work. And vice versa. Some simple examples: It has long been the case that Health and Safety laws often fit hand in glove with environmental concerns. But this one familiar example points to and shows the way in which, for example, the large and current global project of ending the practice of digging coal from beneath the earth's surface to burn in the name of energy consumption is a goal which a human freedom view of labour and environmental law share. So too are the environmental ends, and conditions of work impact, of 'working from home'. The challenge of decarbonizing maritime shipping is another simple example when seen through the lens proposed here, of an engine for improved labour conditions in higher-skilled jobs. But these few and simple examples are underwritten something broad and basic – the idea that if we correctly identify what is of true significance, rather than epiphenomena, we can focus on removing obstacles to them.

There is more for labour lawyers. We can see Sen's insight can make real sense of what is now a very common but very vague idea – that of a 'human centred' labour law. Many speak of such a thing – including the ILO.[25] But the work *of actually having* a human-centred approach in the real world, *actually begins,* where all interesting and important matters have their origin – in the human mind. And this is why the ideas of real human freedom and capability are so important for labour lawyers – they provide our best understanding of what it means to be truly focused, and in the right way, upon people. Such an approach cannot begin with, and will never proceed from, the starting point of our current constituting narrative. We need a new narrative for labour law. Climate change provides further evidence of the truth of this basic point.

24. *Supra.*
25. *See*, for example, *Work for a Brighter Future* (Report of the Global Commission on the Future of Work, ILO 2019).

CHAPTER 12

Energy Poverty, Fair Transition and Labour Law

Pr. Sophie Robin-Olivier

An important notion has emerged in the fair transition context: energy poverty.[1] It aims at taking into account a vulnerable group of individuals, who are or will be, particularly affected by measures to combat climate change (and to face the energy crisis), which include an increase in energy prices, both for transport and heating. This concept sheds light on a category of vulnerable individuals, who, although they are more severely impacted by the energy transition, remain invisible to social law specialists looking through the lenses of more classical analytical grids (socio-professional categories, level of income, geographical situation or place of life, gender, race, disability, religion, or other discriminatory grounds). But blindness, in this matter as in others, is not without consequences. One lesson learnt from the 'gilets jaunes' protests in France is probably that we must not ignore social categories that are at higher risk of facing adverse impacts of climate change reforms if we want the green transition to be both fair and acceptable.

To identify and accommodate individuals most affected by the green transition, energy poverty can thus be seen, prima facie, as a useful concept. This form of poverty affects not only low-income households but also lower middle-income households in many Member States. According to a recent Council Recommendation on ensuring a fair transition towards climate neutrality,[2] energy poverty results from a combination of low income, a high share of disposable income spent on energy, and poor energy

1. On this notion, *see* namely: Steve Pye, and Alii, *Energy Poverty and Vulnerable Consumers in the Energy Sector Across the EU: Analysis of Policies and Measures* (2015) https://ec.europa.eu/energy/sites/ener/files/documents/INSIGHT_E_Energy%20Poverty %20-%20Main%20Report_FINAL.pdf; Neil Simcock, Harriet Thomson, Stefan Petrova and Saskia Bouzarovski (eds), *Energy Poverty and Vulnerability: A Global Perspective* (Oxford: Routledge, 2018).
2. Council Recommendation on ensuring a fair transition towards climate neutrality 2022/C 243/04, OJ C 243, 27.6.2022, p. 35.

efficiency. The risk of energy poverty increases with high and volatile energy prices, which are driven by a number of factors including, in recent times, those related to Russia's war against Ukraine and the subsequent Union policy response.[3] In the context of energy transition, however, there are good reasons to maintain energy prices at a higher level, especially for fossil fuels, for decarbonization purposes. As a result, reducing energy prices or providing income support to allow continued access and consumption cannot be an appropriate solution, at least in the long run, and as a general, undiscriminated, measure.

According to the Council Recommendation on fair transition towards climate neutrality,[4] in 2019/2020, energy poverty affected about 8 % of the Union population, that is more than 35 million people, who were unable to keep their homes adequately warm, with significant differences between Member States and between income groups.[5] Moreover, according to the Recommendation, up to 6.2 % of people living in the Union (i.e., over 27 million people), have arrears in paying their utility bills. But measuring the phenomenon is uneasy. As for it, the Energy Poverty Observatory estimates, based on a combination of indicators, that more than 50 million households in the Union experience energy poverty.[6] As these figures show, the exact prevalence of energy poverty remains uncertain, which is due to methodological divergences in the assessment of the phenomenon. As the Directive on the internal market for electricity (recast Electricity Directive)[7] recognizes, the method to identify persons suffering from energy poverty constitutes a crucial issue.[8] There is no standard definition of energy poverty, and it is therefore left to Member States to develop their own criteria according to their national context.[9] However, under 'the Governance Regulation'[10] and the recast Electricity Directive,[11] the Commission is required to provide indicative guidance on appropriate indicators for measuring energy poverty. To fulfil its obligations, the Commission has ensured that aggregate indicators were

3. *Ibid.*
4. *Ibid.*
5. These figures are based on the latest available data in the EU statistics on income and living conditions for 2019/2020.
6. European Commission, EPOV Annual Report: Addressing Energy Poverty in the European Union: State of Play and Action, 2019, p. 6. *See also*, for similar statistics, Directive 2018/2002 on Energy efficiency, recital 24.
7. Directive (EU) 2019/944 of the European Parliament and of the Council of 5 June 2019 on common rules for the internal market for electricity and amending Directive 2012/27/EU (recast), OJ L 158, 14.6.2019, p. 125.
8. Article 29 of Directive 2019/944 indicates that when assessing the number of households in energy poverty, 'Member States shall establish and publish a set of criteria, which may include low income, high expenditure of disposable income on energy and poor energy efficiency'. On the issue concerning statistics on energy poverty, *see* namely: Harriet Thomson, Stefan Bouzarovski, Carolyn Snell, *Rethinking the Measurement of Energy Poverty in Europe: A Critical Analysis of Indicators and Data*, 26(7) Indoor and Built Environment 879-901 (2017) DOI: 10.1177/1420326x17699260.
9. Commission decision (EU) 2022/589 setting up the Commission Energy Poverty and Vulnerable Consumers Coordination Group, 6 April 2022, OJ L 112, 11.4.2022, p. 67, recital 5.
10. Regulation (EU) 2018/1999 of the European Parliament and of the Council of 11 December 2018, OJ L 328, 21.12.2018, p. 1.
11. Cited at note 6.

available at the European level.[12] Developed by Eurostat and the European Energy Poverty Observatory (EPOV) and derived from harmonized EU data collections, these indicators are meant to ensure monitoring of the situation EU-wide and to allow identification of national specificities. National indicators are supposed to help complement these European indicators, in order to refine the identification of people affected by energy poverty.[13]

Difficult as it is to measure, energy poverty is by no means a minor problem. It has been the topic of important research by social scientists, engineers, and geographers.[14] And it concerns EU social policy: social inclusion requires access to essential services, including energy, as the Solidarity Chapter of the Charter of fundamental rights of the EU,[15] and the European Pillar of social rights indicate.[16] The need for Member States to address energy poverty is also stressed in the integrated Employment Guidelines of 2020,[17] which inform the coordination of Member States' employment and social policies in the framework of the European Semester.[18] Energy poverty also relates to access to decent housing, another domain of social policy, which the European Commission Communication on the Green Deal[19] approaches, namely, through the angle of building renovation.[20]

But this important social issue, tightly related to fair transition, has not yet penetrated into the domain of labour law. Rather, energy poverty illustrates the current persisting divide between the social dimension of climate change law, captured by the notion of fair (or just) transition, and EU labour law. Efforts to address inequalities and poverty at work and efforts to achieve a fair transition continue to exist in parallel, rather than being integrated into each other.[21] Although the concept of energy poverty has to do with the fight against poverty, in which work conditions and work

12. These indicators are listed in the Annex to Commission Recommendation (EU) 2020/1563 of 14 October 2020 on energy poverty *OJ L 357, 27.10.2020, p. 35.*
13. *See* Commission Recommendation on energy poverty, recital 21.
14. Among the authors cited at note 1, Steve Pye is an energy engineer, Stefan Bouzarovski a professor of geography, and Harriet Thomson a professor in global social policy and sociology.
15. Article 36.
16. The European Pillar of Social Rights, proclaimed and signed by the Council, the European Parliament and the Commission at the Gothenburg Summit in November 2017, is the Union's guiding compass to a strong social Europe (https://ec.europa.eu/commission/priorities/deeper-and-fairer-economic-and-monetary-union/european-pillar-social-rights/european-pillar-social-rights-20-principles_en). Its principle 20 concerns 'Access to essential services'.
17. Council Decision (EU) 2020/1512 of 13 October 2020 on guidelines for the employment policies of the Member States, OJ L 344/22, 19.10.2020.
18. Guideline 8: 'Promoting equal opportunities for all, fostering social inclusion and fighting poverty'.
19. Communication from the Commission to the European Parliament, the European Council, the Council, the European Economic and Social Committee and the Committee of the Regions, 'The European Green Deal', 11 December 2019, COM(2019) 640 final.
20. Cf. the Communication from the Commission to the European Parliament, the Council, the European Economic and Social Committee, the Committee of the Regions 'A Renovation Wave for Europe – greening our buildings, creating jobs, improving lives' (COM(2020) 662 final).
21. For the same observation, concerning integration of gender discriminations and climate change, *see* Gill Allwood, *Mainstreaming Gender and Climate Change to Achieve a Just Transition to a Climate-Neutral Europe*, 58(1) Journal of Common Market Studies 182 (September 2020) DOI: 10.1111/jcms.13082.

arrangements play a central role, and with anti-discrimination law, the aim of which is, namely to protect vulnerable individuals and groups, this notion has remained, for now, out of the perspective of labour law.

The purpose of this contribution is to put to test the idea of including energy poverty in labour law, as a means to ensure that labour law contributes to fair transition. What we want to consider is the role that energy poverty could play in the domain of work relations. Is it, in other words, a useful concept to enshrine fair transition objectives in the framework of labour law? Answering this question requires an exploration of the possible role of energy poverty in bringing together threads of law development (labour law and fair transition), which have, so far, remained largely separated. How energy poverty can serve to bridge the gap between labour law developments and fair transition will be considered in only two domains, which, we believe, have narrow connections with energy poverty: poverty at work and anti-discrimination law. We will start by describing the current place and role of energy poverty in the context of fair transition (I), before considering how this concept can find its way into labour law, first, in the fight against poverty at work (II), and, second, in the framework of anti-discrimination law (III).

1 PLACE AND ROLE OF ENERGY POVERTY IN FAIR TRANSITION

Unsurprisingly, energy poverty has become a more and more pivotal notion in the domain of EU Energy legislation (A). This growing importance of energy poverty in EU Energy policy is the consequence of the role it is supposed to play in achieving a fair (or just) transition (B).

A Energy Poverty as a Central Notion of EU Energy Legislation

The recast Electricity Directive[22] devotes one article of its second Chapter, on 'consumer empowerment and protection' to energy poverty.[23] It insists, in particular, on the need (and difficulty) to identify individuals who suffer from energy poverty: Member States are invited to collect the right information to monitor the number of households in energy poverty. One central issue that Member States have to deal with, according to the Directive, concerns adequate instruments allowing the identification of households that are affected by energy poverty, in order to provide targeted support.[24]

In that Directive, which aims at market integration, energy poverty is a criterion to identify 'vulnerable customers' who must benefit from adequate protection from the market, and, in particular, be shielded from disconnection of electricity in critical times.[25] In the same vein, the decision of the Commission setting up the 'Commission Energy Poverty and Vulnerable Consumers Coordination Group'[26] states that energy

22. Cited above.
23. Article 29.
24. Recitals 59 and 60.
25. Article 28 (1).
26. Cited above at note 6.

poverty, a concept consolidated in the 'Clean Energy for All Europeans' legislative package, aims at putting 'consumers' at the heart of a just energy transition.[27] In this decision, vulnerable customers, affected by energy poverty, are not precisely defined but the Commission indicates that they can be identified on the basis of a range of criteria, including income levels, the share of energy expenditure of disposable income, the energy efficiency of homes, critical dependence on electrical equipment for health reasons, age or other criteria. This makes clear, as mentioned before, that the concept of energy poverty brings together different factors of vulnerability: classical discriminatory grounds (health, age ...), low income, and energy needs, which can result from low energy efficiency (of home, or modes of transport ...).

Another central piece of EU Energy legislation refers to energy poverty: the Energy efficiency Directive, amended in 2018.[28] According to this Directive, Member States are required 'to take into account the need to alleviate energy poverty in accordance with criteria established by them (...) by requiring (...) a share of energy efficiency measures under their national energy efficiency obligation schemes, alternative policy measures, or programmes or measures financed under an Energy Efficiency National Fund, to be implemented as a priority among vulnerable households, including those affected by energy poverty and, where appropriate, in social housing'.[29] Member States are also required to include information about the outcome of measures to alleviate energy poverty in the integrated national energy and climate progress reports requested by regulation 2018/1999 on 'the Governance Regulation'.[30]

In the Commission's proposal for a recast Directive on Energy efficiency that was put forward in July 2021, the concept of energy poverty has gained increased importance. The Commission proposes to add a new article on 'Empowering and protecting vulnerable customers and alleviating energy poverty'.[31] It would require Member States to implement energy efficiency improvement measures and related consumer protection or information measures (...) as a priority among people affected by energy poverty, vulnerable customers and, where applicable, people living in social housing, to alleviate energy poverty. The proposal on Energy efficiency also adds this definition of energy poverty: 'a household's lack of access to essential energy services that underpin a decent standard of living and health, including adequate warmth, cooling, lighting, and energy to power appliances, in the relevant national context, existing social policy and other relevant policies'.[32] In this definition, the reference to decent life and health brings energy poverty closer to Human rights and Social rights'

27. Recital 2.
28. Directive 2012/27/EU of the European Parliament and of the Council of 25 October 2012 on energy efficiency, amending Directives 2009/125/EC and 2010/30/EU and repealing Directives 2004/8/EC and 2006/32/EC, *OJ L 315, 14.11.2012, p. 1, Art. 7(7) a)*. Directive 2012/27 was amended by Directive 2018/2002/EU of the European Parliament and of the Council of 11 December 2018 amending Directive 2012/27/EU on energy efficiency, OJ L 328, 21.12.2018, p. 210, which also mentions energy poverty at Art. 7.
29. Article 7 (11) § 1.
30. Cited above, Art. 7 (11) § 2.
31. Article 22 of the proposal.
32. Article 2 (49).

perspectives, somewhat away from a rather technical concept that tends to prevail in Energy legislation.

B Fair Transition and Energy Poverty

The growing importance of energy poverty in EU Energy policy is tightly related to its role in achieving a fair (or just) transition. Fair transition relies on the idea that 'the effects of climate change are not the same for everyone', and that 'existing inequalities affect the impact of climate change and the ability to respond to it'.[33] It also rests on the consideration that, not only climate change itself, but also measures introduced to reduce climate change or to adapt to it have different effects on people, according to their gender, class, wealth, ethnicity, physical ability and other structural inequalities.[34] The ILO Guidelines on just transition[35] highlight the need to secure the livelihoods of those who might be negatively affected by the green transformation and also stress that the emerging low-carbon economy should be inclusive and based on decent work and lower inequality. In order to achieve such an outcome, the transition should be guided by principles of distributional justice,[36] which requires taking into account most affected persons and groups and compensating for the adverse effects of both climate change and measures to address it.

This adverse impact of climate change and climate change laws, that fair transition is meant to address, concerns namely, though not only, people affected by energy poverty. According to the European Commission communication on the Green Deal, the 'socially just transition' requires measures to address energy poverty.[37] That achieving fair transition necessitates action against energy poverty is a key argument of the Commission Recommendation on energy poverty.[38] In a more recent decision, the European Commission underlined once again the role of the concept of energy poverty in facilitating a just energy transition.[39] Similarly, the Council's Recommendation on ensuring a fair transition towards climate neutrality[40] insists on the need to 'prevent and alleviate energy poverty',[41] in one of the 'policy packages'[42] designed to ensure a green transition.

33. *See* namely, Gill Allwood, cited above.
34. *Ibid.*
35. 'Guidelines for a just transition towards environmentally sustainable economies and societies for all', 2015.
36. Cf. Daren McCauley and Raphael Heffron, *Just Transition: Integrating Climate, Energy and Environmental Justice*, 119 Energy Policy 1-7 (2018) DOI: 10.1016/j.enpol.2018.04.014; Peter Newell and Dustin Mulvaney, *The Political Economy of the 'just transition'*, 179(2) The Geographical Journal 132-140 (2013) DOI: 10.1111/geoj.12008.
37. Point 2.2.1.
38. Recommendation (EU) 2020/1563 of 14 October 2020 on energy poverty, OJ L 357, 27 10 2020, p. 35.
39. Decision 2022/589 setting up the Commission Energy Poverty and Vulnerable Consumers Coordination Group, cited above, recital 5.
40. Cited above.
41. Point 7(b).
42. Defined at point 3(h) as 'a comprehensive and coherent set of policy measures that integrates employment, skills and social policies with climate, energy, transport, environmental and other green transition policies (...)'.

Of course, it seems quite evident that energy poverty is a central concern when measures taken in order to combat climate change focus primarily on energy and energy prices. As a result, it comes as no surprise that the Social Climate fund, on which the Council and the European Parliament agreed on 18 December 2022, aims at mitigating the cost of the green transition for 'those most exposed to fossil fuel increases', and is presented as necessary to compensate the impact of the measures adopted to reduce the use of fossil fuels. To this aim, the Fund is meant to finance a series of measures adopted at the national level, including temporary direct income support measures to tackle the increase in road transport and heating fuel prices, and structural investments (for buildings renovation, namely). No labour law instrument is mentioned.

Similarly, the recast Electricity Directive mentions social security benefits to ensure the necessary supply to vulnerable customers, and state measures to support energy efficiency improvements,[43] without any explicit reference to work or labour law. The same is true for the Directive proposal on Energy efficiency, which envisages state encouragement to building renovations, as well as 'replacement of appliances, financial support and incentives for energy efficiency improvement measures, (...) or energy audits'[44] and encourage Member States to set up an Energy Efficiency National Fund.[45]

But quite unexpectedly, the instruments of labour law are not completely forgotten. The role of European social partners is mentioned in the Directive proposal on Energy efficiency, which mentions that the Commission should encourage European social partners in their discussions on energy efficiency, especially for vulnerable customers and final users, including those in energy poverty[46]. More generally, the proposal mentions the participation of people affected by energy poverty in the energy efficiency improvement interventions:[47] to be sure participation is not associated, in the text, with any particular form of workers' representation, but, in the domain of labour law, this would certainly justify the involvement of workers' representative. It thus seems that labour law and the fight against energy poverty are not irremediably distant. This is even more true when looking at labour law developments concerning in-work poverty, and the fight against discrimination.

2 REFINING THE CONCEPT OF IN-WORK POVERTY THROUGH ENERGY POVERTY

One specificity of energy poverty, compared to poverty in general, is that it serves both the objective of social justice and green transition. This dual functionality (A) is a

43. Article 28 (2).
44. Article 9(5) of the Directive proposal on Energy efficiency, 'to protect people affected by energy poverty vulnerable customers and, where applicable, people living in social housing, Member States shall encourage obligated parties to carry out actions such as renovation of buildings, including social housing, replacement of appliances, financial support and incentives for energy efficiency improvement measures in conformity with national financing and support schemes, or energy audits'.
45. Article 28 (9) of the Directive proposal on Energy efficiency.
46. Recital 94.
47. Recital 96.

justification for the inclusion of energy poverty in the framework of labour law, as another aspect of in-work poverty (B).

A The Dual Functionality of Energy Poverty

As we already insisted on, energy poverty, in spite of various, unprecise, dual-level[48] definitions, depends on a combination of factors. Among these factors, some concern individual situations (income, housing), and some are contextual elements affecting individuals but not depending on their individual situation (energy prices, and their fluctuations, namely). Thus, one thing is certain: energy poverty cannot be assessed only in consideration of income level, and should not be combatted only through income support. To be sure, the same is true for poverty, in general: the focus on income is also insufficient to tackle poverty, since the ability of each person to convert income into capabilities differs from individual to individual, depending on personal characteristics and needs.[49] As a result, poverty, just as energy poverty, is defined as a multidimensional phenomenon.[50] It is also true that, as poverty, in general, energy poverty can be both the cause and outcome of deprivations from human rights, including social rights (right to health, dignity, decent housing, mobility ...).[51] In addition, energy poverty, just as poverty in general, creates a vicious circle: deprivation of energy makes it more difficult to escape poverty as it limits mobility (including reaching the workplace), and makes home uncomfortable and improper for various private activities, including work, at a time of increased telework from home.

However, if energy poverty and poverty partly overlap, unsurprisingly, in terms of definition and effects, they are not one and the same thing. Energy poverty is a specific type of poverty. Qualifying poverty, by relating it to a specific, but central, resource, such as energy, is a way to identify a specific harm, for a certain group of persons, that climate change and climate change law, contribute to foster and, for this reason, must be taken into account in the particular context of the green transition. It is indeed a type of poverty highly dependent on a particular context, in which energy is becoming more expensive because energy sobriety is needed. As a result, it is not only social justice purposes that justify action against energy poverty: the goal is also to ensure transition towards a greener economy. As a result, the means to address energy poverty must be specific. For instance, lowering the price (or cost) of energy, across the board, would indeed contribute to solving the problem of energy deprivation, but it would not achieve green transition. The dual functionality of the concept of energy poverty necessitates combining the alleviation of poverty with sustainable development. Instruments capable of integrating this dual functionality are probably what is so far missing, in the toolbox of labour law. It can thus be contended that tackling the specific problems of poverty derived from increased energy costs could not

48. Definition involves both by the EU and Member States.
49. Olivier de Schutter, *Combating Discrimination on Ground of Socio-economic Disadvantage*, 3 European Journal of Human Rights 224 (2022).
50. *Ibid.*
51. *Ibid.*

be done by considering situations of poverty, in general. The same is true for poverty at work.

B Justification for Combatting Energy Poverty, in Addition to Fighting In-work Poverty, in the Framework of Labour Law

The fight against poverty at work has only recently become a concern at the EU level, in the European Pillar of Social Rights, which proclaims that 'in-work poverty shall be prevented'.[52] This evolution has been described as a change of attitude in EU policy towards in-work poverty, no longer seen as a problem of poverty in general, but rather considered as an issue for labour law itself[53] that requires to depart from the idea that flexibility is overall good, both for employers and workers.[54]

Addressing the issue of poverty at work is part of the 2021 Action plan designed to implement the European Pillar of Social Rights. The Action plan proposed three EU headline targets for 2030, namely that the number of people at risk of poverty or social exclusion should be reduced by at least 15 million by 2030. But for now, EU law developments on poverty at work have been limited. The most recent actions focused on wages, and they have indeed led to the adoption of the Directive on minimum adequate wages.[55]

Poverty at work that results from working arrangements that create and maintain situations of precariousness is not ignored at the EU level.[56] But it is not, for the moment, considered a problem in relation to climate change law. Thus, nothing is done to address the particular situation of precarious workers affected by energy poverty, who face specific obstacles: obstacles in terms of mobility, to reach the workplace or clients, for instance, and uncomfortable situations in their private homes, where they may also have to work.

Fighting energy poverty (and its consequences on the ability to work) would require taking into account elements of workers' situations that depend on their living conditions. No doubt, such consideration for the personal situation of workers, their private home, in particular, seems necessary to ensure the protection of all workers, who are requested to telework from home. But the green transition objective also

52. Principle 6(2) of the European Pillar of Social Rights. For a study of in-work poverty in Member States, *see* the 2019 report of European Social Policy Network on in-work poverty: Slavina Spasova et al., *In-Work Poverty in Europe: A Study of National Policies* (Brussels: Publications Office of the European Union 2019).
53. Cf. Luca Ratti and Antonio Garcia-Muñoz, *In-Work Poverty, and Vulnerable Workers*, 1 European Law Open 734 (2022). *See also* our article, *La pauvreté au travail: nouveau sujet et nouvelle méthode de la politique sociale de l'Union*, 2 Revue trimestrielle de droit européen 497 (2021).
54. Which was part of the philosophy of the Commission Green paper 'Modernising labour law to meet the challenges of the XXIst century', COM(2006) 708 final, 22 November 2006. On this document, *see* namely our commentary, *Moderniser le droit du travail pour relever les défis du XXIe siècle, un Livre vert présenté par la Commission européenne*, 2 Revue de Droit du Travail 89 (2007).
55. Directive (EU) 2022/2041 of the European Parliament and of the Council of 19 October 2022 on adequate minimum wages in the European Union, OJ L 275, 25.10.2022, p. 33.
56. On this idea, *see* namely the European Parliament Resolution of 10 February 2021 on Reducing Inequalities with a Special Focus on In-Work Poverty (2019/2188 (INI)).

requires that instruments of labour law take into account the green transition, in addition to the objectives of protection. This means, in particular, as mentioned before, that income support, through allowances granted for teleworkers, for instance, is not an appropriate solution.

This is not out of the reach of labour law. On the one hand, labour has traditionally granted rights or advantages to take into account family status or transportation needs, from home to the office. On the other hand, trying to integrate different objectives, possibly in tension, is something EU labour law is accustomed to doing. The EU social policy was largely been built around the idea of reconciling free markets and economic freedoms with social justice, through the harmonization of working conditions. Now it needs to invent ways to ensure social justice, together with limiting climate change.

To this aim, energy poverty could be one of the useful concepts. For instance, in the negotiations between social partners on remunerations and working conditions, the situation of workers affected by energy poverty could be taken into account in order to carve out adequate compensation. The core question of the definition of energy poverty, to target workers in need would have to be raised, in this context of collective bargaining. Whatever their source, remuneration policies could include specific allowances for energy efficiency improvements, granted to workers affected by energy poverty.

Specific energy needs (both for transport and home heating), and the green transition objective, should be taken into account in labour law policies, at all levels. Such considerations can be justified, if not required, by the Charter of fundamental rights of the EU, which states that working conditions must respect workers' health, safety and dignity.[57] Since energy poverty impacts workers' health, safety and dignity, it should be taken into account, in determining working conditions, including wages. This need for distinctions based on differences in situations suggests that energy poverty might also step into the territory of EU labour law, as a new concept of anti-discrimination law.

3 TRANSPLANTING THE CONCEPT OF ENERGY POVERTY IN EU ANTI-DISCRIMINATION LAW TO ADDRESS A FORM INTERSECTIONALITY

Energy poverty, as a concept to address the situation of a vulnerable group, entertains close relationships with non-discrimination (A). But existing anti-discrimination law is not equipped to envisage this form of intersectional vulnerability (B).

A The Relationship Between Energy Poverty and Non-discrimination

In the new provisions that the Commission suggests adding to the revised version of the Energy efficiency Directive, equality, non-discrimination and energy poverty sit side by side. On the question of empowerment and protection of the most affected by

57. Article 31.

energy transition, in particular, the proposal mentions that 'Member States should empower and protect all people equally, irrespective of their sex, gender, age, disability, race or ethnic origin, sexual orientation, religion or belief, and ensure that those most affected or put at greater risk of being affected by energy poverty, or most exposed to the adverse impacts of energy poverty, are adequately protected'.[58] In addition, Member States 'should ensure that energy efficiency measures do not exacerbate any existing inequalities, notably with respect to energy poverty'.[59] The proposal also recognizes that 'the particular groups at risk of energy poverty or more susceptible to its effects' include' women, persons with disabilities, older persons, children, and persons with a minority racial or ethnic background'.[60] It is thus quite clear, in this text, that energy poverty is a concept tightly associated with discrimination.

Of course, this seems like a rather trivial observation, since both the EU anti-discrimination law and the fight against energy poverty intend to address factors of vulnerability[61] that prevent access to the basic goods, such as energy, considered necessary to a dignified life. Both anti-discrimination law and actions against energy poverty revolve around the need to take into account the precariousness or vulnerability of certain individuals or groups,[62] which is considered particularly necessary in the objective of a fair transition, as mentioned above. Moreover, energy poverty concerns predominantly victims of discrimination, on grounds of old age, disability, or family situation (single parenting), among others.[63]

All in all, people affected by energy poverty emerge, in the context of fair transition, as what could be described as a protected group (or a group in need of protection), in the language of anti-discrimination law. This group, however, is quite peculiar. It does not correspond to any existing group that anti-discrimination law identifies. The factors of 'vulnerability' that determine energy poverty are varied and function in combination. Sociodemographic characteristics;[64] household composition,[65] health,[66] disability, lack of 'energy literacy'[67] or cultural grounds[68] are among

58. Recital 99.
59. *Ibid.*
60. Article 5(3).
61. Directive 2019/944 on the single market for electricity (cited above) explicitly link energy poverty and customer vulnerability in its Art. 28.
62. For an analysis bringing together non-discrimination and vulnerability, *see* namely Martha Albertson Fineman, *Beyond Identities: The Limits of an Antidiscrimination Approach to Equality*, 92 Boston University Law Review 1713-1770 (2012). *See also*, more recently, Jule Mulder, *What is Vulnerability Anyway? Tracing the EU notion of the vulnerable consumer through the eyes of EU non-discrimination Law*, 46(6) *European Law Review* 719-745 (2021).
63. European Commission, Energy Poverty Advisory Hub, *EPAH Handbooks: A Guide to Understanding and Addressing Energy Poverty*, 10 (2022) (accessible on line: https://energy-poverty.ec.europa.eu/system/files/2022-06/EPAH%20handbook_introduction.pdf).
64. Social aid beneficiaries, social housing tenants, people living in a rented home, people with low levels of education, or ethnic minorities are considered at higher risk of energy poverty.
65. Single parents, pensioners, families with people with disabilities, or young students in rental apartments are more affected.
66. Energy poverty tends to affect disproportionately people with illnesses that either require special attention to indoor thermal conditions like cardiovascular, respiratory diseases or other illnesses that weaken the immune system.

the multiple factors considered to contribute to a higher risk of energy poverty.[69] In this regard, energy poverty captures a form of intersectionality: situations of individuals belonging to different disadvantaged groups are concerned.

However, it is not the case that people suffering from energy poverty have been (and continue to be) stigmatized and oppressed on that ground, which is a complex one, not immediately perceptible, compared to sex, race or other prohibited grounds, even if these classical discriminatory grounds are not so simple to get to grips with either. Nor can people affected by energy poverty be considered the victims of stigmatization, as people in poverty.[70] Thus, although the current process of climate change impacts predominantly a group (or groups) of vulnerable individuals, who are the victims of discrimination, discrimination law would have to be adapted to the specific context of fair transition.

B The Impossibility of Dealing with Energy Poverty Through Existing Anti-discrimination Law

If individuals and groups protected by anti-discrimination law have higher chances to be affected by energy poverty, combatting discrimination, through existing legal instruments, would not suffice to address energy poverty. To be sure, actions against discrimination on disability or age, in particular, could contribute to solving the problem of access to energy that members of these discriminated groups may face. Within the existing legal framework, it is arguable that the particular situation of disabled or older people, who are particularly affected by the increase in energy prices, should, already, be taken into account, in the design of measures adopted, whenever they lie in the scope of application of EU law: since these discriminations are prohibited by the Charter of fundamental rights,[71] no legislative instruments should have the object or effect of discriminating on these grounds. In the domain of EU labour law, where the more precise provisions of Directive 2000/78 prohibit discrimination on the ground of age and disability, and require measures to accommodate disabled persons,[72] energy poverty can be combatted, to a certain extent, in the framework of anti-discrimination law. But the entirety of the intersectional category affected by

67. This factor points at the inability to make use of technological, economic or regulatory advancement for the energy transition. For instance, energy poverty can result from lack of awareness of the problem and little knowledge of domestic energy issues, the lack of financial resources, and poor household energy planning.
68. According to the EPAH Handbook (cited above), this factor refers to people whose culture hinders their perception of energy poverty and influences their behaviour in a way that makes it more difficult to tackle the issue. For instance, it concerns people that underestimate the problem due to historic habituation to cold, or have historical and contextual preference for low efficiency equipment.
69. *Ibid.*
70. On discrimination against people in poverty as a major obstacle in the fight against poverty, *see* Olivier de Schutter, *supra*, p. 225.
71. Article 21(1).
72. Directive 2000/78 Council Directive 2000/78/EC of 27 November 2000 establishing a general framework for equal treatment in employment and occupation, OJ L 303, 2.12.2000, p. 16.

energy poverty would not be covered. Recognizing intersectionality would be necessary. But although this concept has drawn a lot of attention in recent times, it has not yet found its way into EU anti-discrimination law.[73]

As it stands, anti-discrimination law is neither conceived nor perfectly adapted, to play the role that the concept of energy poverty could play. But what would it mean to include energy poverty within the framework of anti-discrimination law? One possibility would be to add a new discriminatory ground and prohibit discrimination on energy poverty. That would prevent the adoption of any measures, in the domain of labour law, without verifying that they do not create a particular disadvantage for persons in a situation of energy poverty or at risk of energy poverty. If aligned on the regime of other discriminatory grounds prohibited by EU directives,[74] such an assessment of potential indirect discrimination would not only apply to public policies, in the field of labour law but also to collective agreements, work contracts and other measures unilaterally adopted by employers, private or public.

As a result, for instance, the prohibition of discrimination on energy poverty would imply that employers, or social partners, make sure that, when workers, or a certain category of workers, are required to telework, adjustments are made for those facing energy poverty. Determination of allowances not taking energy poverty into account, would not be acceptable unless justified by overriding reasons. In the same vein, different solutions would become necessary, when deciding on support granted by employers for the cost of transportation to the workplace or for shifting to transportation modes that contribute to decarbonization. Prohibiting discrimination on the ground of energy poverty could also impact the terms of work contracts. For instance, mobility clauses, which impose rapid adaptations of workers to variations of times or places of work may be harder to respect for workers facing situations of energy poverty. Consequences resulting from non-compliance would have to take into account the discriminatory effect of the contract.

However, one concern about energy poverty becoming a new discriminatory ground is that it would create a diversion from more important and long-lasting problems of discrimination, namely against people who have suffered socio-economic disadvantages and stigma based on these disadvantages, long before climate change and climate change reforms led to concerns about energy poverty. In addition, and more importantly, as mentioned earlier, the problem that energy poverty tries to address is not about stigma, conscious or unconscious bias against the member of a social group, that leads to exclusion. It concerns the effects on a category of the population of contemporary transformations of both the conditions of life (resulting from climate change) and the general legal framework (in order to limit climate change).

73. On this situation, *see* in particular Raphaële Xenidis, *Multiple Discrimination in EU Anti-discrimination Law: Towards Redressing Complex Inequality?*, in Uladzislau Belavusau and Kristin Henrard (eds), *EU Anti-discrimination Law Beyond Gende*r (Oxford; Portland: Hart Publishing, 2018) 41.

74. In particular, Directive 2000/43 Council Directive 2000/43/EC of 29 June 2000 implementing the principle of equal treatment between persons irrespective of racial or ethnic origin, OJ L 180, 19.7.2000, p. 22 and 2000/78, cited above.

As a result, instead of a new discriminatory ground, it seems more appropriate to require accommodation for workers facing energy poverty, in order to ensure substantive equality. Developments in the field of anti-discrimination law, where the concept of reasonable accommodation exists, can be a source of inspiration on the possible forms and scope of a duty to accommodate workers affected by energy poverty. The notion of appropriate measures, in particular, could be borrowed from the definition of reasonable accommodation of disabled persons. In this domain, accommodation includes effective and practical measures to adapt to the workplace, for example, adapting premises and equipment, patterns of working time, the distribution of tasks or the provision of training or integration resources.[75] According to the Court of Justice, measures can be organizational and may include reassignment to another position, if that is necessary to allow a person to remain in employment.[76] This model could be a reference for the accommodation of workers facing energy poverty: it would justify specific measures, either individual or collective, to ensure that they can have access to employment, and can remain in employment.

4 CONCLUSION

This contribution has explored how labour law could adjust to fair transition, in one particular way: by making room for the concept of energy poverty, which is a core concept of fair transition in the current package of energy legislation reforms to limit climate change. To this aim, we have considered the relationships that energy poverty entertains with in-work poverty and anti-discrimination law, to identify where that concept could be lodged, and what it would change for labour law.

It must be noted, in conclusion, that the required changes would be significant, and probably uneasy to work out. Transplanting energy poverty in labour law would require taking care of a complex category of workers, at the intersection of different types of vulnerabilities, whose private life and home would have to be considered. It would impose a substantive conception of equality to prevail, which would go along with an extension of reasonable accommodation way beyond its current scope of application. However, one can expect that the necessary transformation of labour law, in the perspective of fair transition, will push new notions, such as energy poverty, to the forefront, and allow expansion of others.

75. Recital 20 of Directive 2000/78, cited above.
76. On this conception of accommodation for disabled workers, *see* recently Case C-485/20, *HR Rail*, 10.02.2022, ECLI:EU:C:2022:85.

STUDIES IN EMPLOYMENT AND SOCIAL POLICY

1. W. Beck, L. van der Maesen & A. Walker (eds), *The Social Quality of Europe*, 1997 (ISBN 90-411-0456-9).
2. R. Blanpain, M. Colucci, C. Engels, F. Hendrickx, L. Salas & E. De Smyter, *Institutional Changes and European Social Policies after the Treaty of Amsterdam*, 1998 (ISBN 90-411-1018-6).
3. V. Lo: *Law and Industrial Relations: China and Japan after World War II*, 1998 (ISBN 90-411-1075-5).
4. A. Den Exter & H. Hermans (eds), *The Right to Health Care in Several European Countries*, 1998 (ISBN 90-411-1087-9).
5. M. Biagi (ed.), *Job Creation and Labour Law from Protection towards Pro- Action*, 2000 (ISBN 90-411-1432-7).
6. W. Beck, L. van der Maesen, F. Thomése & A. Walker (eds), *Social Quality: A Vision for Europe*, 2000 (ISBN 90-411-1523-4).
7. F. Pennings, *Introduction to European Social Law*, 3rd ed., 2001 (ISBN 90-411-1628-1).
8. J. Murray, *Transnational Labour Regulation: The ILO and EC Compared*, 2001 (ISBN 90-411-1583-8).
9. R. Blanpain & C. Engels (eds), *The ILO and Social Challenges of the 21st Century*, 2001 (ISBN 90-411-1572-2).
10. M. Biagi (ed.), *Towards a European Model of Industrial Relations? Building on the First Report of the European Commission*, 2001 (ISBN 90-411-1653-2).
11. J. Clasen (ed.), *What Future for Social Security? Debates and Reforms in National and Cross-National Perspective*, 2001 (ISBN 90-411-1671-0).
12. A. Numhauser-Henning (ed.), *Legal Perspectives on Equal Treatment and Non-Discrimination*, 2001 (ISBN 90-411-1665-6).
13. R. Blanpain (ed.), *Labour Law, Human Rights and Social Justice* 2001 (ISBN 90-411-1697-4).
14. M.-C. Kuo, H.F. Zacher & H.-S. Chan (eds), *Reform and Perspectives on Social Insurance: Lessons from the East and West*, 2002 (ISBN 90-411-1819-5).
15. P. Foubert, *The Legal Protection of the Pregnant Worker in the European Community*, 2002 (ISBN 90-411-1842-X).
16. M. Biagi (ed.), *Quality of Work and Employee Involvement in Europe*, 2002 (ISBN 90-411-1885-3).
17. F. Pennings, *Dutch Social Security Law in an International Context*, 2002 (ISBN 90-411-1887-X).

18. T. Carney & G. Ramia, *From Rights to Management: Contract, New Public Management and Employment Services*, 2002 (ISBN 90-411-1889-6).
19. R. Blanpain & M. Colucci, *European Labour and Social Security Law, Glossary*, 2002 (ISBN 90-411-1905-1).
20. I.U. Zeytinoglu (ed.), *Flexible Work Arrangements: Conceptualizations and International Experiences*, 2002 (ISBN 90-411-1947-7).
21. J. Berghman, A. Nagelkerke, M. Boos, R. Doeschot & G. Vonk (eds), *Social Security in Transition*, 2002 (ISBN 90-411-1969-8).
22. R. Blanpain, *The Legal Status of Sportsmen and Sportswomen under International, European and Belgian National and Regional Law*, 2003 (ISBN 90-411-1980-9).
23. R. Blanpain & M. Weiss (eds), *Changing Industrial Relations & Modernisation of Labour Law, Liber Amicorum in Honour of Professor Marco Biagi*, 2003 (ISBN 90-411-2008-4).
24. J. Malmberg (ed.), *Effective Enforcement of EC Labour Law*, 2003 (ISBN 90-411-2160-9).
25. M. De Vos (ed.), *A Decade Beyond Maastricht: The European Social Dialogue Revisited*, 2003 (ISBN 90-411-2163-3).
26. M. Sewerynski (ed.), *Collective Agreements and Individual Contracts of Employment*, 2003 (ISBN 90-411-2190-0).
27. R. Blanpain & M. Van Gestel, *Use and Monitoring of E-Mail, Intranet and Internet Facilities at Work: Law and Practice*, 2004 (ISBN 90-411-22-66-4).
28. A. C. Neal (ed.), *The Changing Face of European Labour Law and Social Policy*, 2004 (ISBN 90-411-2312-1).
29. E. Sol & M. Westerveld (eds), *Contractualism in Employment Services: A New Form of Welfare State Governance*, 2005 (ISBN 90-411-2405-5).
30. F. Pennings (ed.), *Between Soft and Hard Law – The Impact of International Social Security Standards on National Social Security Law*, 2006 (ISBN 978-90-411-2491-3).
31. L. Dickens & A. C. Neal (eds), *The Changing Institutional Face of British Employment Relations*, 2006 (ISBN 978-90-411-2541-5).
32. G. Sebardt, *Redundancy and the Swedish Model in an International Context*, 2006 (ISBN 978-90-411-2503-3).
33. A.M. Swiatkowski, *Charter of Social Rights of the Council of Europe*, 2007 (ISBN 978-90-411-2608-5).
34. M. Sargeant (ed.), *The Law on Age Discrimination in the EU*, 2008 (ISBN 978-90-411-2522-4).
35. G. Di Domenico & S. Spattini (eds), *New European Approaches to Long- Term Unemployment: What Role for Public Employment Services and What Market for Private Stakeholders?*, 2008 (ISBN 978-90-411-2614-6.)
36. C. Welz, *The European Social Dialogue under Articles 138 and 139 of the EC Treaty: Actors, Processes, Outcomes*, 2008 (ISBN 978-90-411-2744-0).
37. M. Rönnmar (ed.), *EU Industrial Relations v. National Industrial Relations: Comparative and Interdisciplinary Perspectives*, 2008 (ISBN 978-90-411- 2770-9).

38. F. Pennings, Y. Konijn & A. Veldman (eds), *Social Responsibility in Labour Relations: European and Comparative Perspectives*, 2008 (ISBN 978-90- 411-2783-9).
39. F. Pennings & C. Bosse (eds), *The Protection of Working Relationships: A Comparative Study*, 2011 (ISBN 978-90-411-3289-5).
40. S. Devetzi & S. Stendahl (eds), *Too Sick to Work?: Social Security Reference in Europe for Persons with Reduced Earnings Capacity*, 2011 (ISBN 978-90- 411-3426-4).
41. Ulrich Becker, Frans Pennings & Tineke Dijkhoff (eds), *International Standard Setting and Innovations in Social Security*, 2013 (ISBN 978-90-411-3233-8).
42. E. Ales (ed.), *Health and Safety at Work: European and Comparative Perspective*, 2013 (ISBN 978-90-411-4661-8).
43. F. Pennings, T. Erhag & S. Stendahl (eds), *Non-public Actors in Social Security Administration: A Comparative Study*, 2013 (ISBN 978-90-411-4917-6).
44. A. Neal (ed.), *Cross-Currents in Modern Chinese Labour Law*, 2014 (ISBN 978-90-411-4763-9).
45. B. Waas (ed.), *The Right to Strike: A Comparative View*, 2014 (ISBN 978-90-411-5007-3).
46. A. Ojeda-Avilés, *Transnational Labour Law*, 2015 (ISBN 978-90-411-5858-1).
47. A. Numhauser-Henning & M. Rönnmar, *Age Discrimination and Labour-Law: Comparative and Conceptual Perspectives in the EU and Beyond*, 2015 (ISBN 978-90-411-4979-4).
48. A. Perulli & T. Treu (eds), *Enterprise and Social Rights*, 2017 (ISBN 978-90-411-8234-0).
49. Dr F.C.A. van Haasteren, *Decent Flexibility: The Impact of ILO Convention 181 and the Regulation on Temporary Agency Work*, 2017 (ISBN 978-90-411-9236-3).
50. T. Dijkhoff & L.G. Mpedi (eds), *Recommendation on Social Protection Floors: Basic Principles for Innovative Solutions*, 2018 (ISBN 978-90-411-8623-2).
51. A. Perulli & T. Treu (eds), *Sustainable Development, Global Trade and Social Rights*, 2018 (ISBN 978-90-411-9235-6).
52. M. Mironi & M. Schlachter (eds), *Regulating Strikes in Essential Services: A Comparative 'Law in Action' Perspective*, 2019 (ISBN 978-90-411-8997-4).
53. A. Perulli & T. Treu (eds), *The Role of the State and Industrial Relations*, 2019 (ISBN 978-94-035-0661-6).
54. T. Gyulavári & E. Menegatti (eds), *The Sources of Labour Law*, 2020 (ISBN 978-94-035-0284-7).
55. V. Cagnin, *Labour Law and Sustainable Development*, 2020 (ISBN 978-94-035-2074-2).
56. A. Perulli & T. Treu (eds), *The Future of Work: Labour Law and Labour Market Regulation in the Digital Era*, 2021 (ISBN 978-94-035-2853-3).
57. A. Perulli & T. Treu (eds), *Labour Law and Climate Change: Towards a Just Transition*, 2023 (ISBN 978-94-035-0877-1).

www.ingramcontent.com/pod-product-compliance
Lightning Source LLC
Chambersburg PA
CBHW071332230926
51849CB00002B/372
* 9 7 8 9 4 0 3 5 0 8 7 7 1 *